take a hint from the heavens...

1986 is packed with promise. Make the most of it with the predictions, insights, clues and suggestions America's most popular astrologer, Sydney Omarr, has prepared for you!

Learn about the "geometry" of relationships—who you get along with, and why . . . pore over celebrity sun signs and personality profiles . . . discover how and why the movements of the zodiac affect men and women so differently . . . and much, much more. Whatever your desire, whatever your dilemma, let Sydney Omarr's time-tested wisdom guide you through 1986, and watch your dreams become exciting realities!

For Expanding Your Personal Knowledge of Astrology, SIGNET Brings to You

SYDNEY OMARR'S ASTROLOGICAL GUIDES FOR YOU IN 1986

- [ ] **ARIES** .... (136764—$2.75)*
- [ ] **TAURUS** .... (136772—$2.75)*
- [ ] **GEMINI** .... (136780—$2.75)*
- [ ] **CANCER** .... (136799—$2.75)*
- [ ] **LEO** .... (136802—$2.75)*
- [ ] **VIRGO** .... (136810—$2.75)*
- [ ] **LIBRA** .... (136829—$2.75)*
- [ ] **SCORPIO** .... (136837—$2.75)*
- [ ] **SAGITTARIUS** .... (136845—$2.75)*
- [ ] **CAPRICORN** .... (136853—$2.75)*
- [ ] **AQUARIUS** .... (136861—$2.75)*
- [ ] **PISCES** .... (136888—$2.75)*

*Price is $3.25 in Canada

Buy them at your local bookstore or use this convenient coupon for ordering.

NEW AMERICAN LIBRARY
P.O. Box 999, Bergenfield, New Jersey 07621

Please send me the books I have checked above: I am enclosing $_____
(please add $1.00 to this order to cover postage and handling). Send check or money order—no cash or C.O.D.'s. Prices and numbers are subject to change without notice.

Name_____

Address_____

City _____ State _____ Zip Code _____
Allow 4-6 weeks for delivery.
This offer is subject to withdrawal without notice.

SYDNEY OMARR'S
DAY-BY-DAY ASTROLOGICAL GUIDE FOR
Aries
(MARCH 21–APRIL 19)
1986

A SIGNET BOOK

NEW AMERICAN LIBRARY

NAL BOOKS ARE AVAILABLE AT QUANTITY DISCOUNTS
WHEN USED TO PROMOTE PRODUCTS OR SERVICES.
FOR INFORMATION PLEASE WRITE TO PREMIUM MARKETING DIVISION,
NEW AMERICAN LIBRARY, 1633 BROADWAY,
NEW YORK, NEW YORK 10019.

Copyright © 1985 by Sydney Omarr

All rights reserved

Sydney Omarr is syndicated worldwide by Los Angeles Times Syndicate.

SIGNET TRADEMARK REG. U.S. PAT. OFF. AND FOREIGN COUNTRIES
REGISTERED TRADEMARK—MARCA REGISTRADA
HECHO EN CHICAGO, U.S.A.

SIGNET, SIGNET CLASSIC, MENTOR, PLUME, MERIDIAN and NAL BOOKS
are published by New American Library,
1633 Broadway, New York, New York 10019

First Printing, July 1985

1 2 3 4 5 6 7 8 9

PRINTED IN THE UNITED STATES OF AMERICA

CONTENTS

1 **Defining Terms**   7
   - *Astrology*   7
   - *The Zodiac*   8
   - *Sun Sign*   9
   - *Element*   9
   - *Quality*   11
   - *Element and Quality Together*   12
   - *Planet*   13
   - *House*   15
   - *Rising Sign*   16
   - *Horoscope*   17
   - *Aspect*   18
   - *Transiting Planet*   19

2 **Your House of the Sun**   21
   Your "Piece of the Pie"

3 **The Geometry of Relationships**   32
   What Signs You Get Along with—and Why

4 **Twelve Places at the Table**   35
   Personality Profiles of the Signs

5 **Moods of the Moon**   44
   Day-by-Day Changes

6 **Venus and Mars**   55
   Love and Sex ... Peace and War ...
      Cooperating and Competing

7	**Venus Sign Position Chart 1910–1975**	*70*
8	**Mars Sign Position Chart 1910–1975**	*76*
9	**The Planets As "Stars"** Astrological Cast of Characters	*80*
10	**Astrotrivia—Rating Yourself in the Best Game in Town**	*95*
	I Sun Signs of the Rich and Famous	*95*
	II More Celebrity Sun Sign Lore	*97*
	III Fascinating Facts About the Signs	*99*
	IV Where Do You Belong?	*100*
	V Which Animal Best Suits You?	*102*
11	**Sun Sign Changes 1920–1975**	*105*
12	**ARIES: The Big Picture**	*113*
13	**ARIES: Objectives and Obstacles** A Game Plan for Being the Most Successful ARIES Under the Sun	*116*
14	**Pairing Off with ARIES** Your Compatability with Other Signs of the Zodiac	*121*
15	**The ARIES Sex Role Dilemma**	*126*
16	**The ARIES Female** Child . . . Young Woman . . . Mate . . . Mother	*128*
17	**The ARIES Male** Child . . . Young Man . . . Mate . . . Father	*131*
18	**ARIES Help Wanted** Selecting a Career/Your On-the-Job Style	*134*
19	**How "Pure" an ARIES Are You?** Your Moon Sign . . . Your Rising Sign	*137*
20	**Find Your Rising Sign**	*142*
21	**ARIES Astro-Outlook for 1986**	*145*
22	**Fifteen Months of Day-by-Day Predictions**	*147*

1

Defining Terms

What Are Those Astrologers Talking About?

Everyone knows it is more fun to visit another country if you know a bit of the language, and it's a lot easier to find your way around, too. The same idea applies to astrology, which is still foreign territory to many people. Astrology has its very own language, but it really isn't difficult to get a handle on it as long as you understand a few important terms. What follows is a kind of "Astrological Phrase Book," a brief compendium of the most basic words and concepts in the astrological language. Once you've learned them, you'll find you know a lot more about the why of your sun sign as well as information that will help you understand other astrological factors that make you what you are. Best of all, your new language can help you enjoy and explore one of the most exciting, underdeveloped territories under the sun—modern astrology!

Astrology Is an Ancient and Practical "Science"

The first definition of astrology in the standard dictionary is "astronomy," and at one time in history the two studies were synonymous. The word astrology derives from Greek and literally means "the science (or study) of the stars." However, even in earliest times astrology has had much less to do with the "fixed" stars, which appear to remain in one place, than the planets, which move. (The word "planet" means wanderer.) Early man noticed that, as these heavenly bodies moved, their movements coincided with certain earthly events—mainly the changing of the seasons. Gradually, the movement of the planets was observed to coincide with other important worldly events, such as wars, and the science of "divination" (prediction) by the planets was born. Astronomy and astrology lived happily together until the Christian church banned the latter in about 1550, condemning it as mere superstition. Astrology bounced back in the 1700s, when it came into use as an indicator of human personality, as well as a way to foretell future events. However, this so-called modern astrology is based on the same premise the ancients set down thousands of years ago: "As above, so below." Simply put, what it means is that the positions of the planets, which represent the cosmic order, are related in a significant and observable way to both human behavior and events in human life.

The Zodiac Is a "Circle of Signs"

The zodiac ("circle of animals") is an invisible band in the sky which corresponds to the apparent yearly path of the sun, moon, and the major planets around the earth. It is the "apparent" path in the sense that it is what we *observe* from here on earth. Obviously we know that the earth and other planets revolve around the sun, but the study of astrology (and astronomy) takes earth as the reference point.

The 360-degree circle of the zodiac around the earth is divided into twelve thirty-degree segments—the twelve astrological signs. Throughout the year, as the sun appears to move, it passes through each of these segments in about thirty days. Zero degrees Aries, the vernal equinox or beginning of spring, is the beginning of the zodiac and the start of the seasonal year. It is at that point, on or about March 22, that the sun crosses or intersects with the *ecliptic*—another imaginary band that is (in the mind's eye) the extension of the earth's equator. Another major intersection of the sun's path and the ecliptic takes place at the fall equinox about September 22, the beginning of the seventh sign of the zodiac, Libra. (Equinox means equal days and nights, which is what we experience briefly in the early spring and early fall.) The zodiac "finishes" with the end of the twelfth sign Pisces, about March 21, then begins again with Aries.

Though the segments of the zodiac (the astrological signs) are *named* for the constellations of stars in the sky, they do not correspond with them. The constellations served as convenient visual markers for the ancient astrologer/priests, but the zodiac—and astrology—has always been based on the seasonal year, which never changes. The position of the constellations have changed with reference to our point of view here on earth, however, due to the slipping of the earth's axis. The constellations return a couple of degrees every year and have been doing so for centuries. That's why when the modern *astronomer* says "Aries," he is referring to a group of stars that is in a different position in the sky than the segment of the zodiac the *astrologer* calls "Aries."

Your Sun Sign is Determined by the Month and Day You Were Born

The twelve segments of the zodiac are the twelve astrological signs, from Aries through Pisces, and it takes the sun exactly one year to pass through all twelve signs. A person born when the sun is passing through a particular segment of the zodiac is said to be born under that sign, and it is his/her sun sign. For example, a person born October 14 is said to be born under the sign of Libra. Your sun sign is the most important component of your astrological personality, it is the "real you." However, there are nine other planets besides the sun, and at the moment of a person's birth, those planets are passing through certain segments of the zodiac, or signs, as well. You will learn about some of these lesser influences on your personality in this book later on.

An Element Is Part of a Sign

Obviously your sun sign is a lot more than simply a piece of the sky, or it wouldn't have any meaning. The meaning it has is based on two ancient astrological concepts, the *four elements* and the *three modes*. When these two factors are combined they form the basis of all astrological descriptions of human personality. You can't *see* an element or a quality; they are only to be understood in terms of analogy, but they are fundamental to everything else in astrology, so it is important to understand them.

The four elements, defined by ancient philosophers as the basic components of everything and everybody, are *fire, earth, air,* and *water*. It is doubtful that even in earliest times this breakdown was to be taken as a physical reality: The elements are really four different ways we experience both things and people. For instance, if a thing or a person was experienced as hot rather than cold, sharp rather than dull, active rather than passive, it was said to partake of the *fire* element. And it's easy to see the connection.

Later on, during the Renaissance, the four elements were called "humors," starting a whole new way of typing people. *Fire was the humor choler*, and people who were said to have too much of it were those angry, impatient types who are subject to modern-day diseases like high blood pressure and heart attacks. *The earth element was called black bile* and could cause extreme melancholia (depression) in a person who had too much of it. *Air was the sanguine or rosy humor* and meant a lighter personality. *The water element was the humor phlegm*, and people with too much of it had rather "soggy" personalities and tended to be fat, as well. If the relationship between the elements (or humors) and the signs of the zodiac is beginning to ring a bell, it should. Here's the way the twelve signs break down into elements:

Fire signs: Aries, Leo, Sagittarius
Earth signs: Taurus, Virgo, Capricorn
Air signs: Gemini, Libra, Aquarius
Water signs: Cancer, Scorpio, Pisces

The four elements as four primal types of being exist today in the way many psychologists categorize people's thought processes. Once again, the relationship to the ways in which the twelve astrological signs really do perceive and react to the world is uncannily correct:

The fire signs are instant reactors who put it all together very quickly; things rarely have to be spelled out for a fire sign. These types of people also see the future possibilities inherent in the present and want to bring them about *now*. Obviously, fire signs tend to be impatient, but they have strong wills. Fire is the principle of *action*.

The earth signs are more pragmatic and slower to react. If they can't literally see something or touch it, they have difficulty visualizing it. They operate out of *sense perceptions* and are the realists of the zodiac—the builders who provide stability and continuity. Earth is the principle of *sustenance*.

The air signs see everything as connected to everything else. They are sequential thinkers for whom there must be a beginning, a middle, and an end to everything. For the most part these people operate on *logic* and act only when they can see the sense of their actions. The air signs are endlessly curious and represent the principle of *connecting and reasoning*.

The water signs tend to feel their way through life. What is most real to them is what their emotions tell them; they do what their emotions tell them to do as well. They are imaginative thinkers, the poets and artists of the zodiac. The water principle is that of *caring, nurturing, and protecting*.

A Quality Is Part of a Sign

There are only four elements, but there are twelve signs. In astrological arithmetic, the *three qualities* which divide the *four elements* make up the difference. It isn't easy to grasp the concept of the elements, but the qualities (or "modes" as they are sometimes called) help a lot, because they make the elements a lot more tangible. Called *cardinal*, *fixed*, and *mutable*, the three modes can best be understood as *kinds of motion*.

Cardinal motion is start-up movement. It is the principle of bringing into being. Cardinal goes forward, so, the cardinal signs are *initiators*.

The four cardinal signs are those that start the four seasons:
Aries (*spring*)
Cancer (*summer*)

Libra (*fall*)
Capricorn (*Winter*)

Fixed motion means staying in place. Fixed things have come into being, and now simply are. The fixed signs represent stability, and are difficult to move. The four fixed signs represent the middle of each season:

Tarus (*spring*)
Leo (*summer*)
Scorpio (*fall*)
Aquarius (*winter*)

Mutable motion means flexible motion. Things that are mutable are changing, able to turn into something else. The mutable signs represent the *ability to adjust, and to accept change.* The four mutable signs are those that end the seasons:

Gemini (*spring*)
Virgo (*summer*)
Sagittarius (*fall*)
Pisces (*winter*)

Elements and Qualities Together Add Up to Signs

When you put elements and qualities together you begin to get a picture of what they add up to—the twelve astrological signs. Here is how each quality modifies each element.

Fire element/Cardinal quality = Aries
This get-up-and-go sign has all the flash and dash of fire plus an added dose of a pioneering spirit by virtue of its cardinal quality.

Fire element/Fixed quality = Leo
Leo burns with the ardor and enthusiasms of fire, but gives off very steady heat due to its fixed quality.

Fire element/Mutable quality = Sagittarius
Sagittarius represents the kind of fire that spreads, igniting everything and everybody in its path—which is rather erratic because of Sagittarius's mutable quality.

Earth element /Cardinal quality = Capricorn
Capricorn is the most active builder of the earth signs because of its cardinal quality. Capricorn's brand

of reality demands that something be brought into being.

Earth element/Fixed quality = **Taurus**
This strong sign stands and waits, holding things and people together. Taurus is the warmest and most nurturing of the earth signs, and is always "there."

Earth element/Mutable quality = **Virgo**
Virgo's practical sense knows that all things must change. This mutable sign represents the principle of stability with flux; that is, permanence in the face of change.

Air element/Cardinal quality = **Libra**
Libra's air nature moves forward, actively connecting people and things into partnerships via its cardinal quality of initiation.

Air element/Fixed quality = **Aquarius**
Aquarius is the most immovable of the air signs, representing the permanance of ideas and their practical application.

Air element/Mutable quality = **Gemini**
This very movable sign represents changing thoughts and opinions, the breaking up of static ideas so that new ones can come about.

Water element/Cardinal quality = **Cancer**
Cancer is the most initiating of the water signs because of the cardinal quality. Though shy, Cancer generally moves quietly but effectively to the forefront.

Water element/Fixed quality = **Scorpio**
Scorpio's powerful self-control comes from the emotional water element that is contained and compressed because of this sign's fixed quality.

Water element/Mutable quality = **Pisces**
Pisces extreme emotionalism—as well as this sign's creativity—comes from feelings that constantly change and move into new areas, creating new outlets.

Planets Are the Most Important Factor in Astrology
"Planet" is probably an even more important word in the astrological language than "sign." How can that be?

Because it is the placement of the planets in various signs which indicates personality and it is the movement of the planets through the zodiac that indicates events. In other words, without the planets the signs would have no application to people and what happens to them.

As early man noticed that the planets moved in fairly regular patterns, he began to associate certain characteristics with each of the planets, and each planet gradually took on a "personality." In a number of different cultures, certain planets were hooked up with certain gods, because it was the gods who really controlled life on earth. The moon was virtually always a female god—like Diana or Artemis. Jupiter, always a "good guy" planet, was known as Vishnu, the preserver, to the Hindus. Before he got his Roman name of Jupiter, the Greeks knew him as Zeus, a lusty fellow who had a heart of gold. (You'll get a complete rundown on each of the planets in Chapter p, "The Planets As Stars.")

From these planetary "personalities" came the idea that each planet caused a certain kind of behavior or event by virtue of its own nature. For instance, Mars, always the war god, is still regarded by modern astrologers as an indicator of strife and conflict. When predicting events, the astrologer looks at what sign and what house Mars will be passing through at a certain point in time to see what kind of influence it is most likely to bring into a person's life.

When looking at personality, the astrologer determines which sign a person's Mars is in at the time of the person's birth to see how that individual is most likely to assert him-/herself. The sun, the most important planet makes us what we are in totality according to which sign the sun is placed in at our birth; i.e., our sun sign's Venus is the planet of relationships, and its placement in a specific sign shows how a person is likely to relate to others.

In short, planets indicate *action*, and the signs in which the planets are placed indicate *the kind of action*.

Since ancient times, astrologers have recognized seven planets. The sun (which is really a star), the moon (which is really a satellite of our own planet, earth) Mercury, Venus, Mars, Jupiter, and Saturn.

With the development of the telescope, three more planets were discovered (although there is some evidence that early astrologer/priests divined their existence). Uranus was first spotted in 1781, Neptune in 1846, and Pluto as late as 1930. Some astrologers/astronomers anticipate that there are two more to be found, so that there would be twelve planets instead of the current ten.

A House Is an Area of Life—and a Planet's "Home"

Just as there is a great circle in the sky called the zodiac, and it is divided into twelve equal units of *space*, there is another circle which is based on units of *time*. As we all know, the earth makes one complete rotation on its own axis every twenty-four hours. Imagine yourself standing in one place during a twenty-four-hour period and making a mark on the sky every two hours while that sky appears to pass by you as the earth turns. At the end of twenty-four hours, you will have marked off twelve different units of sky. A "house" is simply one of those pieces of sky that has passed by during your day-long vigil. Toward the end of your day of skywatching, twelve houses will have gone by, and "house one" will be coming up again.

When an astrologer draws up a natal horoscope—which is simply a map of the sky when you were born—he/she does it by drawing a picture of the sky as it appeared from the exact place of birth, at the exact time of your birth. What happens is that the twelve houses are lined up in a very specific way—a very different way than if you had been born *in another place at the same time* or *at the same time in another place.*

What is most important about the particular lineup of the houses is that each house represents a different area of human life, and how those areas are positioned *for you* has a tremendous effect on your astrological makeup. For instance, the second house is the house of income and personal possessions and has a lot to do with attitude toward money and how easy or how difficult it will be to come by in your lifetime. The seventh house is the house of partnership and offers clues about who you are likely to marry. If you know the time of your birth within one hour or so, you can add a very important dimension to your astrological self-knowledge by reading the chapter "Your House of the Sun—Your 'Piece of the Pie,'" because the house of the horoscope into which the sun falls in your horoscope usually indicates what area of life will absorb you during your lifetime.

Your Rising Sign Is the One that Starts the First House

Your rising sign is sometimes called the ascendant, because it is the sign of the zodiac that was "ascending" on the eastern horizon at the time of your birth, no matter what time your birth occured. It is the "sunrise sign," corresponding to the nine o'clock position on the face of an ordinary clock. The astrologer's "clock" starts at this position and is read counter-clockwise around the circle of the face. If you were born around sundown, your rising sign will be the one 180 degrees *opposite* the sign you were born under. For instance, if you are an Aries born at sundown, your rising sign will be Libra. If you are an Aries born at sunrise, your rising sign is probably Aries as well.

Why is your rising sign so important? Because it starts the first house of personality, or your very individual way of presenting yourself to the world. No matter what your sun sign is, your rising sign will cover it to a greater or lesser degree (which is why it is so difficult to guess someone's Sun Sign when you first meet them). The rising sign has to do with appearances and can actually influence your physical looks.

If you don't know the time of day you were born, you can't determine your rising sign (although some astrologers can by doing what is called a "rectification," based on the events in your life so far). However, even those who do not know their rising sign can have their horoscopes read; what the astrologer does is put your sun sign on the first house, and do an analysis of what is called a solar horoscope. If you *do* know your birthtime within an hour or so, you can use the rising sign chart in this book to determine yours.

Planets in Signs in Houses Make Up a Horoscope

The whole basis of astrology is that anyone born in a particular moment in time partakes of the qualities of that moment in time. Actually, the same applies for things; for instance, a business that has its beginnings at a precise astrological moment also has a horoscope which can be read, and tells a lot about its potential for success or failure.

An astrologer looks at the particular moment in drawing up a horoscope—or "picture of the hour." A horoscope is basically a map of the sky, showing exactly where the planets were in relation to the signs and the houses, to each other, and from the particular reference point of your birthplace. It is also called a "natal chart" or "natal map."

Everyone's horoscope has ten planets and twelve houses. Those ten planets can be in a variety of signs, and in a variety of houses. Each planet means something different according to its own nature, how that nature operates in a particular sign, and what area of life the planet is most likely to affect by virtue of which house of the horoscope it falls into. Sound complicated? It is, and only a highly trained astrologer can interpret the many factors and put them together for you in a meaningful way. The most exciting part of astrology is the fact that *no two individuals are ever exactly alike*—not even twins, who are born a few minutes apart.

Although you can find out a lot about your astrological personality right in this book, many people like to take the next step and have a personalized horoscope drawn up for them and interpreted by a professional astrologer. There are a number of ways to find a good person to do this for you; in astrology, as in every other profession, there are variations in the level of competence. Two places you can start your search are:

National Astrological
  Society
62 West 39th St.
New York, NY 10018

American Federation of
  Astrologers
Tempe, AZ 85282

An Aspect Is the Distance Between Planets

Among the more sophisticated factors an astrologer looks for in your horoscope are the *aspects*. Within the 360-degree circle of the horoscope (and the zodiac), planets form certain aspects to each other by virtue of the distance between them. Some distances are considered harmonious, and some are inharmonious, in terms of how those two (or more) planets work together. It's all a matter of mathematics. The soft or harmonious aspects are the sextile (60 degrees apart) and the trine (120 degrees apart). The hard or inharmonious aspects are formed when planets are in square to each other (90 degrees apart) or in opposition, 180 degrees or exactly half a circle apart. These are only the major aspects, and there are lots and lots of minor ones between, but you can get a good picture of interplanetary relationships with only these few.

For example, if your sun sign is Aries, and at the time of your birth the planet Saturn was in the sign of Libra, or 180 degrees away from Aries, you are likely to have a more serious (Saturnine) disposition than the typical "happy" Aries. Depending on your point of view, this can be a positive note in your horoscope, because you will have greater powers of concentration than many an Aries—or a negative note, because you will be less happy-go-lucky. In another example, a person with a Capricorn sun sign may have a horoscope in which Jupiter, the planet of expansiveness, is 120 degrees away from the sun—either in the sign of Virgo or Taurus— and therefore in "trine" aspect to his/her sun. The result: a much more outgoing, giving Capricorn than the run-of-the-mill type. On the other hand, such an easy aspect could expand Capricorn's acquisitive nature too much, and make for a megalomanic (someone who craves worldly goods and power).

The ancients separated aspects into "favorable" and "unfavorable," but psychologically-thinking modern astrologers know that it is not that simple; it all depends on the total horoscope, plus the individual's reactions to the particular vibrations of the planets in that horoscope.

A Transiting Planet Affects Your Life Now

When someone goes to an astrologer for the first time, he/she usually has *two* readings—separate, but interrelated. The first will be an interpretation of your natal chart or birth horoscope. This tells you about your given personality—the traits, problems, abilities, and advantages you are most likely to have by virtue of the placement of the planets in the sky at the time of your birth. The second reading will have to do with what you can expect in your life at the present time and the near future. Your birth horoscope always remains the same, but the planets in the sky keep changing their relationships to your birth horoscope throughout your lifetime. The astrologer will acquaint you with the current "transit"—or movements—of the planets and how you, the individual, can expect them to affect you. For instance, if an astrologer notes that Uranus, the "earthquake planet," is approaching your fourth house (the house of emotional security, the place where we really live), the astrologer might alert you to the fact that big changes are in the offing: even a total shaking of the foundations, or a pulling up of roots. This is a major transit, and many people change their residence, partners, or jobs when it occurs. Similarly, but on a less critical note, the astrologer may notice that the planet Venus is going to make a transit over the place in the zodiac occupied by Mars in your birthchart. This could indicate a firey romantic interlude or the rekindling of an old flame.

There are two important things to keep in mind about astrological predictions. The first is that your natal horoscope—your "birth imprint"—really determines how you will react to life's events. To put it even more strongly, your innate personality will really *create* the events of your life, because "character is destiny." There is no doubt that the planets create conditions, but we must take responsibility for how we cooperate with those conditions. The second thing is that *there are very few hard and fast rules.* There are guidelines, to be sure, and most of them have ancient roots; a lot of astrological prediction is based on the case history technique. However, since no two sets of conditions—

the one in the sky and the one in an individual birthchart—are ever *exactly* the same, it is virtually impossible for any astrologer to tell you specifically what is going to happen.

2

Your House of the Sun

Your "Piece of the Pie"

The prime symbol in the very symbolic language of astrology is the perfect circle; it represents the sky around us, the cosmic atmosphere into which we are all born. All astro-math is based on division of the 360-degree figure, which since ancient times has been regarded as having mystical qualities. When thinking about the houses of the horoscope, however, it helps to use a very down-to-earth analogy. Look at that circle as a great "pie in the sky," which is divided into twelve cosmic slices—each slice representing one house and a different facet of human experience.

Just as there are ten planets in everyone's horoscope, there are twelve houses. However, not all those houses may be occupied by a planet; it all depends on where the planets were in the sky at the moment of your birth. The placement of any planet in a specific house is a *very* important factor in your individual horoscope, but the most important is the placement of the sun. No matter what your sun sign, your House of the Sun has a lot to tell you about the life you've been "given" to live on this earth. As your sun sign is the prime indicator of *character and personality,* your house of the sun points to the *area of human affairs* that you are most likely to find yourself concentrating on in your lifetime.

In the sense that it helps define the boundaries of your life, your house of the sun is your "piece of the pie"—that slice of life within which you will live. Does your house of the sun totally box you in? In a way it does, but it is more productive to think of the dimensions of your house of the sun as *guidelines* about where you can most profitably focus your energies.

Here's the way it works:

- The *sun* is the most important planet in your horoscope. It is the planets that do the "acting," and the sun plays the leading role.
- Your sun sign determines *how* your sun (the real you) acts, i.e., the characteristics of the character you play.
- Your house of the sun is the "stage" on which you will play out your role.

For instance, if your sun sign is Scorpio (the great investigator) and your house of the sun is the twelfth (hidden things), you find yourself drawn to some kind of career in which you must "dig" to do your investigating. Ergo, you might make a good psychoanalyst, archeologist, or genetic researcher. Or, your greatest pleasure in life might be reading mystery novels or spy thrillers—or writing or editing them.

In order to figure out which piece of the pie you've been served, you have to know your birth-time within an hour or so. If you were born during Daylight Savings Time or War Time, you have to subtract one hour from your birth time to determine the "real sun time."

Each house is described here from three different angles:

- The matters or principles connected with it
- The people/places/things related to it
- The problems and the possibilities of having your sun in that house.

Birth time, 4 to 6 a.m.: **Sun in First House**

- *First house matters:* Exploration . . . use of the physical body . . . being on the scene . . . breaking new ground . . . independent action . . . emergencies . . . conquest . . . controversy . . . strategy . . . competition . . . being in the vanguard.

- *First house people/places/things:* Entrepreneurs ... acrobats ... cutting instruments ... rock music ... metals ... satire ... hardware ... the head and face ... opticians ... adrenalin ... new products ... commodities ... salesmen ... fighters ... firemen.
- *Problems and possibilities:* With your sun in the first house, your sun sign personality is quite strong. Regardless of what your sun sign is, you should be able to make clear-cut decisions and have a good sense of your own identity. If you are to gain control over your life, you are going to have to banish fear from it and develop both the moral and the physical courage that is available to you. Though your will should be strong, you will have to keep yourself from a tendency to tyrannize others. When you feel most defeated is the time your first house sun will come to your rescue. The one thing that could keep you from living out the very vivid life this house placement gives you is inflexibility and intolerance. Be willing to listen.

Birth time, 2 to 4 a.m.: **Sun in Second House**

- *Second house matters:* Calmness ... conservation ... ability to make grow ... eroticism ... collecting ... comforting ... administrating ... luxury ... stabilizing ... building up ... perpetuating ... patience ... using ... making stronger ... indulging.
- *Second house people/places/things:* Possessions ... money ... the voice ... landscape gardeners ... brokers and bankers ... love/passion ... personal adornment ... life-sustaining skills ... buying and selling ... security needs ... nurses ... food and shelter ... good music ... creature comforts.
- *Problems and possibilities:* You should be able to establish yourself firmly and securely in whatever you choose to do; self-adjustment should come easily to you. Your economic life could be relatively worry-free but you must resist valuing money and

possessions for their own sake and becoming overly materialistic. You must develop the will that is given you and turn it into willpower, or you could lose self-respect. You are a good manager, but if you allow yourself to become too settled, you will fear to take the necessary risks to make your life less limited. Though things come to you fairly easily, do not let yourself over-indulge in any of them, including rich food.

Birth time midnight to 2 a.m.: **Sun in Third House**

- *Third house matters:* Connecting ... associating ... verbalizing ... dexterity ... inquisitiveness ... distribution ... novelty ... thinking and reasoning ... cause and effect ... exchanging ... bringing the news ... being responsive ... "here today, gone tomorrow."
- *Third house people/places/things:* Short journeys ... realatives (especially siblings) ... speech/languages ... high school teachers ... role-playing/entertaining ... computers ... graphic arts ... handwork ... transportation ... the nervous system ... handwriting .. repair men ... gossip ... comedy ... ventriloquists.
- *Problems and possibilities:* You should be an excellent communicator who reports things clearly and accurately. In your desire for information, however, you could become rather superficial and a bit of a talebearer. If you don't focus your mental energies carefully, you may waste the gift of curiosity your third house sun gives you. You must also learn to live with uncertainty, and to keep your opinions flexible. If life scares you, you are likely to become very defensive and locked in to your ideas. Develop your capacity for listening as well as your talent for talking.

Birth time 10 p.m. to 12 a.m.: **Sun in Fourth House**

- *Fourth house matters:* Adaptability ... change ... instinctiveness ... fluctuation ... protecting ...

imagination ... softness ... the subconscious ... survival ... enveloping ... integrating ... fertility ... mothering.
- *Fourth house people/places/things:* Dreams ... the past ... roots ... home and family ... physical sensation ... museums ... caterers ... water and other liquid ... introverts ... obstetrics ... boats ... domestics ... imagination.
- *Problems and possibilities:* Via your fourth house sun, you are given the possibility of understanding yourself and your motivations quite thoroughly. If you handle your life in a mature way, you will establish a warm and comfortable home for you and your family. However, you must strive for real self-knowledge if you are not to become simply self-absorbed and self-centered. Your imagination is considerable, and you could be highly creative; the down side is that you could develop irrational fears that verge on paranoia. Work to see the world clearly at all times and try to conquer your tendency to play the introvert. No mater what your sun sign, the placement of that sun in the fourth house will make you instinctively avoid the limelight. Get out there and shine!

Birth time 8 to 10 p.m.: **Sun in Fifth House**

- *Fifth house matters:* Being at the heart of things ... pleasures ... power ... ambition ... generosity/giving ... "gilding the lily" ... showmanship ... stability ... management ... territorial rights ... self-expression ... autocracy ... organization.
- *Fifth house people/places/things:* Philanthropy ... corporations ... impresarios ... holidays and vacations ... romantic love ... children ... gamblers ... gold ... circuses ... nursery teachers ... fashion and fashion designers ... public life.
- *Problems and possibilities:* Even if you have a "shy" sun sign, your fifth house placement of the sun will force you into some form of self-expression that is possibly very creative. You also have a capability

for approaching life with a joyful, expectant manner; however, your pursuit of pleasure and play could become extreme. Consciously avoid any pleasure that threatens to get out of control. Your affairs of the heart could be many, but it is important to keep alert for anything that smacks of an abusive partner; it's possible you could enjoy the drama of an unhappy situation. Develop your capacity for warmly accepting others.

Birth time 6 to 8 p.m.: **Sun in Sixth House**

- *Sixth house matters:* Competence/skill ... specialization ... refining ... categorizing ... analyzing ... obedience ... realism ... responsibility ... purifying ... invention ... making things work ... ministering ... discriminating.
- *Sixth house people/places/things:* Service ... critics ... crafts ... libraries ... closets ... public health ... the harvest ... small animals ... dependents ... dental hygienists ... research ... diagnosing ... numbers work ... chemists.
- *Problems and possibilities:* With your sun in the sixth house you have the potential of becoming a true master at something; however, if you allow yourself to get bogged down in life's details, you could possibly end up being a wage slave. No matter what your sun sign, your instincts tell you to be of service to others. While you are capable of great self-sacrifice, you must avoid the temptation to be overly humble and to assume the servant role. You are mentally very keen, and can break things and jobs down into smaller parts in order to accomplish them. Do not let the state of your own health become an obsession. With the sun is the sixth house, your basic constitution should be quite strong. Don't worry!

Birth time 4 to 6 p.m.: **Sun in Seventh House**

- *Seventh house matters:* Sharing ... comparing ... give-and-take ... peacemaking ... negotiation ...

making things beautiful ... creating balance ... fairness ... sociability ... gratification ... advocacy ... diplomacy ... aestheticism.

- *Seventh house people/places/things:* Divorce lawyers ... love poetry ... marriage brokers ... the kidneys and lower back ... illustration ... resort managers ... public relations ... fine arts ... receptionists ... boutiques ... jugglers ... tailors ... pianos.
- Possibilities and problems: You have a great need to identify with others, and can create a wonderful rapport with them easily. However, your need for a life partner could make you overly dependent. If you have an independent sun sign, this could create a serious life conflict. With this placement, you are able to adjust to new people and new situations easily, but you must avoid a tendency not to stick with a position when you really believe in it. You have the potential of forming very warm, balanced and intimate relationships; however, if you do not handle this gift in a mature manner, you could develop a fear of intimacy, and shy away from it or become an outrageous and insincere flirt.

Birth time 2 to 4 p.m.: **Sun in Eighth House**

- *Eighth house matters:* Release of blockages ... probing ... anonymity ... procreation ... rejuvenation ... willpower ... endurance ... controlling ... investigation ... aloneness ... demolishing and rebuilding ... crisis ... elimination.
- *Eighth house people/places/things:* Puzzles ... generals ... political parties ... labor lawyers ... the healing arts ... death and dying ... taxes ... spies ... superathletes ... crime detection ... statesmen ... sex symbols ... geologists ... explorers ... mating instinct ... sanitation engineers.
- *Problems and possibilities:* A light sun sign (like Gemini or Libra), the placement of the sun in this house will add depth to your character. You will feel compelled to investigate things that are hidden or

even dangerous. While it is good to probe, you must beware of a tendency to concentrate on what is morbid. All things being equal, you will be highly sexed; however, with insufficient self-knowledge, your healthy sexual instincts could turn into obsession with the subject—or a total advoidance of it. Learn to live with your dynamic physical body and you will live with others quite happily. Also, encourage your religious or mystical feelings, which are quite real. You have the potential of totally transforming your life at one point or another.

Birth time noon to 2 p.m.: **Sun in Ninth House**

- *Ninth house matters:* Anticipating ... aspiring ... moving around ... expanding things ... speculating ... idealism ... advising ... unpredictability ... search for truth ... search for opportunity ... taking aim ... magnanimity ... excess.
- *Ninth house people/places/things* Casinos ... ambassadors ... passport offices ... luck ... international transportation ... trading/high finance ... dancers ... aristocrats ... large animals ... higher studies ... lawmaking ... profiteers ... veterinarians.
- *Problems and possibilities:* Even if you have a routine-loving sun sign (like Virgo), this placement of the sun will give you the desire and the ability to constantly renew your life, and to adapt to new patterns of behavior. You will feel strongly about one religious or ethical system or another, or at least have a very strong personal philosophy. However, you could become rather dogmatic and rigid in your opinions. Your adaptability is admirable, but a desire for the new and novel could be the "downside" of your openness to new experience. Exercise control. With certain sun signs, there may be a tendency toward inner battles between opportunity-seeking and a firm set of principles. You are a spender—of both your money and your physical resources.

Birth time 10 a.m. to 12 a.m.: **Sun in Tenth House**

- *Tenth house matters:* Realism ... structure ... ambition ... rigidity ... integrating ... limitation ... disciplining ... reputation ... social position ... creating the useful ... contraction ... coolness ... convention.
- *Tenth house people/places/things:* Figures ... fame ... common sense ... property ... correctional systems and facilities ... ceramics ... money lenders ... efficiency experts ... the bones ... the elderly ... sculptors ... watches and clocks.
- *Problems and possibilities:* You have the capacity of becoming a respected member of whatever group you move in, because your public image is very important to you. If you play your cards right, you can arrive at a sense that you are fulfilling your destiny. However, if you become obsessed with power and appearances, you could end up living a shallow, meaningless life behind your strong facade. It is most important with this placement of the sun to find the right outlet for you to express yourself and get positive feedback from others. You won't be happy starving in a garret, because both money and recognition are too important to you. This position of the sun often brings fame.

Birth time 8 to 10 a.m.: **Sun in Eleventh House**

- *Eleventh house matters:* Helping ... experimentation ... humanitarianism ... association ... liberalism .. freedom ... suddenness ... awakenings ... combining ... freethinking ... rationality ... caring ... breaking through ... observing coolly ... predicting.
- *Eleventh house people/places/things:* Paradoxes ... stunt men ... electricity ... zealots ... divorce ... fireworks ... the social sciences ... reform ... geniuses ... aviation ... weathermen ... brotherly love ... magnetism ... groups ... friends ... causes.
- *Problems and possibilities:* If you are a very personal

sun sign (like Cancer), you will gain a lot of objectivity with the placement of the sun in this house. You should have very high aims and goals, and some of them will undoubtedly involve helping the less fortunate in some way or another. Though this is admirable, if you don't set yourself on a definite path in life and stick to a definite plan, you could simply drift along, with only vague ideas about where you can shine. It is important to be quite realistic with the sun in this house. Your own crowd is important to you, but you must avoid becoming such a part of the group that you lose a sense of your own individuality—which is potentially very great. Some people with the sun in the 11th house are downright wacky, but often very achieving people.

Birth Time 6 to 8 a.m.: **Sun in Twelfth House**

- *Twelfth house matters:* Dissolving ... ambiguity ... disguising ... retreating ... sensualism ... enchantment ... paying dues ... healing spiritually ... insubstantiality ... confinement ... persuading ... comprehending the incomprehensible ... merging ... pretending.
- *Twelfth house people/places/things:* Makeup ... escapism ... alcohol and drugs ... drama and dramatic actors ... films ... advertising ... pastoral work ... fishing ... astrophysics ... con men ... magicians ... hospitals ... alibis ... myths ... prisons.
- *Problems and possibilities:* Yours is not an easy house of the sun to have—especially if you are a very self-expressive sun sign type like Leo. You may feel that life is confining you in some way or another; what you are really sensing is your gift of the ability to transcend self to a much higher spiritual level. You should be an expert at coping with intangibles and sensing the nuances of any situation. In a sense, you have a kind of ESP which can be developed for life success. However, the real down side of the twelfth house sun is that it

can lead to a very confused, unfocussed attitude toward life. It is essential that you give yourself a definite structure to work within if you are to free yourself from the worries and cares of life. By all means avoid any form of escapism that is dangerous.

3

The Geometry of Relationships

What Signs You Get Along with—and Why

The first thing most people want to know about their sun sign is what other signs they are compatible with. It's a natural question, and a good one to ask an astrologer, because one aspect of astrology, called "synastry" (literally, "stars together") concentrates on the subject of relationships. When practising synastry, the astrologer compares the two birth charts of the two people involved to find what connections there are between them. It is a complicated process, but it provides excellent clues about how two people will relate to each other. What chart comparison does is *describe the nature of the relationship*. Actually, to an astrologer there are no "bad" or "good" relationships; there are just a lot of different kinds and each has a special character. Of course it is true that some relationships end up on the rocks, sometimes devastating one or both parties involved. But, even in such cases, the astrologer looks at it as a "karmic" relationship—one in which people *had* to come together in order to learn some life lessons.

While comparing two complete horoscopes is the ideal way to look at a relationship, there is a very simple method of looking at two sun signs, and coming up with an overall prediction of how two people will relate to each other. This method goes back to the great circle of the zodiac and to the division of the twelve signs into four elements: fire, earth, air, and water.

Here's the lineup of signs in each element:

Fire: Aries, Leo, Sagittarius

Earth: Taurus, Virgo, Capricorn
Air: Gemini, Libra, Aquarius
Water: Cancer, Scorpio, Pisces

The general rules of thumb for element-mixing are as follows:

Great	Good	Semi-tough or Difficult
Fire and air	Fire and fire	Fire and water
Water and earth	Earth and earth	Earth and air
	Air and air	Fire and earth
	Water and water	Air and water

Here's the way it looks mathmatically:

If you divide the 360-degree circle of the zodiac by the twelve signs, you find that each sign is 30 degrees away from the next.

- Signs that are 30 degrees apart—or next to each other—are semi-tough.
- Signs that are 60 degrees (two signs) or 180 degrees (six signs) away from each other are the best combinations. (The latter, 180 degrees away from each other, makes these signs polar opposites, and in astrology polar opposites attract.)
- Signs that are 120 degrees apart—four signs away from each other—are in the same element, and their relationship is good, but far from perfect.
- Signs that are 90 degrees or three signs away from each other have the most difficult relationships of all. They are said to be in "square aspect" to each other.

When you look at the four elements in terms of what they signify in the physical world, you get a good idea why some elements get along more easily.

Fire turns water into steam (hot air).
Water puts fire out.
Fire scorches earth.

Earth smothers fire.
Air fans fire and makes it brighter.
Fire warms up cool air.
Water softens up hard earth.
Earth makes water keep its shape.
Water and air do nothing (unless you add heat).
Air blows earth around.

What about combinations of the same element, such as fire with fire? In effect, they tend to neutralize or cancel each other out. Or, they can simply be too much of one element for comfort.

- Two fire signs together could experience "burn out" fairly quickly.
- Two air signs might analyze each other to the death of the relationship.
- Two earth signs could depress each other a lot.
- Two water signs could make for an overly "heavy" relationship.

4

Twelve Places at the Table

A Mini Astrodrama in Which the Twelve Signs Play Themselves

No matter how accurate or colorful any description of a zodiac sign may be, it is still a description—not the real thing. A sign is simply an abstract concept until it takes form in a living, breathing human being. There are obviously as many different types of people as there are individual horoscopes, and no two are exactly alike. However, the twelve signs of the zodiac are still the best guidelines we have for sorting out human behavior into broad but meaningful categories. There are even fiction writers who use the zodiac signs as prototypes for characters they create because it makes them more realistic, i.e., more like people you are likely to meet.

What follows is fiction, but it gets closer to the truth about each zodiacal sign than a general description ever can. The twelve characters in this docudrama are obviously caricatures, because their behavior is highly exaggerated. But it is exaggeration for emphasis, and for the purpose of bringing to life the twelve signs of the zodiac, which don't really exist except as real people. Like real people, these twelve characters have foibles; but they have fine points too. As you read this drama, you may find yourself drawn to some signs and put off by others. Make mental notes of which signs you find yourself most sympathetic with and check out your findings in the parts of this book about astrological compatibility. It could prove very interesting—

and very revealing. As each sign of the zodiac has a sex or gender, they are portrayed here as male or female accordingly. But the basic behavior pattern is applicable to both sexes.

The twelve signs of the zodiac are invited to dinner at that great dining room in the sky. When they arrive, they find that their host (who shall remain signless) has slipped up, and there are only eleven places set at the table. Since it is a fancy affair, each sign is trying to be on his/her best behavior. However, the situation is a bit unsettling, so in the course of trying to resolve it, they all relapse into their natural zodiacal characteristics.

Aries An energetic young man, he comes bounding into the room, almost tripping on an untied shoelace. He is dressed rather casually for the occasion, and looks as if he got dressed rather quickly. When he realizes what the situation is, there's no doubt in his mind how to handle it.

"Only eleven places? Don't worry; Pisces will probably never show anyway. But, I got here before anybody else (the doorman will prove it) so I should definitely get a seat. In fact, I should sit down *first*. No, I don't need to wash my hands or anything. I'm *starved*, so I hope you aren't having anything like the gooey mess with the French name you had before. A hamburger will do just fine. And don't serve it cold like you did the last time. Hey, there's a great-looking dish over there, ha ha! Seat me next to her, will you Cancer? Well, she looks like a nice warm type, so I think I'll go let her warm me up. By the way, I'm organizing a sky-diving club. Want to join? Seriously, if you can't afford the membership fee, I'll put it up for you, because I'd love to have you join. Oh, you're doing okay now? Glad to hear you're off the rack. Got any pretzels?"

Taurus An attractive young woman with faint dimples in her roundish cheeks and a slightly unruly but pretty mass of curly hair comes sauntering into the room. She is dressed in a soft and pretty outfit that looks expensive, and has her handbag clutched tightly under her arm. She looks around the room with moderate curiosity. As the host walks up to her, she gives him a warm smile; when she speaks, her voice is low and melodious—but firm.

"Only eleven places? You mean, only eleven *chairs*. All you have to do is set another place and give me a pillow to sit on. I don't mind, as long as I'm comfortable. And I smell something wonderful, so I know the food is going to be delicious. To be honest with you, that's really why I came. I don't like to go out much, you know. What I really like is curling up in my warm and comfy bed—with someone warm and comfy, of course. (Are you busy later on?) But, now that I'm *here*, there's no way I'm not going to eat. What's for dessert? Who's that nervous-looking lady over there? Virgo? I'll go try to make her feel comfortable."

Gemini It's hard to tell just how old this fellow is as he springs in the door; he could be any age, though he looks about eighteen. He is dressed in the very latest style, though nothing he has on is really extreme. His eyes dart all over the room, and he is carrying a notebook under his arm. When the host tells him about the eleven places, he is so busy listening to another conversation, he almost misses it. When he reacts, it is in a typically casual way.

"Don't worry about me; I don't need a place. I'll just float around the room, because what I really came here for is the conversation. I'm writing a book, you know—it's called *1001 Opening Conversational Gambits* and tonight I'm researching. I see you've got some really fascinating types here. How did you make up the guest list? Are they all married? Why did they come alone? What's the menu? Who's the chef? Can I see the wine list? Who's that blowsy-looking type over there? Taurus? I'll bet *she's* got a story. Where's the telephone? I've got to make a call."

Cancer A sexy, voluptuous woman of indeterminate age pauses at the door; she seems shy, but conscious of the impression she is making. Her clothes are a bit unusual, and some things are from the thrift shop. However, her antique jewelry is genuine, and the whole effect is glamorous. When she discovers there are only eleven places, she is visibly upset, and there is a touch of a whine in her voice as she speaks.

"I wish I'd known; I could have stayed home with the children. They have colds, you know. If you want, I'll simply leave; but I really don't want to go home by myself; I'll get scared and have bad dreams. Upset? Yes, I am upset, and when I get upset I can't eat. Unless it's really soothing and nourishing. Did you know that a touch of heavy cream in mashed potatoes is simply heavenly? Chicken soup? I make it by the gallon. Say, you look as if you could stand a little fattening up. Well, all right. I *guess* I'll stay—unless I change my mind, of course."

Leo   This is a fine figure of a man—fairly tall, rather muscular, and with a thick crop of curly hair that is somewhere between blond and red. He is elegantly dressed and his gold cufflinks probably put a real drain on Fort Knox. His grand entrance is smooth and practised, and his handshake is hearty and warm. When his host tells him the news, he takes it very personally.

"Well, let me tell you, this is embarrassing! I mean, all these people here to see me, and I may have to stand? I've given bigger parties than this, and they've always gone off without a hitch. Let me handle things for you the next time. For now, just get that chair over there and squeeze someone in—Virgo won't mind. No, *here*; not *there!* While we're all waiting I guess I can entertain everyone with my tantrum act. What? No, I'm only kidding—though I am mad. I'll do my Hamlet number instead. Like my cufflinks? They match my Gold Card. I've ordered another pair with sapphires, too."

Virgo   A rather prim woman stands quietly at the door looking as if she would like to blend into the woodwork. She is dressed very neatly, but conservatively, with flat-heeled sensible shoes. In her handbag she carries a surgical mask to wear in case any of the other guests has a cold. Her reaction to the news that there are only eleven places is swift and shrill.

"Well, it certainly isn't *my* fault. I answered the invitation the minute I got it. I *always* do! Why didn't you check on things more carefully? If you had, this wouldn't have happened, and you wouldn't have all these people standing around thinking terrible things about you. I don't mind for myself, you understand, I don't eat much anyway; you never know what you're going to get. I'll stay in the kitchen and help the cook clean up. You can't be too careful about these things, you know. You wouldn't believe the sanitary conditions I've found in *some* kitchens. Not mentioning any names, of course. Oh, *why* did you mess things up this way; you are simply impossible. . . ."

Intermission: Our host walks away as Virgo continues to complain. As he checks on the guests, he discovers that Libra has just arrived. Sagittarius and Pisces are nowhere to be found, but Scorpio, Capricorn, and Aquarius are waiting to greet him. Because he looks like he's a bit uncomfortable, the host talks to Libra first.

Libra A very attractive male, wearing all the right things, walks tentatively into the room, looking as if he is searching for someone. He is visibly uncomfortable alone. His gaze scans the room, quietly appraising everything and everybody in it. He seems to approve, but in his nervousness, he approaches the table, and starts rearranging one of the settings, then rearranging it again. All this is done very tactfully and gracefully. In fact, he looks as if he couldn't make an awkward gesture if he tried. His host approaches him and breaks the news. Libra's reaction is smooth and unruffled.

"Oh, how *clever* of you to arrange this little puzzle for us. It will make things so much more fun. Of course, we've got to make things absolutely fair; we wouldn't want to hurt anyone's feelings. I could leave if it would help, but . . . Oh, how nice of you to tell me I'll definitely have a place; it makes me feel a lot less awkward. I rarely go places alone, you know. Who would I like to sit next to? Well, the Capricorn lady looks like a sturdy and sensible type. But on the other hand, Scorpio is a *knockout*. Is she attached? Hmmm, Taurus looks like she'd like to chat, but oh, that Cancer! Decisions, decisions; I'll make up my mind later on. Where did you get that *great* painting?

Scorpio A slim and sexy woman dressed totally in black comes slinking into the room. Her style and movement are absolutely magnetic, and every eye turns to look at her. But she gives no visible response that she is aware of it. She doesn't seem to be feeling anything at all, but when her host approaches and tells her what is going on, she is seething with quiet rage.

"Do you really think you are going to get away with this? I suspected something when I got that weird invitation. Who in the world would ever come as they are and let everybody else know what they're really like? No matter how many times you tell me it was an innocent mistake to set only eleven places, I'll never believe it. Nothing in this world is innocent. And when it comes to drawing straws, just remember you owe me one from the last time. You know, the *last* time! Who's that wimpy looking guy over there? Gemini? Maybe I'll amuse myself with him for a while. I need a new conquest; I'm getting out of practice."

Sagittarius While Scorpio has been talking with the host, a tall rather rangy male has come loping into the room carrying a suitcase. He is a bit disheveled because his flight was late. He throws the suitcase in a corner and starts putting himself back together—a bit absentmindedly because he is looking around the room with a big smile and a lot of anticipation. He moves toward the host and gives a slap on his back that is almost *too* hearty.

"Only eleven places? Why worry? We'll work it out somehow. Life's too short to get uptight anyway. Had the greatest trip, and I'm turning right around tomorrow and going to the Orient so I can practice my Chinese. Say, are you serving Chinese food? I love Chinese food—and a good beer to go with it. At least I hope you're serving better wine than you did last time. You're looking a little pale . . . been partying too much lately? Ha ha, only kidding. Who's that guy over there with the flashy cufflinks? And the mouse with the sensible shoes? Think I'll see if I can loosen her up a bit. Did you hear I'm going to win the lottery again? What do you mean, how do I know? I just *know*. And I've got a great idea for an international fast food chain I'm going to bankroll with my winnings. I'm gonna call it 'The Great Gobler' and serve only turkey sandwiches. Hey, I'm thirsty. Where's the bar?"

Aquarius An intellectual-looking gentleman—sort of an absentminded professor type—has been standing in the doorway quietly puffing his pipe and scrutinizing the crowd. His jacket and pants don't match, but he isn't aware of it. An even stranger—but typical—sartorial note is his electric blue tie with orange stripes. He's got his earphones with him; if things get too dull, he'll listen to some hard rock or electronic music and be in seventh heaven. When he finds out about the missing place, he gives a thoughtful answer and makes an impractical suggestion.

"Oh, well, rather than make anyone feel left out, we could cancel the whole dinner and bring the food to the local shelter for the homeless. Ah, you don't care for that idea. Too bad; I'm becoming more and more concerned about poverty in our own backyard. Of course, I'm no bleeding heart like Pisces, but fair's fair. Want to hear about a new invention I'm working on? It's an electronic stamp sorter that will revolutionize the whole philatelic world. Huh? Oh, that's stamp collecting. Glad you asked me to come alone, since I'm free as a bird now. My last attachment got so *sticky!* I've sworn off. At least off those emotional types who want you to get so involved. No, I never get lonely—I've got too many friends for that. By the way, I can just sit on the floor in the lotus position, and get some meditating in at the same time."

Capricorn A rather handsome, perfectly put together woman has been quietly observing the crowd and the room, mentally putting a price tag on everything. What she has on is very expensive, but understated and in excellent taste. In her handbag she carries a petition with her name on it. She wants to run for local office, and is hoping to pick up some supporters tonight. If they are "her kind of people," that is. Her reaction to the host's situation is sober but logical.

"Well, it's obvious someone will have to go, but I

trust your judgment to decide who is most important—if you know what I mean. Your appointments are in excellent taste; I see you like Tiffany as much as I do. Who's that rather tacky looking type over there? Cancer? Where *does* she get her clothes? I have little sympathy for people who can't get their act together and run their lives successfully. She's probably a poet. Ah, well, different strokes for different folks; fantasy has no place in *my* life, you know. By the way, I have some excellent ideas about how to shape things up in the community; will you sign my petition? At dinner, are we going to discuss great books? I just bought a whole series . . . all leather-bound, of course. They look smashing in my living room."

Pisces Meanwhile, a rather wispy but very pretty woman has been wandering in and out of the doorway, looking as if she isn't quite sure she is in the right place. She is dressed in a misty fabric of very pale colors; there doesn't seem to be a clear-cut edge anywhere. In fact, if you don't rub your eyes, you might think you are seeing an apparition. The host knows it's Pisces and catches her just as she's about to drift out the door again. He doesn't bother telling her about the missing place, because he knows she wouldn't understand why that was important.

"Late? Am I late? I lost my watch two weeks ago. Or was it three? Oh well, what's time anyway in the larger scheme of things? Hungry? Not really, though I can't remember the last time I ate. *Love*—it's *love* that's food for the soul, and that's what I care about nourishing. I wonder if any of these people have had any *real* soul food lately. No, don't worry, I won't try to convert anyone tonight. I'm too, too drained because of my current work. What kind? Well, it really isn't a job-job, I mean where you make money, and all. I've started a shelter for homeless animals in my apartment; I cry so much when I see a stray that I can't stand it. Who? Ho, he left some time ago. Something about there being 'other fish in the sea.' What in the world do you suppose he meant by that? By the way, I'm a little short of cash. Do you think you could lend me . . .?"

At this point, things are at a stalemate, but the situation will quickly resolve itself in one of twelve ways. Take your pick: This time *you* can choose the ending you like—and the one you think makes best astrological sense.

A. Aries gets in a fight with Leo and has to go to the emergency room.
B. Taurus gets really tired and hungry and decides to go home, cook a hamburger, and go to bed early.
C. Gemini runs out of note paper and gets laryngitis at the same time.
D. Cancer gets a call from the babysitter and is so worried she goes home to take care of her children.
E. Leo gets so irritated that no one is paying attention to the bruises Aries gave him that he leaves in a huff.
F. Virgo gets a stomach ache and decides to leave. Besides, it's time for her mineral bath.
G. Libra isn't able to make up his mind and gets a headache in the process.
H. Scorpio decides it's definitely a plot to humiliate her, and bows out less than graciously.
I. Sagittarius gets a little drunk and leaves early to get the plane.
J. Capricorn leaves as soon as she gets her petition filled up because there isn't anyone there *really* worth knowing.
K. Aquarius decides to go teach people at the shelter to use his stamp-sorting machine so they can get jobs.
L. Pisces remembers she has a date with her spiritual advisor and that she forgot to feed the animals.

5

Moods of the Moon

How to Successfully Navigate Its Day-by-Day Changes

Never underestimate the power of the moon. It is the closest planet to earth, and the only one whose effect on human life can actually be measured. Even the most skeptical antiastrology person has to admit that the moon rules the tides. If you stand on the beach for even a half hour or so, you can literally *see* how the moon works its magic as the water flows higher or lower, according to the time of day. There are places in the world where the tide rises as much as forty feet from its lowest to its highest point—that's *power*. If you think about the fact that humans are about 98 percent water in our chemical makeup, it's much easier to accept the fact that the moon has the same powerful effect on us as it does on the tides.

Like the "female" she symbolically is, the moon also changes her mind—or her sign—more quickly than any other planet. If you look at the day-by-day predictions in this book, which gives the position of the moon for every day, you will see that this changeable planet moves into a different sign about every two days.

As it moves from sign to sign, the moon brings a different kind of energy to the earth's atmosphere. Those who are particularly sensitive—like Cancers—feel it most strongly. But even the most stolid types are often moved by the effect of the particular sign the moon occupies on any given day, though they may not want to admit it.

Are we then slaves to the moods of the moon? Not if we understand its energies and cooperate with them. If you work *with* the moon and not against her, you can actually make life a lot easier for yourself. For instance, there are certain activities that go more smoothly when the moon is in a particular sign, just as other activities are more difficult to accomplish. Scheduling things accordingly could prevent a lot of frustration. You don't have to become a complete "lunatic" (ancient meaning, "one ruled by the moon") to benefit from its positive vibes, but simply go with the flow. Keep in mind, however, that the moon's effect will be *modified* by your sun sign, so be sure to check out your individual daily prediction. For instance, for *any* sun sign, the days when the moon is in that sign should bring a surge of energy. Whether you handle that energy positively or negatively is up to you.

Here's a rundown of the moods of the moon and the human activities that go with them.

When the Moon Is in Aries There is a very *physical* tone to this day. People may be throwing their weight around in more ways than one. Impatience, independent action, and quick tempers can sprout up all over the place. The good news is that most people will be feeling rather decisive, so some things can be completed. The bad news is that decisions may be totally unilateral; what *you* want may be exactly what someone else *doesn't* want. Similarly, people may be invading each other's territories; "keep off the grass" signs won't mean much today. Rule-breaking is the order of the day, and so are the consequences that go along with it. However, if there's a big mountain to scale, today's the day to begin the climb. If there's a formidable task that requires a lot of get-up-and-go to accomplish, today's the day to plunge in with both feet. If there's something you've been hesitating to tell someone, today you'll get the nerve to say it, but it may be difficult to be tactful. Try, anyway. On the up side, people will be feeling in the mood for some fun and frolic—practical jokes are very "moon in Aries." Even the boss may get in the spirit of things. It's a good day to:

Make a sale
Do heavy housework
Do some baking
Start a diet
Buy a lottery ticket
Get a haircut
Have your eyes checked

Sharpen knives
Stop worrying
Make a clean break
Start an exercise class
Do something on your own
Try a new recipe
Throw a last-minute party

When the Moon Is in Taurus Today, the amber light goes on, and people start to proceed with more caution. Rather than being adventurous, most people will feel like sticking with routine tasks. It is not a good day to try something new. In this more conservative mood, people will tend to hold on to what they have; don't try to borrow money from a friend today. Concentrate on making your own money grow, instead. Speaking of increase, this is an excellent day to "make your garden grow" in every sense of the phrase. Along with a quieter mood of the day, you may feel like pampering yourself a bit; allow yourself at least one luxury. Chocoholics, beware, however; this is a day for food binges and all forms of dietary excess. Creature comforts are a lot on everyone's mind; in fact, it may be difficult to crawl out of that comfortable bed in the morning. And more than a few people will be crawling back into it fairly early—with their favorite person. Sexual cravings are high on the list of "moon moods" today. Enjoy!

It's a good day to:

Put something off until tomorrow
Buy clothes or jewelry
Get your teeth filled
Start a savings account
Stick to your guns
Buy candy
Stay home and watch television

Put up preserves
Have a massage
Start singing lessons
Sell high on the market
Buy a plant
Buy real estate
Hug somebody

When the Moon Is in Gemini There's a touch more energy in the air today, and people will begin moving around a lot more. For some, there will be a lot of nervous energy and the scattery feeling that goes along with it; don't force yourself to concentrate if you can avoid it. It's a day to make connections—call, write, or bump into both new and old friends. Wits are generally sharp today, and people could be cracking jokes all around you. On the other hand, they may also be spilling some secrets. Gossip is easy to start today, and it could spread like wildfire. Mind your mouth! Anything requiring manual dexterity can easily get done today; even those who are usually clumsy may find they have nimble fingers. The tendency today is to do things quickly, if a bit superficially. If there are a couple of things that require a once-over-lightly treatment, get them out of the way now. If you haven't been invited to a party, give your own—or at least plan to get together with some buddies for a little socializing; the time is definitely right.

It's a good day to:

Get your hair cut	Use your hands
Join a club	Pay bills
Have a tooth pulled	Eat out
Sign up for a new course	Take a walk/drive
Send a letter	Call your brother/sister
Try something new	Tell a fib
Learn a language	Do two things at once

When the Moon Is in Cancer   In Cancer, the moon is in her very own sign—and you'll know it. All those "moon" characteristics—like changeableness, sensitivity, and the desire for security—will be heightened. Cancers, of course, will feel it most strongly; and the other water signs, Scorpio and Pisces, may be even moodier than usual. The general tendency today is to do things that make you feel comfortable and feel good. For some, that means eating a lot of food; for others, it could be hitting the bottle a bit. People tend to feel a bit sorry for themselves during the transit of the moon through Cancer. When two people who live together are both feeling that way, the result can be a rather touchy day—and evening. As much as you want the comfort of others, you are better off on your own and working off those anxious feelings by yourself. Not for safety, but for comfort's sake, the best place to go today is no farther than your own backyard. You'll probably be feeling very stay-at-home anyway. However, it's an excellent day for memories. Reminisce with somebody you love, or get out that old photo album by yourself. You might find yourself shedding a tear or two, but it's all in a good cause.

It's a good day to:

Bake something delicious	Hug your children
Buy something old	Take care of somebody
Put up preserves	Go without makeup
Buy property	Call your mother
Start a habit	Buy something for the house
Plant something	Entertain at home
Pamper yourself	Give your hair a treatment

When the Moon Is in Leo Today, everyone feels like "coming out of the woodwork." Just as Cancer moon makes you want to hide, Leo moon makes you want to get out there and be seen. Nothing but the best will do on this day, so it could be a rather expensive one. Most people will be more generous than usual—both with their money and their affections; many a new romance has started under a Leo moon. Leo is also one of the more playful signs, so a lot of you will be in the mood for fun and games. Eating out is very Leo moon—and so is picking up the check. Today, you may have to fight for it. However, the boss may be a lot stricter than usual, and even those with nobody to "boss" will try to push somebody around. If you've got children, today you will appreciate them very much—no matter what they do. Most people find themselves reaching for the newest thing in the closet under this transit of the moon. If they don't have anything new to wear, they'll probably go out and buy it—on credit. No matter what time of the year it is, you'll be looking for a little sunshine or at least a warm place. On the beaches or by the fireplaces are where most people would like to be today—wishing life were one long vacation.

It's a good day to:

Borrow money	Buy jewelry
Get a new hairstyle	Invest in the market
Start building something	Do something creative

Follow a hunch　　　　　　Prepare a gourmet meal
Steal the spotlight　　　　　Dress up
Be brave　　　　　　　　　Kiss somebody new
Be waited on

When the Moon Is in Virgo　　Now it's back to work, and back to reality. There's a sharp distinction between the Virgo moon mood and what precedes it, so you may shock yourself. Perhaps by deciding it's really time to get organized and then actually *doing* it. On the home front it's a great day to rearrange all those sloppy closets and cupboards. On the job, you couldn't pick a better time to wrestle with that nasty detail work you've been avoiding. However, all is not good news under Virgo moon. For one thing, by contrast to Leo moon's generosity, people will be positively stingy today—both with their money and their love. Even the best of situations could deteriorate today when one or the other of the involved parties decides to point out the other's flaws. Your best course under the Virgo moon is to check that impulse to criticize. People can become highly self-critical during this transit, too. One extreme example of the going-over some people can give themselves during a Virgo moon is to develop mysterious maladies or to discover aches and pains they never felt before. Not to worry; they'll be all better by the time the moon moves into the next sign. Virgo moon is also inspection time, so the boss may be particularly sensitive to messy desks today and sloppiness in general. Keep things buttoned up and tidy for best results.

It's a good time to:

Start a diet　　　　　　　　Start a new job
Get a physical　　　　　　　Sew or mend something
Bake bread　　　　　　　　Read a good book
Quit smoking　　　　　　　Get a complete makeover
Buy a pet　　　　　　　　　Call your maiden aunt
Try to do without something　Feel like a martyr
Buy health food　　　　　　Do a puzzle

When the Moon Is in Libra　　Now it's time to kiss and make up. Any relationships that suffered from the ragged nerves of Virgo moon time can be nicely patched up today. Pleasantries should be easy for one and all. In fact, even people who are normally rather gruff should smile a bit more today. Libra moon is one of the most social of moon periods; meeting and greeting should be prevalent activities. Most people will want to put their best foot forward, too, so the impulse to dress up and look your best may come upon you. You may feel rather self-indulgent as well; hard work is not as compatible with the Libra moon period as rest and relaxation are. It's definitely a time of togetherness, so even habitual loners may be looking for company. Most people will feel they need people—possibly one special person. Romance blossoms under the Libra moon in its purest form. It's not so much sex people want now as romantic love and companionship. No one's actually made a count, but it's a fair bet that more flowers get sent under the Libra moon than at any other time. Physical beauty is also highly important, so Libra moon is a great one under which to get yourself a whole new look or to redo anything that needs it. Something that's off-balance will bother you more at this time.

It's a good day to:

Be tactful	Forgive and forget
Redecorate	Add color to your life
Give a party	Luxuriate
Fall in love	Sign up for a dance class
Join a singing group	Buy a stereo
Buy something beautiful	Buy a down comforter
Try a new makeup	Learn about wine

When the Moon Is in Scorpio Things could easily get heavy today, and the tendency will be to go to extremes. Haters will hate more; lovers will love more passionately and physically. The sex drive is stimulated in many people during this transit of the moon. With all those intense emotions flying around, it's not surprising that people easily get hot under the collar—and/or imagine that somebody is out to get them. However, there is an up side to the Scorpio moon, and that is the extra jot of will power it gives the most weak-willed people. If you've got to dig in your heels and clench your teeth to get something done, today's the day you will be able to do it. People *endure* a lot under the Scorpio moon. The only problem is that they may develop some resentment toward those they believe should be enduring with them. However, the tendency is to keep silent. In spite of the intense emotionalism of the Scorpio moon, there isn't a lot of outright complaining. People will let the pressure build up inside of them and then burst out into violent rages. If your temper isn't good under the best of circumstances, control it during the Scorpio moon, by all means. It's also a time when people tend to feel a bit claustrophobic; a good walk in the fresh air can work wonders at this time.

It's a good day to:

See a psychiatrist
Buy a house
Open a secret bank account
Make a firm decision
Do your taxes
Throw away what you don't need
Do some strenuous exercise
Have good sex
Face up to a crisis
Read a good mystery
Take body-building
Get a prescription filled
Buy life insurance
Change your life

When the Moon Is in Sagittarius Things definitely lighten up when the moon moves into Sagittarius—and people loosen up, too. In fact, one danger under this moon is getting too relaxed—with your diet, your money, or your generous spirits. Moderation is not the mood of the day, so you may have to force it on yourself. It is not a good time to try to stop smoking—or to stop doing anything self-indulgent. There's definitely a "live and let live" attitude in the air when the moon is in Sagittarius, so bad relations should be easily improved. A spirit of good will is pervasive, as well as a lighthearted attitude. One thing that means is that even normally conservative people will be willing to take chances; those for whom a more liberal outlook is a natural state of affairs could really go too far out on a limb. If you gamble, bet *only* what you can afford to lose today. The place everyone will want to be today is outdoors. In fact, more than one person will simply disappear from the scene to do something either adventurous or relaxing. It's an excellent day to think big, but you may find the follow-through a bit difficult. The big picture is what's easiest to see right now; leave the fine brush strokes for another time. Enjoy the spirit of fun and generosity that should be in the air.

It's a good day to:

Make a long-distance call	Go to church
Plan a trip	Enjoy a hobby
Buy a dog (or a horse)	Learn a new language
Contribute to a wildlife- foundation	Do something charitable
	Borrow money
Try a new approach	Run away from it all
Sell anything to anybody	Get a bigger place
Try your luck/feel lucky	

When the Moon Is in Capricorn In sharp contrast to the "easy come, easy go" feeling of the Sagittarius moon, the moon in Capricorn brings on a much more serious mood. You could call it the "workaholic's moon," and even those whose work style is less intense will find themselves wanting to get a lot done. It's important to *accomplish something* when the moon is in Capricorn, if you are to feel comfortable. Most people want to tread only on solid ground at this time, so there could be a bit of distrust in the air. No one wants to waste time— and least of all on things or people from whom they are not likely to derive some kind of benefit. Another curious facet of the Capricorn moon mood is a tendency to feel older and more serious; some lighter types dislike the feeling so much they will go out of their way to look young. It's the kind of day that matronly secretary in the office is likely to appear in something rather frilly. People can really handle things under the Capricorn moon too; endurance is *very* Capricorn. That means those who exercise will work out harder and longer; those who normally do not push themselves will do at least a little self-prodding. A good image is paramount to many people when the moon is in this sign, and the tendency is for people to be quite status conscious. Self-control is the order of the day, in every respect.

It's a good day to:

Start a new job	Make a list
Buy antiques	Keep your money

Buy anything for investment	Go to the dentist
Wear anything with a good label on it	Start a diet
	Work late
Bet on a favorite	Ask for repayment of a debt
Go to the chiropractor	
Buy insurance	Clean house

When the Moon Is in Aquarius When the moon moves into the sign of Aquarius from the sign of Capricorn, it's as if somebody took the cork out of the bottle. Suddenly, the rather repressed mood bursts into a desire for change—a *need* for change. This is one of those days when people tend to make rash moves like quit a dull job, call it quits with a clinging person, throw out everything in their closet and start all over again. Reaching this point is easy to do under the Aquarian moon. However, it's usually very positive. What's important at this time is to try something new, not just get rid of something old. Some people decide to experiment with a new recipe, a new lover, or a new hair style. It's the kind of day when a woman with long hair will decide to get a crew cut. On the relationship side, the mood now is one of brotherly love and friendship rather than highly charged sexual encounters. Wanting to be with friends and feeling like part of a group is what's important now. No one is a stranger under the Aquarian moon, and talking to people on the street is very common. The thing to be careful of under this moon is doing something irreparable—like finally telling the boss what you really think of him. He/she could easily decide that it's time for a change of personnel.

It's a good day to:

Do something kinky	Buy/wear something crazy
Try a new food	Color your hair
Do something friendly	Contribute to a charity
Start flying lessons	Move to a new place
Do something impulsive	Buy a television/stereo
Join a club	Make a new friend
Make a speculative investment	Be fair

When the Moon Is in Pisces This is a time when people wear their hearts on their sleeves and feel *very* vulnerable. There's a lot of ultrasensitivity under the Pisces moon, and a lot of crying on shoulders—if you can find one that isn't already occupied. Mixed in with the emotionalism is a real feeling of empathy with others; now's the time people feel that everyone is in the same boat. However, it may be a bit difficult to keep things afloat today, because there isn't a lot of firm direction from anyone or anything. It's confusion time, and even the clearest of messages can get a little garbled. Indecisiveness will spread like the plague, so don't expect to get any clear-cut answers today. Creative people get more creative under the Pisces moon, and anyone could feel just a bit poetic. Romantic relationships are heavenly under the Pisces moon as long as they don't get out of control. Keeping certain other things under control—like drinking and other forms of escapism—is a wise precaution, too. The most satisfying and least dangerous escape is to hold hands with someone you love while you watch a real tearjerker movie. Lots of people call in sick under the Pisces moon, and there's a good reason: Most people don't like to cry in public.

It's a good day to:

Put on weight
Fall in love
Develop ESP
Find God
Buy flowers or perfume
Swear off something
Get hooked on something

Write a poem
Take in a stray dog or cat
Visit the sick
See a therapist
Stay home and read
Pamper yourself
Buy a camera

6

Venus and Mars

**Love and Sex
Peace and War
Cooperating and Competing**

Next to your sun sign, your moon sign, and your rising sign, the positions of Venus and Mars in your horoscope are probably the most important indicators of your personal psychology. This is because Venus shows your affectional nature and Mars shows your sexual nature. To put it another way, *Venus shows your wants and needs in romantic love while Mars shows your sexual style and your manner of expressing it.*

In a broader sense, Venus and Mars are the principles of peace and war. Venus wants to cooperate and relate to others, to share life experiences. Mars is totally concerned with self and getting what you want. Everybody's got a Venus and Mars in their horoscope because every human being has to both live with others and assert him-/herself. It's all a matter of degree. If you want to, you can think of Venus as the "higher" side of human relationships; Mars the "lower." However, you've got to keep in mind that—like all other opposites in the universe—both *cooperating* and competing are necessary if the world is to continue going round.

Because Venus has to do with the need to share, the sign in which it is placed will tell a lot about how you attract people you want to share with. It will also show what attracts you to others. Beyond the love arena, the position of Venus in your horoscope shows your attitudes toward money and personal possessions, creature comforts, and things of beauty. Venus is "feminine" in nature, and women tend to relate to their Venus sign more than men. But for *both* sexes, it is an available energy.

The good side of Venus is:
Sharing, beautifying, peacemaking
The bad side is:
acquisitiveness, self-indulgence, laziness

Because the position of Mars shows how you go about getting what you want, it will tell a lot about your personal drive—how *much* you want what you want. It is the desire principle, and will indicate just how passionate your passions are. Ambition, assertiveness, and anger are just a few steps away from each other, so Mars will also reveal what makes you angry or what gets you going. The planet Mars is "masculine" in nature—highly so—and men will find it easier to get in touch with their Mars energy. However, every woman's got a Mars too, and sooner or later a woman's Mars energy will present itself.

The "good" side of Mars is:
Dynamic energy, courage, sexual drive
The "bad" side is:
manipulation, cowardice, sexual abuse

No matter what area of life you are relating these planets to, it is useful to think of them in sexual terms, and of our human sexual organs. Venus is open and receptive; Mars thrusts forward and penetrates. Because we normally attract someone or are attracted to someone before we get sexually involved, Venus energy precedes Mars energy. In other words, Venus shows how *receptive* you are; Mars shows how *active* you are. Venus also has a lot to do with our ideas and images of romance, our romantic fantasies, while Mars is an indicator of sexual fantasies—which may or may not be acted out, depending on the individual's degree of inhibition.

Just as some combinations of people can coexist in constant harmony while others are in constant conflict,

Venus and Mars in an individual person can work well together, or at cross-purposes. When your Venus doesn't get along well with your Mars, you've got a problem. Sometimes a sexual problem, but always an inner conflict. How can you tell if your Venus and Mars are "friends" or "foes"? First, by looking up the positions of your personal Mars and Venus in the charts provided at the end of this chapter, reading the descriptions of those planets in the signs they fall in for you. But, just to make things a bit clearer, here's a rundown of easy Mars/Venus relationships and difficult ones. (By the way, you can also apply this principle in comparing your Venus/Mars positions to those of someone else, as well.)

Venus and Mars are "at war" when:

- One is in a fire sign, and one is in an earth sign. Here you've got a conflict between the practical and the experimental sides of yourself.
- One is in a fire sign and one is in a water sign. One part of you says "let's do it"; the other side says, "I might get hurt," so you might be stalled.
- One is in an earth sign and one is in an air sign. Air likes to think about things a little; earth needs to know it will work. Once again, it may hold you back.
- One is in an air sign and one is in a water sign. Yours is a conflict between the mental relationship and the emotional one; you may find it hard to decide what you want.

Venus and Mars are on good terms when:

- One is in a fire sign, one is in an air sign.
- One is in an earth sign and one is in a water sign.
- Both are in the same element.

Venus and Mars in The Signs

Venus in Aries (fire element)

While this position of Venus in a man or a woman indicates the kind of person who falls in love impulsively, both sexes want to be conquered, when they have Venus in Aries. They may be outrageously flirtatious, but can lead others on a merry chase before they give in. There is a tendency to look for trouble when Venus is in ths position; actually, it is excitement Venus in Aries people crave. Their personal likes and dislikes will be quite clearly defined, and they will be vocal about them. In matters of taste, there is less refinement than when Venus is in a softer sign. Both the males and the females may play up their sexuality in the way they dress; they like very loud things like rock music and bright colors. There is also an impish charm in these people and a tendency to play love games. The *real* goal is to be swept away by a romantic lover who lives up to a mediaeval code of chivalry and/or chastity.

Mars in Aries (fire element)

This is a highly competitive position for Mars; people with Mars in Aries leave no doubt about the fact that they want it, and they want it *now*—whatever "it" is. Mars in Aries can cut through a lot of life's red tape. When it comes to courtship, Mars in Aries people are equally able to disregard the small talk and get right down to business. However, this position of Mars often makes for a rather selfish lover—one who is so concerned with getting that he/she doesn't do an awful lot of giving. Mars in Aries people are likely to turn off as quickly as they turn on. Passion burns brightly, but is often short-lived. They are highly independent and likely to leave if a romantic partner gets too possessive or demanding. Mars in Aries is also always ready for a fight, so relationships are a bit stormy.

Venus in Taurus (earth element)

This is a highly sensual position for Venus to be in. People with Venus in Taurus are turned on by sweet words and soft music—and any form of touching. They like all kinds of nice and beautiful things, and will be attracted by someone who dresses well and has expensive taste. Venus in Taurus people can be a little self-indulgent, but in the main their desire is to make the object of their affection comfortable. And they will do it in very tangible ways; Venus in Taurus people of both sexes like to do things for others. When someone with Venus in Taurus is attracted, he/she is loyal. Love does not come in a flash, as it does with Venus in Aries people, but when it comes, it usually stays. At least as far as the person with Venus in Taurus is concerned. These people are generally so devoted that a breakup is extremely unsettling. You can always make a Venus in Taurus person happy with candy or flowers. The best kind of love feels good, tastes good, looks good, and smells good.

Mars in Taurus (earth element)

This Mars can express itself as ambition with a definite direction—or as controlled sexuality. Mars in Taurus people of both sexes can appear rather lazy, but actually their slow movements are usually on a deliberate course. Some people with Mars in Taurus are really looking for a safe position in a job or with a partner. Their manner of sexuality is highly sensual though they may be slow to get aroused. When a Mars in Taurus person enters into an affair, however, there is usually the intention to make it a long and serious one. These people are certainly capable of quick affairs, but they generally prefer a comfortable relationship where they do not constantly have to keep proving their love. There is a certain giving quality to Mars in Taurus, and the men are exceptionally considerate lovers. The women are fairly passive, but passionate and giving when they get going.

Venus in Gemini

Venus in Gemini people of both sexes tend to be turned on more by *talk* than by physical stimulation. Relationships have to have a mental dimension in order for them to get involved. In fact, Venus in Gemini people are likely to make better friends than lovers. When their affections *are* engaged, the connection is likely to be a little tenuous, and the Venus in Gemini's feelings may not run as deep as his/her partner's. Fickleness is a reality with these people— they like a lot of changes, and that goes for people as well as environments. Job-hopping is a trait of Venus in Gemini, and so is a constant changing of the guard in their romantic lives. However, Venus in Gemini people make wonderful romantic partners, because they are really *interested* in the people they get involved with. Never tell a Venus in Gemini person to "shut up and make love"; he/she will be very likely to shut the door on the relationship.

Mars in Gemini

Mars in Gemini people assert themselves rather erratically; there isn't a lot of staying power, in jobs or in relationships. The "alternating current" of Mars in Gemini energy makes for a rather on again, off again sexual life. People with Mars in this position are capable of having a number of purely mental relationships in between their sexual ones. These are the kind of people who talk their way into things, including a job and someone's bed. Their approach is a bit on the delicate side, and one may wonder when the Mars in Gemini person is really going to get started. However, once their passion is aroused, Mars in Gemini people like a lot of variety; sex can get quite original with these people. The tendency to bore easily goes both for their attitudes toward their sexual partners and the manner in which they have sex. Both sexes are real charmers, however, and sometimes get their way in a rather devious manner.

Venus in Cancer (water element)

The overriding thing that people with Venus in Cancer want is *security*, really the emotional kind, but since a secure home base goes along with their needs, the material kind is important too. Venus in Cancer people can be highly traditional in their romantic values—home, mother, and apple pie are symbols of the things that turn these people on. If you want to engage the emotions of a Venus in Cancer person, all you have to do is look as if you *need* somebody—preferably a mother. Venus in Cancer people need to be needed, but sometimes can go overboard by totally taking over the other person's life. With Venus in this sign, people respond strongly to all kinds of romantic things, from the card that says "I love you" to a little token of affection for no special occasion. However, Venus in Cancer people are highly self-protective, so you first have to break down their natural reserve and fear of getting hurt. Once you do, you won't find a more faithful lover. Except perhaps Taurus.

Mars in Cancer (water element)

Mars in Cancer people can sneak up on you when they've decided they want you; their approach is a bit sideways, like the locomotion of the crab that is the Cancer symbol. They are soft and subtle lovers and said by some to be among the best sexual partners in the zodiac. However, as sensitive and understanding as they tend to be in the sexual area, they can be overly possessive with people they love, and even turn rather cruel when they are rejected. Cancer is a water sign, and it is as if that water starts boiling—invisibly—then the lid totally pops off when the explosion comes. Mars in Cancer people tend to be a little blind to their sexual/ambition drive and can even pretend to themselves that it doesn't exist. For this reason, they make formidable enemies, because while they look as if they are asking for peace they are really preparing for battle.

Venus in Leo (fire element)

There's a pretty simple way to get a Venus in Leo person to like you. Give him/her a lot of attention—*positive* attention. Venus in Leo people do want love, but they want admiration and adulation to come along with it. A bit like Venus in Aries, Venus in Leo wants a *courtly* lover—someone who will swear absolute loyalty. When it's a Leo sun sign person who also has Venus in Leo, you've got the absolute monarch of them all. Venus in Leo also goes only for the best, and is attracted to what looks expensive or rewarding—in both jobs and people. Venus in Leo expects you to dress and look your best, no matter what the circumstances. It is not a "casual" Venus. Demonstrations of love are very important, too. Words are great, of course, and so is a lot of hugging and the rest of the physical love spectrum. However, candy—or some other tangible token of affection—is expected. Venus in Leo has fierce pride, so if you even slip once and appear not to *respect* this person, he/she is likely to brush you off—with a very grand gesture of course.

Mars in Leo (fire element)

Speaking of grand gestures, Mars in Leo wrote the book. This kind of person is the one who will lavish the object of his/her affection with all kinds of luxurious things. Mars in Leo is a real showy person and expects to be appreciated for it. Both the males and the females are aggressive about going after what they want, and once they are happily ensconced—with a lover or a job—they are loyal and steady. However, the down side of the Mars in Leo position is a violent temper: a *really* violent temper. Both sexes can get quite physical in expressing anger. This is the position of the female who throws plates and the man who slaps his faithless lover on the cheek. Mars in Leo is unrelentingly honest—and will expect you to be too. One devious move, and it's over

Venus in Virgo (earth element)

Venus in Virgo wants a love that *works*. Pure sex or romance may appeal to Virgo's desire for the unadulterated, but there's got to be an element of the practical in it too. People with Venus in Virgo often actually fall in love with their jobs faster than they do with people. When Venus is in the sign, you often find the dedicated, loyal, "number two" person who spends a lifetime catering to the needs of a powerful boss. He/she is likely to be just a little bit in love with that boss too. As for sex, the Venus in Virgo person has a very healthy attitude toward it—possibly too healthy in the sense that it is sometimes regarded as an excellent form of exercise. Venus in Virgo people are not really cold—in fact, when they love someone they can't do enough for them, particularly in attending to their physical comfort. The problem is that this position of Venus makes a person overly analytical in determining what he/she wants. If the Venus in Virgo person keeps his/her mouth shut, and doesn't openly criticize, there is a much better possibility that he/she will make good, solid relationships.

Mars in Virgo (earth element)

Virgo's inventive sexuality is one of the best-kept secrets in the zodiac; Mars in Virgo turns out some of the most experimental and skillful lovers of all. That is, if you can attract one of these people in the first place. Mars in Virgo people are far from promiscuous; in fact, their standards are likely to be a bit too high. They are constantly questioning their *own* desires and drives, picking them apart instead of acting upon them. Mars in Virgo is ideal for success in just about any job or profession. With any sun sign, it adds to the ability to cooly analyze problems and solve them with a reasonable amount of dispatch. When it comes to romantic involvement, this is not one of the more "romantic" Mars positions (unless the sun sign is Libra). You may feel as if your Mars in Virgo lover is checking you over first for anything that might turn him/her off. This is the sign that usually says "let's shower together" before he/she says "let's go to bed."

Venus in Libra (air element)

First off, remember that when the planet Venus is in Libra, it's in its "home sign." When it comes to beauty, harmony, and balance, Venus in Libra people want it all. When Venus is in Libra, the most attractive things in life are the *nicest*—people, places, jobs, clothes, you name it. Venus in Libra people want it nice, but they also want it *easy*. In fact, this sometimes "cold" position of Venus can make for a person who marries for status or money. If you look comfortable in every sense of the word, you've got a shot at attracting that Venus in Libra person who catches your eye. And he/she will, because this position of Venus usually confers a great-looking body. Even if the Venus in Libra person loves or marries for convenience, he/she gives an awful lot in return. Once you've engaged his/her love the Venus in Libra person considers you the best, the most beautiful/handsome, and the brightest person in the universe and will treat you accordingly.

Mars in Libra (air element)

This position of Mars often makes for a passive/aggressive type of individual—a specific psychological pattern. The Mars in Libra person rarely goes directly after what he/she wants, but more or less lingers in front of it, waiting for the other person to make the right move. Mars in Libra people don't get hired as quickly as other types because they don't seem to *care* enough about whether or not they get the job. When it comes to love, Mars in Libra can be quite frustrating. You really don't know what's going on here—does or doesn't he/she want to get involved? This is also a rather "refined" position for brash Mars. Mars in Libra people usually have excellent manners, and never appear to get ruffled. They will just sit and smile while you rant and rave. Suddenly, however, they can turn on their heel and walk out the door. The technique Mars in Libra people use to go about making their subtle conquests is *talk*—but it can easily fool you because it seems so casual.

Venus in Scorpio (water element)
A lot of people with sun sign Scorpio have Venus in Scorpio too; (one's Venus sign is often one's sun sign because Venus is so close to the sun in the solar system). These double-whammy Scorpios are extraordinarily intense in all their emotional needs, but anyone with Venus in Scorpio is going to be touched by the madness of this intense sign. The curious paradox is that Venus in Scorpio people are either totally *turned on* by someone or something—or totally *turned off*. There are very few halfway deals in their lives. Venus in Scorpio can also be highly manipulative, adjusting his/her emotions to suit other needs—like money. When Venus is in Scorpio, people are attracted to what seems mysterious, dangerous, or hard-to-get. They love puzzles, and can be a bit of a puzzle themselves to prospective romantic partners. When they do get involved, however, they have a great deal of staying power—emotionally at least. They can fairly easily separate their physical *actions* from their mental states, however.

Mars in Scorpio (water element)
People with Mars in Scorpio have a very strong "energy field" surrounding them; you can almost see it and feel it. What they want, they want passionately—and will seek in no uncertain terms. They are equally positive about what they *don't* want—so you will know whether you've got a shot with them right away. No waiting with *this* aggressive sign. The legendary super-sexuality of Scorpio is real with Mars in Scorpio people. However, they may use their sexual power to control

other people and situations. And, if they are rejected against their will (which doesn't happen too often) they are capable of the worst kind of venomous reactions. Jealous lovers who are violent to their former partners are a parody of the Mars in Scorpio type of intensity. One way Mars in Scorpio people can hurt or simply tease others is by withholding their love—and their physical passion. They have great powers of self-control.

Venus in Sagittarius (fire element)

People with Venus in the restless, mobile sign of the Centaur often get the reputation for being fickle, and there is more than a grain of truth in that label. But the reason a Venus in Sagittarius person may move around or not become committed is that he/she is so vulnerable to deceit and dishonesty. As the saying goes, "once burned, twice shy," and openhearted, friendly Sagittarius is likely to get burned very early in life. When Venus in Sagittarius people do get involved, they are absolutely delightful to love. Broadminded, unpossessive, full of fun, they really want to enjoy romance. Sagittarius is also a very intellectual sign, so in order to get Venus in Sagittarius people to stick with you for a while, you've got to keep them interested. Sex is great, but sex with talk is even greater for these people. Venus in Sagittarius is also highly idealistic, so you've got to be a higher type to appeal to someone with Venus in this sign. Love is gallantry and honor and all those things that are so hard to find in life.

Mars in Sagittarius (fire element)

Sagittarius is a sign that thinks in global terms, so when Mars is in the sign of Sagittarius, you find a person who wants it all—and often has to be satisfied with nothing. People with Mars in Sagittarius assert themselves bluntly and get right to the point. However, they tend to be so optimistic in their expectations that they may just as quickly decide they have made a mistake. Better luck next love. Mars in Sagittarius doesn't deliberately hurt people; this sign is kind to all—both animals and humans. Their sexual nature can also be rather "animalistic" because this is a lusty sign, and so fond of all outdoor sports that they often want to do it anywhere, anytime. One way Mars in Sagittarius people get to your heart is through your sense of humor; they really know how to make people laugh. It is a powerful weapon in their professional lives too; it's hard to fire someone who is such a delight to have around—even if he/she isn't around that much. The big problem with Mars in Sagittarius people is that they sometimes don't want to take responsibility for their own actions, and lay things on other people. Even if Mars in Sagittarius is the one to break things up, he/she will somehow or other get you to believe that it's *your* fault.

Venus in Capricorn (earth element)

Appearances count a lot to Venus in Capricorn people—in every sense of the word. In order to appeal to them, you've got to look solid and substantial—and fairly rich as well. Because there is a natural reserve to Capricorn, people with Venus in this sign will dislike public displays of affection; the cooler you are in your approach, the better. Their public image and their private one are not too far apart, either. Not that Venus in Capricorn isn't normal; he/she can be quite passionate in bed. But very, very *serious,* too. If you mistake this sign's sober approach to life for coldness, you will not be the first person who has. Once again, like those with Venus in Virgo, Venus in Capricorn is attracted to *practical* people—people who can really work for them in one way or another. While some do actually consciously go after a financially comfortable marital situation, what the vast majority will settle for is someone who is willing to help handle a lot of the more serious aspects of life. Male or female, Venus in Capricorn people want you to be *useful.* Unfortunately, some people with Venus in this sign have such a low sense of self-worth, that they will try to buy love—or sell it—because they don't feel anyone will accept them for what they are.

Mars in Capricorn (earth element)

Mars in Capricorn people always want to know the rules before they enter the game; they assert themselves with extreme caution. However, when they *know* what they want, they have incredible powers to help them get it. One is patience; Mars in Capricorn can wait very well. Another thing they have going for them is self-control; their timing is excellent because they can hold themselves back when they want to. All this makes for a rather sexually confusing type, and sometimes one who is sexually confused. Mars in Capricorn people can go without sex for amazing lengths of time if nothing seems worth the effort. When they do go for it, their approach can be extremely lusty and earthy, as befits the earth element of Capricorn. Even more than someone with Mars in Scorpio, the person with Mars in Capricorn can be a user. In love or business, he/she can easily fake it to get the carrot on the end of the stick. Then, before you know it, the person who seemed so hot for you has now turned stone cold. Sad, but true.

Venus in Aquarius (air element)

The best way to attract someone with Venus in Aquarius is to be a bit unconventional; these people love anyone or anything that is off-beat. However, you may find that you are considered a specimen rather than a romantic partner—or at least that's how it's likely to feel. People with Venus in Aquarius seem to have a real problem with deep involvement; often they really *want* it, but somehow or other their deepest wells of emotion are very difficult to tap.

Their habitual reaction to love is often "easy come, easy go." Are they cruel people? Generally not, and often Venus in Aquarius people suffer a lot from their difficulty with feeling. They will rarely tell you, however, because there is a real need for distance there. And distance is what they seek in one-on-one relationships. If you become possessive with, or jealous of a person with Venus in Aquarius, you will lose him/her very quickly. As with some of the other mental signs like Gemini and Libra, you have got to keep the affair or the marriage *interesting* in one way or another. This is a Venus position that often likes kinky sex, porno movies, and other forms of artificial stimulation. However, they usually don't care enough about sex-for-the-sake-of-sex to be unfaithful.

Mars in Aquarius (air element)

When Mars is in this erratic sign, people tend to go through periods of feast and famine, largely because they can fluctuate between being extremely assertive and sure about what they want or totally inactive. During the latter periods you could actually call the Mars in Aquarius person lazy. In love, the Mars in Aquarius person tends to go after the unusual or difficult; involvements with people who are already attached are quite common. In many cases it is because the Mars in Aquarius person really is terribly afraid of deep involvement. There is a detachment about Mars in Aquarius people that sometimes works against permanent attachment to people or professional situations. Mars in Aquarius really prefers to go it alone. Perhaps the reason is that they always want to be free to experiment with the new. In sex, the Mars in Aquarius person is hung up on technique; he/she likes intelligent sex, and sometimes wants to prove how clever he/she is via this rather bizarre route.

Venus in Pisces (water element)

For people with Venus in Pisces, what's attractive is often bound up with some kind of sacrifice. This is the position of Venus that leads to martyrdom of all kinds. Some Venus in Pisces people find it impossible to get involved with anything or anyone normal and healthy; their instinctive need is to care for the lame and needy. Therefore, many Venus in Pisces people are rather easily taken advantage of by unscrupulous types who use them or take them for all they're worth. By the same token, Venus in Pisces people can put a real *drain* on the object of their affections—demanding more and more proofs of undying love, soulful demonstrations, sometimes even more tangible support. However, in the broadest, most universal sense of the word, Pisces is the "best" position for Venus as it represents the principle of *true love*. True love is totally unselfish, totally self-sacrificing. Though few normal mortals are capable of such "divine" love, Venus in Pisces people come closest to being able to make it. On the more mundane side, people wth Venus in Pisces are attracted by all kinds of sentimental and often impractical things. They will love you most if you spend your last penny on a bouquet of violets rather than bread for the table. So what? You'll just live on love.

Mars in Pisces *(water element)*

Mars in Pisces people can easily lose their way; the sign of Pisces is not stable enough for the aggressive energy of Mars, so Mars in Pisces people tend to scatter their energies in too many places. On the other hand, they are the most subtle and devious people in the zodiac when it comes to going after what they really *do* want. Their come-on is usually to be rather weak and helpless. Both the males and the females snare you by making you think they really *need* you. There's a lot of poetry to Mars in Pisces people, so the start of an affair is likely to be all moonlight and roses. However, you may find that once you are entangled, you can't get yourself out when you want out. Mars in Pisces people have a way of snarling you up in their webs of erratic energy. Just when they've agreed that you should go, they'll become helpless again and make you feel you have to stay. However, Mars in Pisces people do offer a very wonderful kind of love—soft, sensitive, and caring. The object of their desires is often someone similar or someone involved with art or music in some way. However, Pisces types are best off hooking up with a strong partner—someone who can keep their Mars energy on a straight and even course. The best part of Mars in Pisces people is that they are rarely, if ever, cold.

VENUS SIGN 1910–1975

	Aries	Taurus	Gemini	Cancer	Leo	Virgo
1910	5/7-6/3	6/4-6/29	6/30-7/24	7/25-8/18	8/19-9/12	9/13-10/6
1911	2/28-3/23	3/24-4/17	4/18-5/12	5/13-6/8	6/9-7/7	7/8-11/8
1912	4/13-5/6	5/7-5/31	6/1-6/24	6/24-7/18	7/19-8/12	8/13-9/5
1913	2/3-3/6 5/2-5/30	3/7-5/1 5/31-7/7	7/8-8/5	8/6-8/31	9/1-9/26	9/27-10/20
1914	3/14-4/6	4/7-5/1	5/2-5/25	5/26-6/19	6/20-7/15	7/16-8/10
1915	4/27-5/21	5/22-6/15	6/16-7/10	7/11-8/3	8/4-8/28	8/29-9/21
1916	2/14-3/9	3/10-4/5	4/6-5/5	5/6-9/8	9/9-10/7	10/8-11/2
1917	3/29-4/21	4/22-5/15	5/16-6/9	6/10-7/3	7/4-7/28	7/29-8/21
1918	5/7-6/2	6/3-6/28	6/29-7/24	7/25-8/18	8/19-9/11	9/12-10/5
1919	2/27-3/22	3/23-4/16	4/17-5/12	5/13-6/7	6/8-7/7	7/8-11/8
1920	4/12-5/6	5/7-5/30	5/31-6/23	6/24-7/18	7/19-8/11	8/12-9/4
1921	2/3-3/6 4/26-6/1	3/7-4/25 6/2-7/7	7/8-8/5	8/6-8/31	9/1-9/25	9/26-10/20
1922	3/13-4/6	4/7-4/30	5/1-5/25	5/26-6/19	6/20-7/14	7/15-8/9
1923	4/27-5/21	5/22-6/14	6/15-7/9	7/10-8/3	8/4-8/27	8/28-9/20
1924	2/13-3/8	3/9-4/4	4/5-5/5	5/6-9/8	9/9-10/7	10/8-11/12
1925	3/28-4/20	4/21-5/15	5/16-6/8	6/9-7/3	7/4-7/27	7/28-8/21
1926	5/7-6/2	6/3-6/28	6/29-7/23	7/24-8/17	8/18-9/11	9/12-10/5
1927	2/27-3/22	3/23-4/16	4/17-5/11	5/12-6/7	6/8-7/7	7/8-11/9
1928	4/12-5/5	5/6-5/29	5/30-6/23	6/24-7/17	7/18-8/11	8/12-9/4
1929	2/3-3/7 4/20-6/2	3/8-4/19 6/3-7/7	7/8-8/4	8/5-8/30	8/31-9/25	9/26-10/19
1930	3/13-4/5	4/6-4/30	5/1-5/24	5/25-6/18	6/19-7/14	7/15-8/9
1931	4/26-5/20	5/21-6/13	6/14-7/8	7/9-8/2	8/3-8/26	8/27-9/19

VENUS SIGN 1910–1975

Libra	Scorpio	Sagittarius	Capricorn	Aquarius	Pisces
10/7-10/30	10/31-11/23	11/24-12/17	12/18-12/31	1/1-1/15	1/16-1/28
				1/29-4/4	4/5-5/6
11/19-12/8	12/9-12/31		1/1-1/10	1/11-2/2	2/3-2/27
9/6-9/30	1/1-1/4	1/5-1/29	1/30-2/23	2/24-3/18	3/19-4/12
	10/1-10/24	10/25-11/17	11/18-12/12	12/13-12/31	
10/21-11/13	11/14-12/7	12/8-12/31		1/1-1/6	1/7-2/2
8/11-9/6	9/7-10/9	10/10-12/5	1/1-1/24	1/25-2/17	2/18-3/13
	12-6/12-30	12/31			
9/22-10/15	10/16-11/8	1/1-2/6	2/7-3/6	3/7-4/1	4/2-4/26
		11/9-12/2	12/3-12/26	12/27-12/31	
11/3-11/27	11/28-12/21	12/22-12/31		1/1-1/19	1/20-2/13
8/22-9/16	9/17-10/11	1/1-1/14	1/15-2/7	2/8-3/4	3/5-3/28
		10/12-11/6	11/7-12/5	12/6-12/31	
10/6-10/29	10/30-11/22	11/23-12/16	12/17-12/31	1/1-4/5	4/6-5/6
11/9-12/8	12/9-12/31		1/1-1/9	1/10-2/2	2/3-2/26
9/5-9/30	1/1-1/3	1/4-1/28	1/29-2/22	2/23-3/18	3/19-4/11
	9/31-10/23	10/24-11/17	11/18-12/11	12/12-12/31	
10/21-11/13	11/14-12/7	12/8-12/31		1/1-1/6	1/7-2/2
8/10-9/6	9/7-10/10	10/11-11/28	1/1-1/24	1/25-2/16	2/17-3/12
	11/29-12/31				
9/21-10/14	1/1	1/2-2/6	2/7-3/5	3/6-3/31	4/1-4/26
	10/15-11/7	11/8-12/1	12/2-12/25	12/26-12/31	
11/3-11/26	11/27-12/21	12/22-12/31		1/1-1/19	1/20-2/12
8/22-9/15	9/16-10/11	1/1-1/14	1/15-2/7	2/8-3/3	3/4-3/27
		10-12/11-6	11/7-12/5	12/6-12/31	
10/6-10/29	10/30-11/22	11/23-12/16	12/17-12/31	1/1-4/5	4/6-5/6
11/10-12/8	12/9-12/31	1/1-1/7	1/8	1/9-2/1	2/2-2/26
9/5-9/28	1/1-1/3	1/4-1/28	1/29-2/22	2/23-3/17	3/18-4/11
	9/29-10/23	10/24-11/16	11/17-12/11	12/12-12/31	
10/20-11/12	11/13-12/6	12/7-12/30	12/31	1/1-1/5	1/6-2/2
8/10-9/6	9/7-10/11	10/12-11/21	1/1-1/23	1/24-2/16	2/17-3/12
	11/22-12/31				
9/20-10/13	1/1-1/3	1/4-2/6	2/7-3/4	3/5-3/31	4/1-4/25
		10/14-11/6	11/7-11/30	12/1-12/24	12/25-12/31

VENUS SIGN 1910–1975

	Aries	Taurus	Gemini	Cancer	Leo	Virgo
1932	2/12-3/8	3/9-4/3	4/4-5/5 7/13-7/27	5/6-7/12 7/28-9/8	9/9-10/6	10/7-11/1
1933	3/27-4/19	4/20-5/28	5/29-6/8	6/9-7/2	7/3-7/26	7/27-8/20
1934	5/6-6/1	6/2-6/27	6/28-7/22	7/23-8/16	8/17-9/10	9/11-10/4
1935	2/26-3/21	3/22-4/15	4/16-5/10	5/11-6/6	6/7-7/6	7/7-11/8
1936	4/11-5/4	5/5-5/28	5/29-6/22	6/23-7/16	7/17-8/10	8/11-9/4
1937	2/2-3/8 4/14-6/3	3/9-4/17 6/4-7/6	7/7-8/3	8/4-8/29	8/30-9/24	9/25-10/18
1938	3/12-4/4	4/5-4/28	4/29-5/23	5/24-6/18	6/19-7/13	7/14-8/8
1939	4-25/5/19	5/20-6/13	6/14-7/8	7/9-8/1	8/2-8/25	8/26-9/19
1940	2/12-3/7	3/8-4/3	4/4-5/5 7/5-7/31	5/6-7/4 8/1-9/8	9/9-10/5	10/6-10/31
1941	3/27-4/19	4/20-5/13	5/14-6/6	6/7-6/1	7/2-7/26	7/27-8/20
1942	5/6-6/1	6/2-6/26	6/27-7/22	7/23-8/16	8/17-9/9	9/10-10/3
1943	2/25-3/20	3/21-4/14	4/15-5/10	5/11-6/6	6/7-7/6	7/7-11/8
1944	4-10/5-3	5/4-5/28	5/29-6/21	6/22-7/16	7/17-8/9	8/10-9/2
1945	2/2-3/10 4/7-6/3	3/11-4/6 6/4-7/6	7/7-8/3	8/4-8/29	8/30-9/23	9/24-10/18
1946	3/11-4/4	4/5-4/28	4/29-5/23	5/24-6/17	6/18-7/12	7/13-8/8
1947	4/25-5/19	5/20-6/12	6/13-7/7	7/8-8/1	8/2-8/25	8/26-9/18
1948	2/11-3/7	3/8-4/3	4/4-5/6 6/29-8/2	5/7-6/28 8/3-9/7	9/8-10/5	10/6-10/31
1949	3/26-4/19	4/20-5/13	5/14-6/6	6/7-6/30	7/1-7/25	7/26-8/19
1950	5/5-5/31	6/1-6/26	6/27-7/21	7/22-8/15	8/16-9/9	9/10-10/3
1951	2/25-3/21	3/22-4/15	4/16-5/10	5/11-6/6	6/7-7/7	7/8-11/9
1952	4/10-5/4	5/5-5/28	5/29-6/21	6/22-7/16	7/17-8/9	8/10-9/3
1953	2/2-3/13 4/1-6/5	3/4-3/31 6/6-7/7	7/8-8/3	8/4-8/29	8/30-9/24	9/25-10/18

VENUS SIGN 1910–1975

Libra	Scorpio	Sagittarius	Capricorn	Aquarius	Pisces
11/2-11/25	11/26-12/20	12/21-12/31		1/1-1/18	1/19-2/11
8/21-9/14	9/15-10/10	1/1-1/13	1/14-2/6	2/7-3/2	3/3-3/26
		10/11-11/5	11/6-12/4	12/5-12/31	
10/5-10/28	10/29-11/21	11/22-12/15	12/16-12/31	1/1-4/5	4/6-5/5
11/9-12/7	12/8-12/31		1/1-1/7	1/8-1/31	2/1-2/25
9/5-9/27	1/1-1/2	1/3-1/27	1/28-2/21	2/22-3/16	3/17-4/10
	9/28-10/22	10/23-11/15	11/16-12/10	12/11-12/31	
10/19-11/11	11/12-12/5	12/6-12/29	12/30-12/31	1/1-1/5	1/6-2/1
8/9-9/6	9/7-10/13	10/14-11/14	1/1-1/22	1/23-2/15	2/16-3/11
	11/15-12/31				
9/20-10/13	1/1-1/3	1/4-2/5	2/6-3/4	3/5-3/30	3/31-4/24
	10/14-11/6	11/7-11/30	12/1-12/24	12/25-12/31	
11/1-11/25	11/26-12/19	12/20-12/31		1/1-1/18	1/19-2/11
8/21-9/14	9/15-10/9	1/1-1/12	1/13-2/5	2/6-3/1	3/2-3/26
		10/10-11/5	11/6-12/4	12/5-12/31	
10/4-10/27	10/28-11/20	11/21-12/14	12/15-12/31	1/1-4/4	4/6-5/5
11/9-12/7	12/8-12/31		1/1-1/7	1/8-1/31	2/1-2/24
9/3-9/27	1/1-1/2	1/3-1/27	1/28-2/20	2/21-3/16	3/17-4/9
	9/28-10/21	10/22-11/15	11/16-12/10	12/11-12/31	
10/19-11/11	11/12-12/5	12/6-12/29	12/30-12/31	1/1-1/4	1/5-2/1
8/9-9/6	9/7-10/15	10/16-11/7	1/1-1/21	1/22-2/14	2/15-3/10
	11/8-12/31				
9/19-10/12	1/1-1/4	1/5-2/5	2/6-3/4	3/5-3/29	3/30-4/24
	10/13-11/5	11/6-11/29	11/30-12/23	12/24-12/31	
11/1-1/25	11/26-12/19	12/20-12/31		1/1-1/17	1/18-2/10
8/20-9/14	9/15-10/9	1/1-1/12	1/13-2/5	2/6-3/1	3/2-3/25
		10/10-11/5	11/6-12/5	12/6-12/31	
10/4-10/27	10/28-11/20	11/21-12/13	12/14-12/31	1/1-4/5	4/6-5/4
11/10-12/7	12/8-12/31		1/1-1/7	1/8-1/31	2/1-2/24
9/4-9/27	1/1-1/2	1/3-1/27	1/28-2/20	2/21-3/16	3/17-4/9
	9/28-10/21	10/22-11/15	11/16-12/10	12/11-12/31	
10/19-11/11	11/12-12/5	12/6-12/29	12/30-12/31	1/1-1/5	1/6-2/1

VENUS SIGN 1910–1975

	Aries	Taurus	Gemini	Cancer	Leo	Virgo
1954	3/12-4/4	4/5-4/28	4/29-5/23	5/24-6/17	6/18-7/13	7/14-8/8
1955	4/25-5/19	5/20-6/13	6/14-7/7	7/8-8/1	8/2-8/25	8/26-9/18
1956	2/12-3/7	3/8-4/4	4/5-5/7 6:24-8/4	5/8-6/23 8/5-9/8	9/9-10/5	10/6-10/31
1957	3-26/4-19	4/20-5/13	5/14-6/6	6/7-7/1	7/2-7/26	7/27-8/19
1958	5/6/5/31	6/1-6/26	6/27-7/22	7/23-8/15	8/16-9/9	9/10-10/3
1959	2-25/3-20	3/21-4/14	4/15-5/10	5/11-6/6	6/7-7/8 9/21-9/24	7/9-9/20 9/25-11/9
1960	4-10/5-3	5/4-5/28	5/29-6/21	6/22-7/15	7/16-8/9	8/10-9/2
1961	2-3/6-5	6/6-7/7	7/8-8/3	8/4-8/29	8/30-9/23	9/24-10/17
1962	3/11-4/3	4/4-4/28	4/29-5/22	5/23-6/17	6/18-7/12	7/13-8/8
1963	4/24-5/18	5/19-6/12	6/13-7/7	7/8-7/31	8/1-8/25	8/26-9/18
1964	2/11-3/7	3/8-4/4	4/5-5/9 6/18-8/5	5/10-6/17 8/6-9/8	9/9-10/5	10/6-10/31
1965	3/26-4/18	4/19-5/12	5/13-6/6	6/7-6/30	7/1-7/25	7/26-8/19
1966	5/6-6/31	6/1-6/26	6/27-7/21	7/22-8/15	8/16-9/8	9/9-10/2
1967	2/24-3/20	3/21-4/14	4/15-5/10	5/11-6/6	6/7-7/8 9/10-10/1	7/9-9/9 10/2-11/9
1968	4/9-5/3	5/4-5/27	5/28-6/20	6/21-7/15	7/16-8/8	8/9-9/2
1969	2/3-6/6	6/7-7/6	7/7-8/3	8/4-8/28	8/29-9/22	9/23-10/17
1970	3/11-4/3	4/4-4/27	4/28-5/22	5/23-6/16	6/17-7/12	7/13-8/8
1971	4/24-5/18	5/19-6/12	6/13-7/6	7/7-7/31	8/1-8/24	8/25-9/17
1972	2/11-3/7	3/8-4/3	4/4-5/10 6/12-8/6	5/11-6/11 8/7-9/8	9/9-10/5	10/6-10/30
1973	3/25-4/18	4/18-5/12	5/13-6/5	6/6-6/29	7/1-7/25	7/26-8/19
1974						
1975	5/5-5/31 2/24-3/20	6/1-6/25 3/21-4/13	6/26-7/21 4/14-5/9	7/22-8/14 5/10-6/6	8/15-9/8 6/7-7/9 9/3-10/4	9/9-10/2 7/10-9/2 10/5-11/9

74

VENUS SIGN 1910–1975

Libra	Scorpio	Sagittarius	Capricorn	Aquarius	Pisces
8/9-9/6	9/7-10/22	10/23-10/27	1/1-1/22	1/23-2/15	2/16-3/11
	10/28-12/31				
9/19-10/13	1/1-1/6	1/7-2/5	2/6-3/4	3/5-3/30	3/31-4/24
	10/14-11/5	11/6-11/30	12/1-12/24	12/25-12/31	
11/1-11/25	11/26-12/19	12/20-12/31		1/1-1/17	1/18-2/11
8/20-9/14	9/15-10/9	1/1-1/12	1/13-2/5	2/6-3/1	3/2-3/25
		10/10-11/5	11/6-12/16	12/7-12/31	
10/4-10/27	10/28-11/20	11/21-12/14	12/15-12/31	1/1-4/6	4/7-5/5
11/10-12/7	12/8-12/31		1/1-1/7	1/8-1/31	2/1-2/24
9/3-9/26	1/1-1/2	1/3-1/27	1/28-2/20	2/21-3/15	3/16-4/9
	9/27-10/21	10/22-11/15	11/16-12/10	12/11-12/31	
10/18-11/11	11/12-12/4	12/5-12/28	12/29-12/31	1/1-1/5	1/6-2/2
8/9-9/6	9/7-12/31		1/1-1/21	1/22-2/14	2/15-3/10
9/19-10/12	1/1-1/6	1/7-2/5	2/6-3/4	3/5-3/29	3/30-4/23
	10/13-11/5	11/6-11/29	11/30-12/23	12/24-12/31	
11/1-11/24	11/25-12/19	12/20-12/31		1/1-1/16	1/17-2/10
8/20-9/13	9/14-10/9	1/1-1/12	1/13-2/5	2/6-3/1	3/2-3/25
		10/10-11/5	11/6-12/7	12/8-12/31	
10/3-10/26	10/27-11/19	11/20-12/13	2/7-2/25	1/1-2/6	4/7-5/5
			12/14-12/31	2/26-4/6	
11/10-12/7	12/8-12/23		1/1-1/6	1/7-1/30	1/31-2/23
9/3-9/26	1/1	1/2-1/26	1/27-2/20	2/21-3/15	3/16-4/8
	9/27-10/21	10/22-11/14	11/15-12/9	12/10-12/31	
10/18-11/10	11/11-12/4	12/5-12/28	12/29-12/31	1/1-1/4	1/5-2/2
8/9-9/7	9/8-12/31		1/1-1/21	1/22-2/14	2/15-3/10
9/18-10/11	1/1-1/7	1/8-2/5	2/6-3/4	3/5-3/29	3/30-4/23
	10/12-11/5	11/6-11/29	11/30-12/23	12/24-12/31	
	11/25-12/18	12/19-12/31		1/1-1/16	1/17-2/10
10/31-11/24					
8/20-9/13		1/1-1/12	1/13-2/4	2/5-2/28	3/1-3/24
		10/9-11/5	11/6-12/7	12/8-12/31	
			1/30-2/28	1/1-1/29	
10/3-10/26	10/27-11/19	11/20-12/13	12/14-12/31	3/1-4/6	4/7-5/4
			1/1-1/6	1/7-1/30	1/31-2/23
11/10-12/7	12/8-12/31				

MARS SIGN 1910–1975

	Jan.	Feb.	Mar.	Apr.	May	June	July	Aug.	Sept.	Oct.	Nov.	Dec.
1910	AR	TA	GE	GE	CA	CA	LE	VI	VI	LI	SC	SC
1911	SA	CP	AQ	AQ	PI	AR	TA	TA	GE	GE	GE	TA
1912	TA	GE	GE	CA	CA	LE	LE	VI	LI	LI	SC	SA
1913	CP	CP	AQ	PI	AR	AR	TA	GE	CA	CA	CA	CA
1914	CA	CA	CA	CA	LE	LE	VI	LI	LI	SC	SC	SA
1915	CP	AQ	PI	PI	AR	TA	GE	GE	LI	LE	SA	SA
1916	LE	LE	LE	LE	LE	VI	GE	GE	CA	LE	LE	LE
1917	AQ	AQ	PI	AR	AR	VI	VI	LI	SC	SC	SA	CP
1918	LI	LI	VI	VI	VI	GE	GE	CA	LE	LE	VI	VI
1919	AQ	PI	AR	TA	GE	CA	LE	LE	SC	SA	CP	CP
1920	LI	SC	SC	SC	LI	LI	CA	LI	SC	VI	VI	LI
1921	PI	AR	AR	TA	GE	GE	CA	LE	SA	SA	CP	AQ
1922	SC	SC	SA	SA	SA	SA	SA	SC	LE	VI	VI	LI
1923	PI	AR	AR	TA	GE	CA	CA	LE	CP	CP	CP	LI
1924	SC	SA	CP	CP	AQ	AQ	PI	LE	VI	VI	LI	AQ
1925	AR	TA	TA	GE	CA	CA	LE	VI	VI	LI	PI	LI
1926	SA	CP	CP	AQ	PI	AR	AR	TA	TA	TA	SC	SC
1927	TA	TA	GE	GE	CA	LE	LE	VI	LI	LI	TA	TA
1928	SA	SA	AQ	PI	PI	AR	TA	GE	GE	CA	CA	CA

MARS SIGN 1910–1975

	Jan.	Feb.	Mar.	Apr.	May	June	July	Aug.	Sept.	Oct.	Nov.	Dec.
1929	GE	GE	CA	CA	LE	LE	VI	VI	LI	SC	SC	SA
1930	CP	AQ	AQ	PI	AR	TA	GE	GE	CA	CA	LE	LE
1931	LE	LE	CA	LE	LE	VI	VI	LI	LI	SC	SA	CP
1932	CP	AQ	PI	AR	TA	TA	GE	CA	CA	LE	VI	VI
1933	VI	VI	VI	VI	VI	VI	LI	LI	SC	SA	SA	CP
1934	AQ	PI	AR	AR	TA	GE	GE	CA	LE	LE	VI	LI
1935	LI	LI	LI	LI	LI	LI	LI	SC	SC	VI	CP	LI
1936	PI	PI	AR	TA	GE	GE	CA	LE	LE	SA	LI	AQ
1937	SC	SC	SA	SA	SC	SC	SC	SA	SA	VI	AQ	LI
1938	PI	AR	TA	TA	GE	CA	CA	LE	VI	VI	LI	SC
1939	SC	SA	SA	CP	CP	AQ	PI	CP	CP	AQ	AQ	PI
1940	AR	AR	TA	GE	GE	CA	LE	LE	VI	VI	LI	SC
1941	SA	SA	TA	GE	CA	PI	AR	AR	AR	AR	AR	AR
1942	TA	TA	GE	GE	CA	LE	LE	VI	VI	LI	SC	SC
1943	SA	CP	AQ	AQ	PI	AR	TA	TA	GE	GE	GE	GE
1944	GE	GE	GE	CA	CA	LE	VI	VI	LI	SC	SC	SA
1945	CP	AQ	AQ	PI	AR	TA	TA	GE	CA	CA	LE	LE
1946	CA	CA	CA	CA	LE	LE	VI	LI	LI	SC	SA	SA
1947	CP	AQ	PI	AR	AR	TA	GE	CA	CA	LE	LE	VI

77

MARS SIGN 1910–1975

	Jan.	Feb.	Mar.	Apr.	May	June	July	Aug.	Sept.	Oct.	Nov.	Dec.
1948	VI	LE	LE	LE	LE	VI	VI	LI	SC	SC	SA	CP
1949	AQ	PI	PI	AR	TA	GE	GE	CA	LE	LE	VI	VI
1950	LI	LI	LI	VI	VI	LI	LI	SC	SC	SA	CP	CP
1951	AQ	PI	AR	TA	TA	GE	CA	CA	LE	VI	VI	AQ
1952	LI	SC	SC	SC	SC	SC	CA	SC	SA	CP	CP	LI
1953	AR	AR	AR	TA	GE	GE	CA	LE	VI	VI	LI	LI
1954	SC	SA	SA	CP	CP	CP	SA	LE	SA	PI	AQ	PI
1955	PI	AR	TA	GE	GE	CA	LE	LE	VI	LI	LI	SC
1956	SA	SA	TA	AQ	AQ	PI	PI	PI	PI	PI	PI	AR
1957	AR	TA	TA	GE	CA	AR	LE	VI	VI	LI	SC	SC
1958	SA	CP	CP	AQ	PI	AR	AR	TA	TA	GE	TA	SA
1959	TA	GE	GE	GE	LE	LE	TA	VI	LI	LI	SC	SA
1960	CP	CP	AQ	AQ	CA	AR	VI	GE	GE	CA	CA	CA
1961	CA	CA	CA	CA	CA	LE	VI	VI	LI	SC	SA	SA
1962	CP	AQ	PI	PI	AR	TA	GE	GE	CA	LE	LE	LE
1963	LE	LE	LE	LE	LE	VI	VI	LI	LE	LE	SA	CP
1964	AQ	AQ	PI	AR	TA	TA	VI	CA	SC	SC	VI	VI
1965	VI	VI	VI	VI	VI	VI	LI	LI	LE	SA	CP	CP
1966	AQ	PI	AR	AR	TA	GE	CA	CA	LE	VI	VI	LI

MARS SIGN 1910–1975

	Jan.	Feb.	Mar.	Apr.	May	June	July	Aug.	Sept.	Oct.	Nov.	Dec.
1967	LI	SC	SC	LI	LI	LI	LI	SC	SA	SA	CP	AQ
1968	PI	PI	AR	TA	GE	GE	CA	LE	LE	VI	LI	LI
1969	SC	SC	SA	SA	SA	SA	SA	SA	SA	CP	AQ	PI
1970	PI	AR	TA	TA	GE	CA	CA	LE	VI	VI	LI	SC
1971	SC	SA	CP	CP	AQ	AQ	AQ	AQ	AQ	AQ	PI	PI
1972	AR	TA	TA	GE	CA	CA	LE	LE	VI	LI	SC	SC
1973	SA	CP	CP	AQ	PI	PI	AR	TA	TA	TA	AR	AR
1974	TA	TA	GE	GE	CA	LE	LE	VI	LI	LI	SC	SA
1975	SA	CP	AQ	PI	PI	AR	TA	GE	GE	GE	CA	GE

AR—Aries   LE—Leo   SA—Sagittarius
TA—Taurus   VI—Virgo   CP—Capricorn
GE—Gemini   LI—Libra   AQ—Aquarius
CA—Cancer   SC—Scorpio   PI—Pisces

9

The Planets As "Stars"

The Astrological Cast of Characters in Order of Their Appearance

As you learned in the chapter "Defining Terms," the planets are the *sine qua non* of astrology—the factor without which there would be no such study. It is the placement of the planets in the signs of the zodiac that give those signs meaning in human terms, and the placement of the planets in an individual horoscope that "spell out" that individual's character/personality. As for forecasting, it is the movement (transits) of the planets throughout our lifetime that activate one part of our chart or another and bring out certain life conditions.

Those planets are moving bodies and not "stars" in the astrological sense, though they are sometimes referred to with that word. In Shakespeare's play, *Julius Caesar*, Cassius, one of the conspirators, states, "The fault, dear Brutus, is not in our stars but in ourselves that we are underlings." Shakespeare (Cassius) actually knew what he was talking about because astrology was part and parcel of daily life in Elizabethan times when the play was written, as well as in Caesar's ancient Rome. However, Shakespeare seems to have preferred "stars" as a more poetic word than "planets." He also was right about another thing: The "stars" (planets) don't push people around unless you let them. The key is to understand the role each planet plays in your basic astrological makeup through your natal chart and to get to know yourself via this ancient and pragmatic science. Then you will better understand how the transits of the different planets are most likely to affect you.

Though the planets are not stars by astronomical definition (except for the sun), they do play the starring roles in the great cosmic drama that is acted out every day of our lives, and has been since the beginning of life on earth. There are other heavenly bodies—like the asteroids—that play supporting roles, but most astrologers take the Big Ten into consideration when they do a chart or a personal forecast: the sun, the moon, Mercury, Venus, Mars, Jupiter, Saturn, Uranus, Neptune, and Pluto. (Some of these planets, like the Moon, Venus, and Mars, are touched on in other parts of this book, and you may want to read those sections to get a better understanding of their characteristics.)

Each planet rules one or more signs of the zodiac—i.e., is very closely associated with that sign or signs. The one that rules your sun sign is your own personal planet, so to speak, and its description will fill in more of the background of your sign.

The following is a rundown of the planetary cast of characters, presented in their order of appearance, their actual position in our solar system As you know, the sun is the center of our solar system, and the orbits of the planets form rings around it. Looking at the planets this way underscores the fact that the *closer* planets influence us much more strongly as individuals. Planets farther out in the solar system are not only farther away, they also move much more slowly. While a transit of the moon lasts two days, for instance, a transit of Uranus (which takes eighty-four years to circle the zodiac) may influence your life for many months. However, even with these distant planets, their position in a specific *house* of your own horoscope will greatly influence your astrological makeup.

The Sun

Vital Statistics: 864,000 miles in diameter; average distance from earth, 93 million miles; gaseous nature. Appears to circle the zodiac in 365 days.

Rules: The sign of Leo
Fourth period of life: ages 23 to 41
Role: The true "star" ... the male lead ... the doer ... the activator.

Facts and Foibles: The position of the sun in anyone's horoscope is the central fact about that person, astrologically speaking. Your sun sign is your core—your individuality. It is your ego in the best sense of the word, the part of you that moves you in a certain life direction. No matter what your sun sign is, true self-development means developing the highest potential of that sign. People really grow into their sun signs as they mature, and the sun symbolically governs that stage of life (23 to 41) at which we are (or should be) mature individuals who are concerned with creating something in our own right. The sun is considered a masculine planet, because it is the fiery, animating force of life. We are meant to *express* our sun sign; those who do not can literally have a lifeless quality about them.

Those born under the sign of Leo have been said to be favored because of their rulership by the most important "planet" of them all. In ancient times, the sun was often the chief deity and was worshipped for its extraordinary power. It was recognized that without the sun, life on earth could not exist, and the dimming of its light via an eclipse was a terrifying experience for early civilizations that recognized their dependence upon its warmth and vitalizing nature. Whether or not Leo is a special sign is debatable, but there is no doubt that there is a tendency in some Leo sun sign people to become overly self-centered. Perhaps even unconsciously, they sense that it is a heady destiny to be ruled by the sun, but they are unable to handle its tremendous energies properly.

The Moon

Vital Statistics: 238,857 miles from the earth; 2,160 miles in diameter (one-fourth earth's size). Revolves around the earth (circles the zodiac) in about 27 ½ days

Rules: The sign of cancer
The first four years of human life

Role: The leading lady ... the "feeler" ... the mother ... the reactor.

Facts and Foibles: The moon is not exactly a planet, either; it is a satellite of our own planet, earth. However, it is the largest satellite with respect to its parent planet anywhere in the solar system that we know of. It has a tremendous gravitational pull, which is demonstrated on earth by the changing of the tides and other natural phenomena.

The moon has no light of its own, and we can see it shining only because it reflects the sun. Therefore, the moon is considered a *receptive* or "feminine" planet, rather than an active one like the sun. The moon in mythology has always been a woman—often the "Great Mother" to ancient peoples who saw the sun as the "Great Father." Accordingly, the moon rules the first four years of human life, when we are totally dependent on our mothers, and the motherly sign of Cancer, which is closely associated with nurturing and growth. In an individual horoscope, the position of the moon indicates our ability to feel and to respond emotionally. It is our impressionability and sensitivity, i.e., our subjective rather than our objective sign. The moon reacts to experience and remembers it. All our memories are stored in our subconscious, which is the part of the human psyche the moon signifies. In a sense, as the moon rules the night, it rules our dark or hidden side. As it takes some time for us to develop or grow into our sun sign, the moon sign manifests itself much more strongly in young children than the sun sign does. The moon represents the instinctual nature connected with infantile responses; our moon sign acts from habit, often without thinking.

Mercury

Vital Statistics: 36 million miles away from the sun; 2,900 miles in diameter; orbits sun at 108,000 miles per hour; goes through zodiac in 88 days.

Rules: The signs of Gemini and Virgo
Age of curiosity: 4 through 14

Role: The young male lead ... the observer ... the messenger ... the communicator.

Facts and Foibles: Mercury is the hottest, quickest, and smallest of the planets, and is closest to the sun. It is so closely associated with the sun in an astronomical sense, that Mercury is very often in the same sign as the sun in a natal chart. In any horoscope, it is never more than two signs away from your sun sign.

In ancient times Mercury was regarded as the sun's messenger, and the gods with whom it was associated always had some kind of communicating function. In Egypt, Mercury was Thoth—scribe to the gods, keeper of the divine books. The Greeks called him Hermes, the messenger; the Romans renamed him Mercury, but assigned similar functions. Hermes/Mercury always had a golden tongue, and was regarded as the great persuader. Quickness and deftness also associate Mercury with all kinds of human skills requiring manual and mental dexterity.

Mercury has a double role to play as ruler of the signs of Gemini and Virgo. In a sense, Mercury is two-faced; the communicative side in Gemini, his precise specialist side in Virgo. No matter what your sun sign is, in your horoscope Mercury symbolizes your style of thinking and communicating—not so much how intelligent you are as how you tend to put things together mentally.

Mercury is a very human planet, and has a very human foible; occasionally he gets things all mixed up and causes a lot of trouble. About three times a year, for about three weeks at a time, Mercury seems to be going *backwards*. (That appearance is caused by the varying rates of speed of various planets—like two trains traveling in the same direction that can seem as if they are traveling in two different directions.) During these periods Mercury is said to be *retrograde*, it is known to cause problems in all kinds of human interactions. People get the wrong message, or don't get it at all. People who are supposed to meet on a street corner never find each other. Trains and planes are missed, luggage is lost, orders simply never get transmitted or seem to vanish in thin air. There has been quite a bit of research on Mercury retrograde, and it all proves out. Even if people don't know *why* retrograde Mercury

makes things go wrong, they sure know it does. In 1986 Mercury will be retrograde during these periods:
  March 7 through March 30.
  July 9 through August 3.
  November 2 through November 22.

Venus

Vital Statistics: 67.2 million miles from the sun; 26 million to 160 million miles from earth; approximately the same size and volume as earth. Goes through all twelve signs of the zodiac in about 225 days.

Rules: The signs of Taurus and Libra
       Period of developing sexuality: ages 14 to 21

Role: The young, nubile female lead . . . the love interest . . . the artist.

Facts and Foibles: Like Mercury, Venus follows the sun very closely, so in anyone's horoscope it is never very far away from your sun sign. Symbolically, Venus represents your capacity to love and relate, and the capacity to appreciate beauty. In ancient myth, Venus was seen as the daughter of the moon, a feminine planet associated with many of the earthly things traditionally associated with women: the providing of food and shelter, the beautifying of the home, the harmonizing of opposites and settler of strife. Venus is a peaceful planet in every sense of the word. Aphrodite to the Greeks, Venus to the Romans, this goddess/planet was seen as the bounteous giver of life's gifts and pleasures—the personification of beauty. She is supposed to inspire us with the desire for both material and spiritual growth.

Like Mercury, Venus has two faces, but, strangely, one rules a feminine sign, Taurus, and one rules a masculine sign, Libra. In Taurus, Venus shows her earthier side, more concerned with creature comforts, sex, and material prosperity. In Libra, a more refined Venus shines forth as the graceful "hostess," the one who beautifies things and relates to others.

Though most Libra males are quite virile, their rulership by the planet Venus often manifests itself in extremely good looks and a great appreciation of beauty. The virile male hairdresser or interior decorator is the personification of this side of Venus. Because Venus seeks peace rather than war, harmony rather than discord, she rules lawyers, mediators, and arbitrators.

Since Venus rules one feminine earth sign and one masculine air sign, she is sometimes seen as a symbol for the fact that all things in the universe can be made to work in harmony—even the incompatible elements of air (Libra) and earth (Taurus) and the often antagonistic principles of male and female—in real life as in astrology. Divorce courts come under the rulership of Venus.

Mars

Vital Statistics: 14 million miles from the sun; 35 million miles from earth; 10 percent of earth's size; circles the zodiac in about 687 days.
Rules: The sign of Aries
       Ages 42 to 56
Role: The virile male antagonist ... the lover ... the warrior.
Facts and foibles: Mars is a rather small planet and has sometimes been called "Earth's little brother." However, since ancient times Mars has been attributed with great powers—possibly because of its fiery red color. Even the earliest peoples associated Mars with strife and sex and a warriorlike attitude. In fact, Mars has had a rather bad reputation in astrology and was sometimes known as the "lesser malefic." But some groups assigned Mars another role and gave him a different dimension. The Egyptians called Mars Artes, and connected him with personal creative expression; to the Hebrews he played a similar role. When you think about it, sex, strife, and creative expression are only a few steps away from each other. Certainly, the act of procreation is a creative one, as it gives new life. War and strife are divisive, but often a new order comes out of them as well.

Mars is pure masculine energy—sometimes a bit rough, but always determined. In a personal horoscope, the sign position of Mars tells how you tend to assert yourself, how aggressive you are likely to be when going after what you want, even how much you will want it. Mars is our desire nature. (See the chapter on Venus and Mars to find out more about Mars in your own horoscope.) As the god of war, Mars is associated with courage and bravery, traits that are available to the Aries sun sign person if he/she cares to develop them. Mars is moral courage too, and the Mars-ruled Aries sun sign person at his/her best will never desert a cause or a person—no matter how rough the going gets.

About once every two years Mars returns to the same place it occupied on the day of your birth; to astrologers this is known as the "Mars return." It is a period of time during which one can make great strides, because Mars is stimulating that area of the natal chart connected with taking on the world. People often feel a great surge of energy during their Mars return, but if that energy is not directed in a productive channel, it can cause a lot of problems in relationships. You are far better taking out your Mars return aggressiveness on another job or another creative project rather than another person.

Jupiter

Vital Statistics: Largest planet in the solar system, 318 times larger than earth; 365 million to 600 million miles from earth; gaseous nature; circles the zodiac in about 12 years.
Rules: The sign of Sagittarius
        Ages 57 to 68
Role: The hero ... the "father confessor" ... the one who saves the day.
Facts and Foibles: From earliest times, Jupiter was assigned a role in the "cosmic drama" almost as important as that of the sun. Huge and luminous, Jupiter was easily visible to the naked eye eons before the age of the telescope. The sun may have been god in the all-encompassing sense, but Jupiter was *the* god who could make things happen, even interfere in human affairs if he was needed. And he has always been a "good guy." The Hindus, whose roots lie in antiquity, call him Vishnu, the preserver. To the Greeks, he was Zeus, the god

who reigned supreme on Mount Olympus; he became Jupiter under the Romans. The important thing about this masculine god-planet is that it has always been very godly but very human at the same time. Zeus frequently came down from Mount Olympus to bestow his favors on people—particularly women who caught his fancy (causing his wife Hera to become jealous). Jupiter-Zeus is the god who keeps one foot in heaven and one foot firmly planted on the earth. Since the planet itself is large and impressive-looking, it has always been associated with benevolence and expansiveness. Our English word "jovial" has its roots in the name Jove, by which name Jupiter was sometimes called.

Joviality is one of the characteristics that is available to people born under the sign of Sagittarius, which Jupiter rules. Some Sagittarians are jovial, they spend all their money and all their energy on making life one long party.

But Jupiter has a serious side, too. Jupiter is associated with the divine law, and the ability to make that law known to men on earth. The higher Sagittarian, ruled by Jupiter, has a sense of this mission, and often takes the real-life role of priest-missionary or teacher of higher studies. While Venus and Libra, the sign Venus rules, are associated with the *practice* of law, Jupiter and Sagittarius are connected with the *making* and *interpretation* of laws.

Saturn

Vital Statistics: 75,000 miles in diameter, 95 times as big as earth; 886 million miles from the sun; takes 29 years to circle the zodiac.
Rules: The sign of Capricorn
Ages 68 on
Role: The "older man" ... the taskmaster ... the disciplining father.
Facts and Foibles: Like Jupiter, Saturn is so large it can be seen with the naked eye from earth and was watched carefully by early peoples. It was quickly observed that certain transits of Saturn brought trials and troubles on earth and so the planet earned itself the name of the

"greater malefic" by the time astrologers had begun to record their findings. Is Saturn really a "bad guy" as so many astrology books will tell you? There is no question that Saturn represents the principle of limitation; when you go too far out on a limb or get over expansive, Saturn is always there to teach you that there are rules and restrictions. However, as Saturn also represents the principle of contraction, this planet can and does bring periods of time in which we can consolidate our forces and make a secure place for ourselves in this world.

Saturn is also sometimes called the "lord of Karma." Translated into human terms, that means that Saturn represents our inevitable responsibilities, our "fated" duties in this world. Once again, there is a positive side. When Saturn is strongly placed in an individual's chart, that individual is exceptionally able to handle responsibility and achieve worldly success. As ruler of the sign of Capricorn, Saturn brings to that sign an extraordinary talent for working long and hard as well as reaping the material rewards that come with dedication to a task.

Kronos (or Chronos) was the ancient Greek god who is generally regarded as the prototype for Saturn's particular personality or role, and his story sheds a lot of light on the perceptions of this planet. Kronos was born to the very highest ancient god, Ouranos, and to the original earth mother, Ge. Kronos got a little carried away with this position and overthrew his father (castrating him) to take over the throne. When Kronos was told one of his own children would do the same to him, he swallowed them all—except Zeus, who was miraculously saved and became the "avenger." Later on, Zeus banished Kronos into exile. We know Kronos as Father Time—that shadowy old man who reminds us that it's later than we think. Kronos/Saturn also cautions against runaway ambitions, which is often punished by a downfall like his.

One of the most fascinating aspects of Saturn is that it is an uncannily accurate cosmic clock. Taking about 29 years to make a full circle of the zodiac, Saturn returns to the same place it occupied in your horoscope at your birth when you are about 29 years old. The "Saturn return" is regarded by astrologers as the true end of childhood (astrology is kind to us weak mortals by giving us more time to "grow up" than conventional earthly wisdom does). When Saturn begins to creep up on us in our late twenties, we generally begin to feel that it's time to settle down and do something big in the way of taking on earthly responsibility. Many people go through a "life crisis" at this time, because they feel the push that Saturn is giving them, but have trouble knowing what to do about it. Many, many people resolve the dilemma by getting married, buying a home, having a child, or getting divorced. The point is that it is time to *do something decisive* and to take responsibility for our own lives and actions. There are an incredible number of "Saturn return babies" because having a child is probably the most joyful as well as the biggest responsibility a person can assume.

On its second return—at about the human age of 58—people are generally ready to start relaxing their responsibilities and enjoying the fruits of their labors. It is a wise precaution to make ready for the second Saturn return, because just as Saturn tells us we have to *work*, he also tells us when it is time to *stop* working. But remain a productive human being, with real interests and the wherewithal to pursue them.

Uranus

Vital Statistics: 1.7 billion miles from earth; 29,300 miles in diameter, 15 times larger than earth; takes 84 years to circle the zodiac; has an erratic orbit.
Rules: The sign of Aquarius
Teenagers
Role: The rebel ... the home-wrecker ... the visionary.
Facts and Foibles: Uranus is the first of the "modern" planets, i.e., those unknown to the ancients, and only discovered via the telescope. Uranus, the first planet to be discovered in this manner, was thus a shock to both astronomers and astrologers. Both groups believed the orbit of Saturn defined the limits of our solar system,

and both had to revise their thinking at this discovery. Astrologers took things in their stride by calling Uranus a "planet of the higher octave" and interpreting it as a breakthrough from the realm of purely earthly influences (with Saturn as the dividing line) to the "cosmic" or "higher" order of things. They decided that Uranus—an unconventional planet in many respects—must be the ruler of the quirky sign of Aquarius (which had been formerly ruled by Saturn). In a way it is uncanny that the sudden discovery of Uranus in 1781 heralded all the breakthrough discoveries of the 19th and 20th centuries. In a sense, Uranus ushered in the modern world; it also rules our current Age of Aquarius. As that age (approximately 2000 years long) will continue to shock us with discovery after discovery, it hopefully will also bring us the sense of brotherhood of humanity that is the hallmark of the sign of Aquarius.

As Uranus takes 84 years to circle the zodiac, it stays in each sign about seven years. (It is currently about two-thirds of the way through the sign of Sagittarius.) Whatever Uranus touches as it transits a person's natal chart gets a real jolt. Sometimes very suddenly. Uranus hates the status quo and almost always shakes it up. That means that a lot of changes take place when Uranus comes along, but for most people those changes are eventually positive ones. Uranus gets you out of whatever rut you happen to be in and does it quite forcefully. However, those who resist the changes Uranus "suggests" can cause themselves a lot of trouble. If you aren't willing to bend, Uranus can really "break you up."

Uranus is appropriately associated with the teen years, during which young people are often in a state of rebellion. However, here too, it is a *necessary* fact of life that people must eventually rebel against the strictures of childhood in order to become separate individual human beings. Uranus is associated not only with teenagers, but also with many of the things that represent their rebellion, like rock music, blaring radios, and all that goes with them. In essence, Uranus is the symbol of the electronic modern world.

Neptune

Vital Statistics: 2.6 billion miles from earth; 2.7 billion miles from the sun; takes about 165 years to circle the zodiac.

Rules: The sign of Pisces
No specific age.

Role: The fascinating stranger ... the poet ... the one who confuses the issue... the dreamer of great dreams.

Facts and Foibles: As it is difficult to get a handle on people heavily influenced by Neptune (like Pisceans), it took astronomers a while to figure out what Neptune really was. At first they observed nothing but some rather weird abberations in the orbit of Uranus as they began to plot that planet's orbit. In the early 1840s, some of them proved mathematically that there *must* be another planet out there, although it couldn't be seen. Finally, using all the data at hand, a German astronomer spotted Neptune in 1846.

There is a rather "sneaky" character to Neptune, but what this nebulous planet really symbolizes is the love that passes all understanding, the all-encompassing universal love that is virtually impossible for mortals to feel and give. Venus represents two-way love, the sharing kind. Neptune's love goes only in one direction. Neptune gives in a sense of self-sacrifice, and takes nothing in return.

There is evidence that even though no one really *saw* Neptune until 1846, the ancients knew all about its principles, and embodied them in the mythical figure of Poseidon (later called Neptune), the lord of the seas, master of the deep. When you think that more than three-quarters of the earth's surface is covered by water, you realize that Neptune was pretty important in the overall scheme of things. In fact, according to the Greeks, when the universe was created, it was divided among Zeus-Jupiter, who took the heavens, Hades-Pluto who took the underworld, and Poseidon-Neptune who took the oceans.

Just as water is difficult to contain, it is difficult for many people to get in touch with Neptune's higher qualities in their own charts. Water is soul and spirit, metaphysically speaking, so Neptune should make us aspire to much higher things. Not only universal love, but poetry, music and art in its purest forms. However, what Neptune touches in most people's natal charts often turns into an area of confusion rather than creativity. Neptune rules liquid in all its forms and, unfortunately, some people react to Neptune's confusing vibes by turning to alcohol or drugs. For many drug and alcohol abusers, however, the real goal of their vice is to attain a kind of "cosmic consciousness" which is the real realm of Neptune.

Since Neptune takes 165 years to circle the zodiac, it stays in one sign for 13 years or more. Therefore, it is the zodiacal *sign* Neptune makes to the "personal planets" in your chart that really count. People positively influenced by Neptune make the true artists and poets of this world—as well as the visionaries who interpret its meaning in more philosophical and metaphysical terms.

Pluto

Vital Statistics: 3,666 billion miles from the sun; takes about 242 years to circle the zodiac.
Rules: The sign of Scorpio
Prenatal
Role: The "heavy" . . . the transformer . . . the tragic hero.
Facts and Foibles: As you will note, Pluto is a little light on vital statistics. That's because this immensely distant planet, only discovered in 1930, has yet to reveal some of its secrets to astronomers. Like Neptune, it was discovered only because of the erratic nature of the orbit of Uranus. But, even when Pluto was conclusively sighted in 1930, its small size relative to its extremely strong gravitational pull didn't make sense to astronomers. Either Pluto is much larger than we now think or it is so dense that it exerts a force much greater than its size should account for.

Either way, there's no doubt that Pluto represents *power*. In fact, many astrologers connect the discovery of Pluto with the discovery by man of the extraordinary power in matter itself—the power of the atom. As with Neptune, Pluto's "realm" had been staked out in myth and astrology long before its actual discovery. Pluto is Hades, lord of the underworld—the place of darkness that all men fear. However, since most older religions regard life and death as a cycle, Pluto represents rebirth as well. We die only to be reborn. One of the symbols for Pluto is the Phoenix that rises triumphantly from its own ashes. Pluto—and the sign of Scorpio that it rules—hold onto their secrets, but have an incredible power to endure and triumph over life's circumstances. The extremes of life and death that Pluto/Scorpio is associated with connect neatly with the extremism of this astrological sign. "Plutonic" Scorpios often regard the world as totally black and white, with very few grays in between. They can also be the "best" of people, like reformers and religious leaders, or the "worst" of people, like criminals and those who manipulate others for their own purposes.

10

Astrotrivia

How Do You Rate in the Best Game in Town?

The ancient art of astrology is loaded with bits and pieces of miscellaneous information—all of it fascinating, and some of it more useful than you may think. For instance, did you know that every zodiac sign has a special day of the week and certain colors assigned to it? And, how good are you at guessing sun signs of celebrities—those larger-than-life models of sun signs in the flesh? The Astrotrivia that follows is partly in quiz form, partly in short-take astrological facts. In the first part, you can test your own astrological perceptivity; in the second, you can add a lot to your fund of astrological information—and maybe even learn a few things, you can use in your daily life.

Astrotrivia Part I
Sun Signs of the Rich and Famous

Try to answer the following questions yourself; if you're stumped you'll find the answers on page 103–104.

1. What famous stripper and the famous actress who played her mother in a Broadway show have the sign of Capricorn in common?

2. What two show biz buddies—who run in the same pack—are both Sagittarians?

3. What do these people have in common: Joseph Stalin, Richard Nixon, Herman Goering, Al Capone, and Mao Tse Tung?

4. What two handsome male movie stars, both known for their progressive ideas, have the same sun sign? And, what is it?

5. What highly Scorpionic actor had an on-again, off-again lifetime romance with a glamourous Pisces actress?

6. What two female tennis pros are both athletic Sagittarians?

7. What U.S. president had a "show-me-I'm-from-Missouri" personality, and what was his sun sign?

8. What two famous "lonely hearts" columnists get their soft Cancerian shoulders cried on all the time?

9. What two "greats" of American popular music were both thoroughly American, and both born on the Fourth of July?

10. Under what sign were these warrior peacemakers all born: Dwight D. Eisenhower, David Ben Gurion, Jimmy Carter, Mohandus Ghandi, and Eleanor Roosevelt?

11. What anti-American villainess of World War II was born on the Fourth of July?

12. What sun sign do these people have in common: Oscar Wilde, Truman Capote, and Gore Vidal?

13. What two famous rock stars—one early, one late—were born not only under the same sign, but on the same day?

14. Which of the following is/was not a Scorpio?
    Charles Manson   Robert Kennedy
    Bo Derek   Pablo Picasso
    Katherine Hepburn   Indira Ghandi
    Princess Grace   Johnny Carson
    Henry Kissinger   Billy Graham

15. All of the following were born under the two most musical signs of the zodiac. What are they?

Judy Collins	Michael Jackson
Barbra Steisand	George Gershwin
Stevie Wonder	Luciano Pavarotti
Fred Astaire	Paul Simon
Irving Berlin	Julie Andrews
Bing Crosby	Anthony Newly
Beverly Sills	John Lennon
Bobby Darin	Guiseppe Verdi

16. All the following ladies of the stage and screen are masters of their craft. Which craftsman-like sun sign were they all born under?

Lauren Bacall	Celeste Holm
Anne Bancroft	Greer Garson
Ingrid Bergman	Twiggy
Greta Garbo	Jo Ann Worley
Sophia Loren	Claudette Colbert
Lilly Tomlin	Raquel Welch

17. What sun sign do the following famous rebels and rule-breakers have in common: Marlon Brando, Warren Beatty, Eddie Murphy, Charlie Chaplin, Hugh Hefner?

18. What sun sign do these medical and research geniuses have in common: Madame Curie, Jonas Salk, Christian Bernard?

19. What present-day famous Leo "princess" lived in Camelot with her Gemini "prince"?

20. What two great ballet stars were both born in the same country, and share the graceful sun sign, Pisces?

Answers on p. 103–104

Astrotrivia Part II
More Celebrity Sun Sign Lore

Just a handful of the many, many stage/screen-struck Leos:

Robert DeNiro	Julia Child
Mike Jagger	Arlene Dahl
Lucille Ball	Alfred Hitchcock
Dustin Hoffman	Mae West
Cecil B. Demille	George Bernard Shaw
John Derek	Dino D. Laurentis
Mike Douglas	Robert Mitchum
Robert Redford	Peter O'Toole
Jason Robards Jr.	Roman Polanski
Esther Williams	Jill St. John
Stanley Kubrick	Robert Taylor
Shelly Winters	Keenan Wynn

And here are some Leos who make/made the international scene their stage:

Fidel Castro	Henry Ford
Jackie Onassis	Alex Haley
Coco Chanel	Lawrence of Arabia
Benito Mussolini	Mata Hari
Rasputin	Napoleon
Neil Armstrong	Andy Warhol
Mike Conners	

Librans are often lovely, like Catherine Deneuve and Brigitte Bardot. Barbara Walters is the ultimate "cool" Libra.

Cancer is the second fame sign, because Cancer rules the public. Cancers who have made it somehow or other are:

Bill Cosby	Ringo Starr
Jimmy Cagney	John Glenn
Ernest Hemingway	Arthur Ashe
Gerald Ford	The Mayo brothers (of the Mayo clinic)

Some outspoken, inventive Aquarians whose opinions have not always been popular, but were always ahead of their time:

Norman Mailer	Ralph Nader
Charles Darwin	Thomas Edison
Jules Verne	Betty Friedan
Ayn Rand	Vanessa Redgrave
Galileo	Franklin D. Roosevelt

Astrotrivia Part III
Fascinating Facts About the Signs

Here are the colors that, by tradition, match each of the signs of the zodiac:

1. Aries: bright red, scarlet, magenta

2. Taurus: pastels in most shades, especially pink and turquoise

3. Gemini: beiges and light gray

4. Cancer: shimmery and irridescent shades of gray and silver; anything luminous

5. Leo: bright golds and yellows

6. Virgo: dark navy, brown, gray

7. Libra: cloudy pales, especially blue-green

8. Scorpio: murky colors, especially blood red and black

9. Sagittarius: rich blues, purples, greens

10. Capricorn: black, "no-color" colors

11. Aquarius: checks, stripes, patterns, electric blue

12. Pisces: deep lilac, mauve, sea green

Each Sign/Planet owns a day of the week:

Sunday = Sun/Leo

Monday = Moon/Cancer

Tuesday = Mars/Aries, Mars/Scorpio

Wednesday = Mercury/Gemini, Mercury/Virgo

Thursday = Jupiter/Sagittarius, Neptune/Pisces

Friday = Venus/Taurus, Venus/Libra

Saturday = Saturn/Capricorn, Saturn/Aquarius

(Since there are only seven days and twelve signs, some of the signs double up. Also, since the ancients only knew seven planets, there are only enough days to match seven of the ten planets we now recognize.)

Astrotrivia Part IV
Where Do You Belong?

Each sign is said to have certain places where it belongs. Long ago, the world was divided up according to astrological tradition, so there are certain countries, cities, and areas that have the vibrations of certain signs. Tradition divides up other kinds of spaces, too, as you will see.

- *Aries places:* In the world: Birmingham, Oldman, Leicester, and Blackburn, *England* ... Florence, Naples, Verona and Padua *Italy* ... Marseilles and Burgundy *France* ... *Denmark, Germany, Palestine, Syria, Japan.*

    Anywhere: sheepfolds, forges, tool houses, fireplaces, on sandy soil, kilns, ceilings, fire houses, emergency rooms.

- *Taurus places:* In the world: Dublin, *Ireland* ... Mantua, Parma, Palermo, *Italy* ... St. Louis, *U.S.A.* ... *The Greek Islands, Asia Minor,* the *Caucasus.*

    Anywhere: banks, dairies, pastures, shady places, corn fields, middle rooms of houses, altars, maypoles.

- *Gemini places:* In the world: San Francisco, *U.S.A.* ... London and Plymouth, *England* ... Bruges, *Belgium* ... Versailles and Louvaine, *France* ... Nurenburg, *Germany* ... *Lower Egypt, Armenia, Wales.*

    Anywhere: buildings with pillars, bookcases, hills and mountains, upper back rooms, graineries.

- *Cancer places:* In the world; St. Andrews, *Scotland* ... Amsterdam, *Holland* ... New York City, *U.S.A.* ... Stockholm, *Sweden* ... Genoa, Venice, Milan, *Italy* ... *Paraguay, North and West Africa.*

Anywhere: lakes and brooks, salt marshes, pubs, kitchens, cellars, corner houses facing north.
- *Sagittarius places:* In the world: Avignon, *France* ... Stuttgart, Cologne, *Germany* ... Nottingham, Sheffield, Bradford, *England* ... Provence, *France* ... *Hungary, Arabia, Tuscany.*

   Anywhere: highest place around, topmost room in house, stables for racing horses, obelisks, places near fire, where incense is burned.
- *Capricorn places:* In the world: Brussels, *Belgium* ... Port Said, *Egypt* ... *India, Afghanistan, Mexico, Lithuania, Orkney Islands, Macedonia.*

   Anywhere: vaults, convents, thick forests, gates and hinges, old trees, jails, cattle barns, door knockers, game preserves.
- *Aquarius places:* In the world: Brighton and Trent, *England* ... Salszburg, *Austria* ... Hamburg, *Germany* ... the Piedmont, *Italy* ... *Prussia, Red Russia, Westphalia.*

   Anywhere: buses, bridges, ladders, garages, airplanes, power transmitters, fountains, springs and streams, sleds, ice caps.
- *Pisces places:* In the world; Alexandria, *Egypt* ... Seville, *Spain* ... Southport, Lancaster, Bournemouth, Tiverton, *England* ... *Portugal, Calabria, Normandy, Sahara.*

   Anywhere: fish ponds, oceans, oil fields, submarines, séances, flooded areas, bars, aquariums, boat yards, swimming pools, hospitals.
- *Leo Places:* In the world: Rome, Ravenna, *Italy* ... Bath, Bristol, Portsmouth, Blackpool, *England* ... Philadelphia, Chicago, *U.S.A.* ... *Bohemia, Sicily, the Alps, Damascus.*

   Anywhere: wild animal preserves, deserts and forests, castles, furnaces, gold mines, porches, forts.
- *Virgo places:* In the world: Paris, Lyons, Toulouse, *France* ... Boston, Los Angeles, *U.S.A.* ... Heidelberg, *Germany* ... *Turkey, West Indies, Brazil, Silesia, Switzerland.*

   Anywhere: pantries, restaurants, refrigerators, medicine cabinets, desks, malt houses.

- *Libra places:* In the world: Dover, Liverpool, Newcastle, *England* ... Messina, *Italy* ... Halifax, *Nova Scotia* ... *China, Norway, The Transvaal, the Barbary coast.*

    Anywhere: windmills, wood sheds, harbors, tops of mountains, garrets and lofts, guest rooms, tops of dressers, domed buildings.
- *Scorpio places:* In the world: Copenhagen, *Denmark* ... Leeds, Nottingham, *England* ... Johannesburg, *South Africa* ... Burma, *India* ... *Tibet, North China, Argentina.*

    Anywhere: junk yards, meat markets, laboratories, low gardens and streams, vineyards, deepest part of ocean.

Astrotrivia Part V
Which Animal Best Suits You?

Each sign is said to have an affinity with certain kinds of pets. Here's the rundown.

Aries: No animal that needs a lot of taking care of; but if Aries has one pet, he/she will usually have two, so the animals can take care of each other.

Taurus: Almost any kind of soft, warm creature. Taurus is a great nature lover, so even a skunk would be welcome.

Gemini: Anything with fascinating habits, like bees or ants, or anything that talks, like a parrot or a minah bird.

Cancer: Anything in need of a mother is welcome in Cancer's house, no matter how sloppy or in need of care.

Leo: Cats, of course, preferably with good breeding. Peacocks or anything with bright colors or plumage are fine too.

Virgo: Cats are preferable, because they are clean animals, but any animal in distress brings out Virgo's warmth.

Libra: This sign would just as soon do without, but if a pet is preferred, it's the perfectly groomed poodle or other refined breed of dog or cat.

Scorpio: This sign goes for rather dangerous pets, such as snakes, or anything with a sting. Basically, animals are creatures to be observed, not coddled.

Sagittarius: Horses—at home or at the race track. Any very large dog in the city, almost anything of immense size in the country.

Capricorn: Capricorns *need* pets to help pull them out of their frequent depressions. The friendliest kind of animals are the best bet, like sheepdogs.

Aquarius: This sign needs a very smart animal, so is picky about the breed of dog or cat. Actually, birds are preferable to this cool sign.

Pisces: Many people born under this sign will take in any stray that strays into their path, no matter how scraggly or ugly. They often put animals before humans in their scheme of things.

Astrotrivia Part I answers

1. Gypsy Rose Lee and Ethel Merman (who played Gypsy's mother in *Gypsy*).
2. Frank Sinatra and Sammie Davis, Jr.
3. They were all born under the calculating sign of Capricorn.
4. Paul Newman and Alan Alda were both born under the sign of Aquarius.
5. Richard Burton was the Scorpio; Liz Taylor the Pisces.
6. Billie Jean King and Chris Evert.
7. Harry S. Truman, a Taurus.
8. Abigail Van Buren ("Dear Abby") and Ann Landers.

9. George M. Cohan ("Yankee Doodle Dandy") and Louis "Satchmo" Armstrong.
10. Libra.
11. Tokyo Rose.
12. Libra.
13. Elvis Presley and David Bowie (January 5—Capricorn).
14. Henry Kissinger. He's a wily Gemini, but he could easily fool you, because his moon sign is Scorpio.
15. The column on the left are Taureans; those on the right are Librans.
16. Virgo.
17. Aries.
18. Scorpio.
19. Jackie Kennedy Onassis is a Leo; John F. Kennedy was a Gemini.
20. Rudolph Nureyev and Vaslav Nijinsky.

11

Sun Sign Changes. 1920–1975

If you were born "on the cusp" (very near the end or the beginning of a sign) you can find out what your sign really is by using the chart that follows. Many people do not realize that the sun does not "change signs" on the same day every year—or, for that matter, at the same time. For this reason the chart of sun sign changes is calculated to the minute.

How to Use the Chart

Locate your year of birth, then the month in which you were born. Let's say you were born in April of 1942. In the box for that month and year you will see

20–Tau
12:30 P.M.

That means if you are born *after* 12:30 p.m. on April 20 in 1942, you are a Taurus. If you were born before that date and time, your sun sign is the preceding one, Aries.

In this chart (as well as in the rising-sign chart) the signs are abbreviated as follows:

Ar = Aries
Tau = Taurus
Gem = Gemini
Can = Cancer
Leo = Leo
Vir = Virgo
Lib = Libra
Sc = Scorpio

Sag = Sagittarius
Cap = Capricorn
Aq = Aquarius
Pis = Pisces

NOTE: All times given in the sun sign changes chart are Eastern Standard. You must correct for daylight savings time (subtract one hour) and for time zone. For Central Standard Time subtract one hour; for Mountain Standard Time subtract two hours; for Pacific Standard Time subtract three hours.

	1920	1921	1922	1923	1924	1925	1926	1927	1928	1929
Jan	21–Aq 4:05 am	20–Aq 8:55 am	20–Aq 2:48 pm	20–Aq 8:35 pm	21–Aq 2:29 am	20–Aq 8:20 am	20–Aq 2:13 pm	20–Aq 8:12 pm	21–Aq 1:57 am	20–Aq 7:42 am
Feb	19–Pis 5:29 pm	18–Pis 11:21 pm	19–Pis 5:16 am	19–Pis 11:00 am	19–Pis 4:51 pm	18–Pis 11:43 pm	18–Pis 4:35 am	19–Pis 10:35 am	19–Pis 4:20 pm	18–Pis 10:07 pm
Mar	20–Ar 5:00 pm	20–Ar 10:51 pm	21–Ar 4:49 am	21–Ar 10:29 am	20–Ar 4:20 pm	20–Ar 11:13 pm	21–Ar 4:01 am	21–Ar 11:59 am	20–Ar 3:44 pm	20–Ar 9:35 pm
Apr	20–Tau 4:39 am	20–Tau 10:32 am	20–Tau 4:29 pm	20–Tau 10:06 pm	20–Tau 3:59 am	20–Tau 10:51 am	20–Tau 3:36 pm	20–Tau 9:32 pm	20–Tau 3:17 am	20–Tau 9:11 am
May	21–Gem 4:22 am	21–Gem 10:17 am	21–Gem 9:11 am	22–Gem 9:45 am	21–Gem 3:41 am	21–Gem 10:33 am	21–Gem 3:15 pm	21–Gem 9:08 pm	21–Gem 2:53 am	21–Gem 8:48 am
June	21–Can 12:40pm	21–Can 6:36 pm	22–Can 12:27 am	22–Can 6:03 am	21–Can 12:noon	21–Can 5:50 pm	21–Can 11:18 pm	22–Can 5:07 am	21–Can 11:07 am	21–Can 5:01 pm
July	22–Leo 11:40 pm	23–Leo 5:31 am	23–Leo 11:20 am	23–Leo 5:01 pm	22–Leo 11:58 pm	23–Leo 4:45 am	23–Leo 10:25 am	23–Leo 4:17 pm	22–Leo 11:02 pm	23–Leo 3:54 am
Aug	23–Vir 6:22 am	23–Vir 12:15 pm	23–Vir 6:04 pm	23–Vir 11:52 pm	23–Vir 5:48 am	23–Vir 11:33 am	23–Vir 5:14 pm	23–Vir 11:06 pm	23–Vir 4:53 am	23–Vir 10:41 am
Sept	23–Lib 3:25 am	23–Lib 11:20 am	23–Lib 5:10 am	23–Lib 9:04 pm	23–Lib 2:58 am	23–Lib 8:43 am	23–Lib 2:25 pm	23–Lib 8:17 pm	23–Lib 2:36 am	23–Lib 7:52 am
Oct	23–Sc 12:31 pm	23–Sc 6:03 pm	23–Sc 11:53 pm	24–Sc 5:51 am	23–Sc 11:44 am	23–Sc 5:31 pm	23–Sc 11:18 pm	24–Sc 5:07 am	23–Sc 10:55 am	23–Sc 4:41 pm
Nov	22–Sag 9:15 am	22–Sag 3:21 am	22–Sag 8:55 pm	23–Sag 2:54 am	22–Sag 8:46 am	22–Sag 2:36 am	22–Sag 8:28 am	23–Sag 2:14 am	22–Sag 8:00 am	22–Sag 1:48 pm
Dec	21–Cap 10:17 pm	22–Cap 4:08 am	22–Cap 9:57 pm	22–Cap 3:53 pm	21–Cap 10:45 pm	22–Cap 3:37 am	22–Cap 9:34 am	22–cap 3:18 pm	21–Cap 9:04 pm	22–Cap 2:53 am

	1930	1931	1932	1933	1934	1935	1936	1937	1938	1939
Jan	20–Aq 1:33 pm	21–Aq 7:18 am	20–Aq 1:07 am	20–Aq 6:53 am	20–Aq 10:37 am	20–Aq 6:29 pm	21–Aq 12:12am	20–Aq 6:01 am	20–Aq 11:59 am	20–Aq 5:51 pm
Feb	19–Pis 4:00 am	19–Pis 9:06 am	19–Pis 3:29 pm	19–Pis 9:16 pm	19–Pis 3:02 am	19–Pis 8:52 am	19–Pis 2:33 pm	18–Pis 3:21 pm	19–Pis 2:20 am	19–Pis 8:10 pm
Mar	21–Ar 3:30 am	21–Ar 9:40 am	20–Ar 2:54 pm	21–Ar 8:43 pm	21–Ar 2:28 am	21–Ar 8:19 am	20–Ar 1:58 pm	20–Ar 7:45 pm	21–Ar 1:43 am	21–Ar 7:29 am
Apr	20–Tau 3:06 pm	20–Tau 8:40 pm	20–Tau 2:28 am	20–Tau 8:19 am	20–Tau 2:00 pm	20–Tau 7:50 pm	20–Tau 1:31 am	20–Tau 7:20 am	20–Tau 1:15 pm	20–Tau 6:55 pm
May	21–Gem 2:42 pm	21–Gem 8:15 pm	21–Gem 2:07 am	21–Gem 7:57 am	21–Gem 1:35 pm	21–Gem 7:25 pm	21–Gem 1:08 am	21–Gem 6:57 am	21–Gem 12:51 pm	21–Gem 6:27 pm
June	21–Can 11:53 pm	23–Can 4:28 am	21–Can 10:23 am	21–Can 4:12 pm	21–Can 9:48 pm	22–Can 3:32 am	21–Can 9:22 am	21–Can 3:12 pm	21–Can 9:04 pm	22–Can 2:40 am
July	23–Leo 10:42 am	23–Leo 3:21 pm	22–Leo 9:18 pm	23–Leo 3:06 am	23–Leo 8:42 am	23–Leo 2:33 pm	22–Leo 8:18 am	23–Leo 2:07 am	23–Leo 7:57 am	23–Leo 1:37 pm
Aug	23–Vir 4:27 pm	23–Vir 10:10 pm	23–Vir 4:06 am	23–Vir 9:53 am	23–Vir 3:32 pm	23–Vir 9:24 pm	23–Vir 3:11 am	23–Vir 8:58 am	23–Vir 2:46 pm	23–Vir 8:31 pm
Sept	23–Lib 1:35 pm	23–Lib 7:23 pm	23–Lib 1:16 am	23–Lib 7:01 am	23–Lib 10:45 am	23–Lib 6:38 pm	23–Lib 12:26 am	23–Lib 6:13 am	23–Lib 12:noon	23–Lib 5:50 pm
Oct	23–Sc 11:25 pm	24–Sc 4:15 am	23–Sc 10:04 am	23–Sc 3:48 pm	23–Sc 9:35 pm	24–Sc 3:29 am	23–Sc 10:18 am	23–Sc 3:06 pm	23–Sc 8:54 pm	24–Sc 2:46 am
Nov	22–Sag 7:34 pm	23–Sag 1:25 am	22–Sag 7:10 am	22–Sag 10:53 am	22–Sag 6:44 pm	23–Sag 12:35 am	22–Sag 6:25 pm	22–Sag 12:17 am	22–Sag 6:06 pm	22–Sag 11:59 pm
Dec	22–Cap 8:40 am	22–Cap 2:30 pm	21–Cap 8:14 pm	22–Cap 1:58 am	22–Cap 5:49 pm	22–Cap 1:37 pm	21–Cap 7:27 pm	22–Cap 1:22 am	22–Cap 7:13 am	22–Cap 1:05 pm

	1940	1941	1942	1943	1944	1945	1946	1947	1948
Jan	20–Aq 11:44 pm	20–Aq 5:34 am	20–Aq 11:16 am	20–Aq 5:20 pm	20–Aq 11:09 pm	20–Aq 4:55 am	20–Aq 10:44 am	20–Aq 4:23 pm	20–Aq 10:18 pm
Feb	19–Pis 2:04 pm	18–Pis 7:59 am	19–Pis 1:39 am	19–Pis 7:41 am	19–Pis 1:28 pm	18–Pis 7:15 pm	19–Pis 1:10 am	19–Pis 6:53 am	19–Pis 12:37 pm
Mar	20–Ar 1:24 pm	20–Ar 7:21 pm	21–Ar 1:03 am	21–Ar 7:03 am	21–Ar 12:49 pm	20–Ar 6:38 pm	21–Ar 12:34 am	21–Ar 6:13 am	20–Ar 11:57 am
Apr	20–Tau 12:51 pm	20–Tau 6:51 pm	20–Tau 12:30 pm	20–Tau 6:32 pm	20–Tau 12:18 am	20–Tau 6:08 am	20–Tau 12:03 pm	20–Tau 5:40 pm	19–Tau 11:25 pm
May	21–Gem 12:23 am	21–Gem 6:23 pm	21–Gem 12:01 pm	21–Gem 6:03 pm	20–Gem 11:51 pm	22–Gem 5:41 am	21–Gem 1:34 am	21–Gem 5:04 pm	20–Gem 10:58 pm
June	21–Can 8:37 am	21–Can 2:33 am	21–Can 8:08 pm	22–Can 2:13 am	21–Can 9:03 am	21–Can 1:52 pm	21–Can 7:45 pm	22–Can 1:19 am	21–Can 7:11 am
July	22–Leo 7:34 pm	23–Leo 1:26 am	23–Leo 6:59 am	23–Leo 1:05 pm	22–Leo 6:55 pm	23–Leo 12:48 am	23–Leo 6:37 am	23–Leo 12:12 pm	22–Leo 6:06 pm
Aug	23–Vir 2:21 am	23–Vir 8:30 am	23–Vir 1:50 pm	23–Vir 7:55 pm	23–Vir 1:47 am	23–Vir 7:36 am	23–Vir 1:23 pm	23–Vir 7:09 pm	23–Vir 1:03 am
Sept	22–Lib 11:46 pm	23–Lib 5:33 am	23–Lib 11:10 am	23–Lib 5:12 pm	22–Lib 11:02 pm	23–Lib 4:50 am	23–Lib 10:41 am	23–Lib 4:29 pm	22–Lib 10:22 pm
Oct	23–Sc 8:39 am	23–Sc 2:22 pm	22–Sc 8:01 pm	24–Sc 2:09 am	23–Sc 7:57 am	20–Sc 1:45 pm	23–Sc 7:37 pm	24–Sc 1:27 am	23–Sc 7:19 am
Nov	22–Sag 5:49 am	22–Sag 11:38 pm	22–Sag 5:23 pm	22–Sag 11:22 pm	22–Sag 5:09 pm	22–Sag 10:56 pm	22–Sag 4:47 pm	22–Sag 10:38 pm	22–Sag 4:29 pm
Dec	21–Cap 6:55 pm	22–Cap 12:44 am	22–Cap 6:31 am	22–Cap 12:30 pm	21–Cap 6:15 pm	22–Cap 12:04 am	22–Cap 5:54 pm	22–Cap 11:44 am	21–Cap 5:23 pm

	1949	1950	1951	1952	1953	1954	1955	1956	1957
Jan	20–Aq 4:11 am	20–Aq 10:00 am	20–Aq 3:53 pm	20–Aq 9:38 pm	20–Aq 3:22 am	20–Aq 9:14 am	20–Aq 3:03 pm	20–Aq 8:49 pm	20–Aq 2:43 am
Feb	18–Pis 6:27 pm	19–Pis 12:16 am	19–Pis 6:10 am	19–Pis 11:57 am	18–Pis 5:41 pm	19–Pis 11:33 pm	19–Pis 5:19 am	19–Pis 11:05 am	18–Pis 5:01 pm
Mar	20–Ar 5:49 pm	20–Ar 11:30 pm	21–Ar 5:26 am	20–Ar 11:14 am	20–Ar 5:01 pm	20–Ar 10:54 pm	21–Ar 4:36 am	20–Ar 10:21 am	20–Ar 4:17 pm
Apr	20–Tau 5:18 am	20–Tau 11:00 am	20–Tau 4:49 pm	20–Tau 10:37 pm	19–Tau 4:26 am	20–Tau 10:20 am	20–Tau 3:58 pm	19–Tau 9:44 pm	20–Tau 3:45 am
May	21–Gem 4:51 am	21–Gem 10:27 am	21–Gem 4:15 pm	20–Gem 10:04 pm	21–Gem 3:53 am	21–Gem 9:48 am	21–Gem 3:25 pm	20–Gem 9:13 pm	21–Gem 3:09 am
June	21–Can 1:03 pm	21–Can 6:37 pm	22–Can 12:25 am	21–Can 6:13 am	21–Can 12:noon	21–Can 5:55 pm	21–Can 11:32 pm	21–Can 5:24 am	21–Can 11:21 am
July	22–Leo 1:58 pm	23–Leo 5:30 am	23–Leo 11:29 am	22–Leo 5:05 pm	22–Leo 10:53 pm	23–Leo 4:45 am	23–Leo 10:25 am	22–Leo 4:20 pm	22–Leo 10:13 pm
Aug	23–Vir 6:49 pm	23–Vir 12:24 pm	23–Vir 6:22 pm	23–Vir 12:03 am	23–Vir 5:46 am	23–Vir 11:37 am	23–Vir 5:19 pm	22–Vir 11:15 pm	23–Vir 5:07 am
Sept	23–Lib 4:05 am	23–Lib 9:44 am	23–Lib 3:38 pm	22–Lib 9:24 pm	23–Lib 3:07 am	23–Lib 8:56 am	23–Lib 2:42 pm	22–Lib 8:30 pm	23–Lib 2:27 am
Oct	23–Sc 1:04 pm	23–Sc 6:48 pm	23–Sc 12:37 am	23–Sc 6:22 am	23–Sc 12:07 pm	23–Sc 5:58 pm	22–Sc 11:44 pm	23–Sc 5:35 am	23–Sc 11:33 am
Nov	22–Sag 10:17 am	22–Sag 4:03 pm	22–Sag 9:52 pm	22–Sag 3:36 am	22–Sag 9:23 am	22–Sag 3:14 pm	22–Sag 9:02 pm	22–Sag 2:51 am	22–Sag 8:45 am
Dec	21–Cap 11:24 am	22–Cap 5:14 am	22–Cap 11:01 am	21–Cap 4:44 pm	21–Cap 10:22 pm	22–Cap 4:25 am	22–Cap 10:12 am	21–Cap 4:00 pm	21–Cap 9:49 pm

	1958	1959	1960	1961	1962	1963	1964	1965	1966
Jan	20–Aq 2:20 pm	20–Aq 2:20 pm	20–Aq 8:11 pm	20–Aq 2:02 am	20–Aq 7:49 am	20–Aq 1:55 pm	19–Aq 7:43 pm	20–Aq 1:30 am	20–Aq 8:21 am
Feb	18–Pis 10:49 pm	19–Pis 4:38 pm	19–Pis 10:26 am	18–Pis 6:27 pm	18–Pis 10:16 pm	19–Pis 4:09 am	19–Pis 10:25 am	18–Pis 3:49 pm	18–Pis 9:39 pm
Mar	20–Ar 10:06 pm	21–Ar 3:55 am	20–Ar 9:43 am	20–Ar 5:27 am	20–Ar 9:30 am	21–Ar 3:20 pm	20–Ar 9:43 am	20–Ar 3:05 pm	20–Ar 8:53 pm
Apr	20–Tau 9:28 am	20–Tau 3:17 pm	20–Tau 10:06 pm	20–Tau 2:33 am	20–Tau 8:51 am	20–Tau 2:37 pm	19–Tau 9:00 pm	20–Tau 2:27 am	20–Tau 8:12 am
May	21–Gem 8:52 am	21–Gem 2:38 pm	20–Gem 8:33 pm	21–Gem 1:51 am	21–Gem 8:17 am	21–Gem 1:59 pm	20–Gem 8:33 pm	21–Gem 1:27 am	21–Gem 7:33 am
June	21–Can 4:57 pm	21–Can 10:50 pm	21–Can 4:43 am	21–Can 10:12 am	21–Can 4:24 pm	21–Can 11:04 pm	21–Can 4:43 am	21–Can 9:56 am	21–Can 3:33 pm
July	23–Leo 3:51 am	23–Leo 9:45 am	22–Leo 5:38 pm	22–Leo 8:12 pm	23–Leo 3:19 am	23–Leo 9:00 am	22–Leo 3:38 pm	22–Leo 8:49 pm	23–Leo 2:24 am
Aug	23–Vir 10:47 am	23–Vir 4:44 pm	22–Vir 10:35 pm	23–Vir 3:46 am	23–Vir 10:13 am	23–Vir 3:58 pm	22–Vir 10:35 pm	23–Vir 3:43 am	23–Vir 9:18 am
Sept	23–Lib 5:10 am	23–Lib 2:09 pm	22–Lib 8:00 pm	23–Lib 1:26 am	23–Lib 7:35 am	23–Lib 1:24 pm	22–Lib 8:00 pm	23–Lib 1:06 am	23–Lib 6:43 am
Oct	23–Sc 5:12 am	23–Sc 11:12 pm	23–Sc 5:03 am	23–Sc 10:46 am	23–Sc 4:41 pm	23–Sc 11:30 pm	23–Sc 5:03 am	23–Sc 10:11 am	23–Sc 3:52 pm
Nov	22–Sag 2:30 pm	22–Sag 8:23 pm	22–Sag 2:19 am	22–Sag 8:10 am	22–Sag 2:02 pm	22–Sag 7:50 pm	22–Sag 2:19 am	22–Sag 7:30 am	22–Sag 1:15 pm
Dec	22–Cap 3:40 am	22–Cap 9:35 am	21–Cap 5:27 pm	21–Cap 9:25 pm	22–Cap 3:15 am	22–Cap 9:02 am	21–Cap 3:27 pm	21–Cap 8:41 pm	22–Cap 2:29 pm

	1967	1968	1969	1970	1971	1972	1973	1974	1975
Jan	20–Aq	20–Aq	20–Aq	20–Aq	20–Aq	20–Aq	19–Aq	20–Aq	20–Aq
	1:05 pm	6:54 pm	12:30 am	6:25 am	12:14 pm	6:00 pm	11:49 pm	5:47 am	11:37 am
Feb	19–Pis	19–Pis	18–Pis	18–Pis	19–Pis	19–Pis	18–Pis	18–Pis	19–Pis
	3:25 am	9:11 am	2:47 pm	8:43 pm	2:28 am	8:12am	2:02 pm	8:00 pm	1:51 am
Mar	21–Ar	20–Ar	20–Ar	20–Ar	21–Ar	20–Ar	20–Ar	20–Ar	21–Ar
	2:37 am	8:22 am	2:08 pm	7:59 pm	1:28 am	7:22 am	1:13 pm	7:08 pm	12:58 am
Apr	20–Tau	19–Tau	20–Tau	20–Tau	20–Tau	19–Tau	20–Tau	20–Tau	20–Tau
	1:56 am	7:42 pm	1:18 am	5:16 am	12:54 pm	6:38 pm	12:31 am	5:19 am	12:08 pm
May	21–Gem	20–Gem	21–Gem	21–Gem	21–Gem	20–Gem	21–Gem	21–Gem	21–Gem
	1:19 pm	7:07 pm	12:41 am	6:32 am	12:16 pm	6:00 pm	11:54 pm	5:37 am	1:25 pm
June	21–Can	21–Can	21–Can	21–Can	21–Can	21–Can	21–Can	21–Can	21–Can
	4:23 pm	1:13 am	6:55 am	2:43 pm	8:21 pm	2:07 am	8:01 am	1:38 pm	7:27 pm
July	23–Leo	22–Leo	22–Leo	23–Leo	23–Leo	22–Leo	22–Leo	23–Leo	23–Leo
	8:16 am	2:13 pm	8:05 pm	1:38 am	7:15 am	1:03 pm	6:56 pm	12:30 am	7:23 am
Aug	23–Vir	22–Vir	23–Vir	23–Vir	23–Vir	22–Vir	23–Vir	23–Vir	23–Vir
	3:13 pm	9:52 pm	2:35 am	6:35 am	2:16 pm	8:04 pm	1:55 am	7:29 am	1:24 pm
Sept	23–Lib	22–Lib	23–Lib	23–Lib	23–Lib	22–Lib	22–Lib	23–Lib	23–Lib
	12:38 pm	6:26 pm	12:07 pm	5:59 am	11:47 am	5:34 pm	11:22 pm	4:59 am	10:56 am
Oct	23–Sc	23–Sc	23–Sc	23–Sc	22–Sc	23–Sc	23–Sc	23–Sc	23–Sc
	9:44 pm	1:30 am	9:03 am	3:05 pm	8:53 pm	2:42 am	8:31 am	2:12 pm	8:07 pm
Nov	22–Sag	22–Sag	22–Sag	22–Sag	22–Sag	22–Sag	22–Sag	22–Sag	22–Sag
	7:05 pm	12:59 am	6:23 am	12:25 pm	6:15 pm	12:04 am	5:55 am	11:39 am	5:32 pm
Dec	22–Cap	21–Cap	21–Cap	22–Cap	22–Cap	21–Cap	21–Cap	22–Cap	22–Cap
	8:17 am	2:00 pm	7:44 pm	1:36 am	5:26 am	1:14 pm	7:09 pm	12:57 am	7:47 am

12

Aries: The Big Picture

Because the twelve signs of the zodiac represent twelve ways of being in the world, you will know more about yourself and why you tend toward certain types of behavior and attitudes by knowing more about Aries. If you read about the elements and qualities in "Defining Terms," for instance, you'll find out that you are one of the impulsive, enthusiastic *fire signs,* and, as one of the *cardinal signs,* you should be able to get things and people moving. You can "meet yourself" in the Aries prototype described in "Twelve Places at the Table," and your feisty planetary ruler, Mars, provides some excellent clues about the Aries style.

However, even with these broad brush strokes, your Aries portrait is still a bit abstract; to see yourself in totality, you need more of the background filled in. That means going back to some very important basics: your first-place position in the zodiac, your picture/symbol, the ram, and th glyph that astrologers use to indicate Aries when they draw up a horoscope. In Aries, as in every astrological sign, these three factors link together, forming a strong chain of meaning that holds together everything that is Aries.

When the sun reaches zero degrees Aries—in the imaginary band in the sky that is the zodiac—the earth tips its North Pole toward the sun, the world begins to warm up after the long cold winter, and the cycle of the seasonal year begins again. The first day of Aries—the vernal equinox—is the first day of spring, honored since ancient times as the "birthday" of the whole earth. As the first sign of the zodiac, Aries is the beginning, the starting point of everything. Aries represents the infancy stage of human life, and it is true that many Aries people do possess a childlike quality. At its best, this quality allows them to experience joy and wonder throughout their entire lives; at its worst, Aries first-place or "infant" zodiac status can manifest itself as a perpetual childishness marked by lack of self-control.

In the Christian calendar, the date of Easter is determined by the entry of the sun into the sign of Aries; Easter falls on the first Sunday after the first full moon after the vernal equinox. Though the celebration of the resurrection is far older, and has its roots in ancient rites of spring and rebirth, the symbol of the risen Christ has strong connections with the characterization of Aries. Aries represents the chance to begin again, to renew one's life, to look forward with hope. Aries' legendary enthusiasm and optimism spring from these roots, and—unless totally canceled out by other astrological factors—are two of Aries' strongest weapons against adversity.

The ram, like most ancient symbols, has many layers of meaning, and many prototypes in myth, legend, and history. Again, in Christian tradition, Christ is the "lamb of God," sacrificed for all mankind. For the Jews, the lamb was also a sacrificial animal, and connected with their spring festival of Passover; it is also said that the release of the Jews from bondage in Egypt took place in the Jewish month of the ram. That which is sacrificed is always innocent because purity of heart is a prerequisite to satisfy the gods. Anyone who comes to know and love an Aries will eventually see this sterling quality come shining through. And, once again, the unsullied innocence of the lamb underscores Aries' tendency or ability to see the world through the eyes of the child.

The Aries ram turns up in the legend of the Golden Fleece, in which the god Hermes (Mercury) sends a sacred golden ram to Phrixus, threatened by his evil stepmother with a sacrificial death. Phrixus escapes by flying through the air on the magical beast, which is eventually sacrificed in celebration of the escape, its golden fleece hung in the grove of Aries—later called Mars, the god for whom Aries' ruling planet is named.

The Aries symbol took the form of a powerful weapon in the battering rams of the Greeks and Romans, which was used to knock down the walls of besieged cities. The force of the battering ram was greatly feared and often caused the enemy to capitulate. The Aries person, too, has a power and a force that can allow him/her to ride roughshod over opponents.

The Aries glyph or symbol used by astrologers (see illustration) is said to represent the head and the horns of the ram, which links it neatly with the Aries picture/symbol. But there is more to be read from this glyph that helps to explain where Aries is coming from. Some see in it the sprouting seed of spring pushing up through the earth; the full-blown Aries can push him/herself almost anywhere. Others say the glyph represents an eruption of fire, which can—like Aries—be either a source of light or a force for destruction. Yet another interpretation says the symbol is the upward gushing of water, a kind of hydraulic power or fountain of youth. Either way—as a sign of Aries' outpouring energy or eternal youthfulness—this reaching of the symbol is very apt. Perhaps the simplest picture anyone sees is the arched eyebrows and nose of the human face; not so incidentally, the face and head are the parts of the body traditionally "ruled" by the sign of Aries.

13

Aries: Objectives and Obstacles

A Game Plan for Being the Most Successful Aries Under the Sun

Every astrological sign is a set of possibilities; being born under a particular sign does not guarantee you *are* or *will be* all those things that sign is capable of being. Nor would you want to. There are positive characteristics to be cultivated, as well as negative ones you can avoid or overcome. Living "á la carte"—selecting what you want from all the options available—is open to you, within the overall context of your sign.

You can, of course, order the "prix fixe" dinner by living your life as it comes without attempting to direct it. The choice is yours, which is one good reason it is incorrect to regard your astrological destiny as preordained. You are responsible for how you embody your sign, and what results from that embodiment.

Astrologically speaking, your life as a sign is a journey with a starting point, the raw or primitive end of the sign, and a destination, the evolved or ideal realization of that sign. Once again, you don't have to take the full trip; there are plenty of exits if you choose to use them, and few people are every totally finished. But if you at least know where you are going, and what potential booby traps lie along the way, you will be ahead of the game.

Regard the following as a map and use it in charting

your course. The most successful way to be the best of your astrological sign is to work with it, in full knowledge of its up side and its down side. The most successful and happy people of any astrological sign are those who aim high and are not afraid to stretch their understanding of themselves in order to reach their goal.

Where Aries Starts

In the sign's most primitive form, Aries is like a speeding car with no one at the wheel; it can cause a lot of damage, and the unevolved Aries often does. Because Aries represents the original life force, the will to exist, the sign by necessity possesses a great deal of physical and psychic energy. After all, it takes a lot of power to get the whole world moving. The problem is that Aries often does not have the patience to refine that energy; the "warrior" Aries often uses a sword of untempered steel, and it is easily broken. As children many Aries exhibit a brashnes and willfulness that intimidates children of gentler signs; when Aries says "me first," others often step aside. The behavior is less acceptable when Aries reaches adulthood. Fierce, unyielding, often uncaring, the primitive Aries type rushes headlong at the object of his/her desires, knocking others down in the process. Explosive and sometimes violent, the unstructured Aries is capable of quite uncivilized behavior. Rudeness, a tendency to interrupt when others speak, and sometimes even rough-edged table manners are the mark of many an unfinished Aries.

Here are some buzz words by which you can recognize the primitive Aries type:

Thoughtless	Unsubtle
Crude	Impatient
Selfish	Hurtful/satirical
Hostile	Quick-tempered
Aggressive	Pugnacious

Where Aries Can Go

Of all the signs, Aries possesses the greatest potential for a life of true freedom, where personal choices can be made confidently and fearlessly. An evolved Aries has the courage to face and deal with whatever may come along with his/her freely chosen conviction. Because Aries is the sign of action, the evolved Aries will make his/her own life happen by engaging him/herself with it, and not passively accepting what life doles out. Nothing stands between the mature Aries and life as he/she chooses it to be. However, instead of "me first," the Aries watchword is now "I am in charge of my own life." While primitive Aries tilts with windmills, the finished Aries applies his/her sterling courage and fierce will to realistic and productive challenges. More important, when Aries reaches a high point, there is no more wonderful team leader, no braver or harder working champion of the less fortunate. Aries heart is very big; when a particular Aries grows into that heart, he/she has learned that an important part of the Aries' mission in life is to protect and fight for the rights of those who have been given less courage.

Some buzz words to recognize the evolved Aries type:

Confident	Adventurous
An initiator	Enterprising
Decisive	Resourceful
Resilient	Capable of concentration
Goal-oriented	Warmhearted

How Aries Can Get There

The sign of Aries has been endowed by the cosmos with some excellent resources with which to "fight the good fight." Two that go hand in hand are an instinct for survival and a willingness to take risks. Under pressure, Aries' intensity and fighting spirit rise automatically; it is very rare to see an Aries retire from the fray before he/she has given it the best shot. What in its primitive form is a daredevil instinct and a cocky attitude can be nurtured into nerves of steel with which to defend oneself—and others—when the chips are down.

However, life is a scary place, and even Aries gets scared at times; then, there is no more pitiable sight or embittered human being. Instinctively Aries knows that the "lesson" of his/her sign is to refuse to give up and when he/she does, there is a feeling of total failure. Since achievement-against-odds is the Aries destiny, Aries' best life strategy is to seek out challenges in spite of his/her fears and surmount them, one by one, without impetuous behavior or false bravado. Even scaling a mountain need not be dangerous with the proper amount of preplanning and sensible caution. With each victory Aries will gain in courage, and be able to take on a bigger challenge. For the Aries in search of his/her destiny, life will rarely be dull, because there will always be the necessity to move on to even higher mountains. The fully equipped Aries has no excuse for being an underachiever: If crisis doesn't seek him/her out, Aries should seek out crisis. However, the smarter Aries knows there is a big difference between doing that and simply looking for trouble. Crisis means change, and the change that you bring about yourself is almost always positive.

Potential Pitfalls

It is all too easy for those born under the high-intensity sign of Aries to dissipate their energy in meaningless activity. Aries *must* be constantly on the move, constantly in the middle of things. However, he/she should always be alert to the possibility that the current situation may just not be worth the effort. Selectivity is something most Aries people must learn the hard way; making intelligent choices among experiences and people is a bit hard for those born under the sign of the gamboling ram.

With all that fighting spirit, Aries must also take care not to argue for the sake of arguing. Here's a tip: When you find yourself irritated, annoyed, even incensed by someone or something, ask yourself what the anger is really about. Chances are in many cases that Aries is simply railing internally at him-/herself because of a loss of nerve, and is suffering for it. One part of Aries is shouting "charge," while another part is calling "retreat." The way to reconcile these internal enemies is for Aries to take direct, but constructive action, and make a clear-cut decision. Even if that means recognizing the fact that not even Aries wins them all. However, none of the fire signs, except possibly Sagittarius, is particularly introspective. So, underlying all the potential problems Aries may face is the danger of living an unexamined life. For success, Aries above all should heed those words of wisdom: "Know thyself."

14

Pairing Off with Aries

Your Compatibility with Other Signs of the Zodiac

Since there are only twelve signs of the zodiac, it would be unusual to go through life without having to interact with each of them at one time or another. Obviously, your astrological makeup is more complex than your Aries sun sign, but there are some basic truths about how you tend to react when face to face with someone of another sun sign. If you have read about "The Geometry of Relationships," you already know that being a fire sign means Aries relates more easily to certain elements than to others. Now, getting more specific, you will see what the odds are on your match-ups with each of the other signs, including your own.

When people talk about "relationships," they are usually referring to the romantic kind, and there is no doubt that since time immemorial love has been observed to have a great deal to do with keeping the earth revolving in its orbit. However, we also have a lot of other interpersonal interactions, from important ones, like boss-employee and parent-child to more casual ones, like waitress-patron, cabdriver-rider, and buddy-buddy. The general rules that follow apply in all cases; just change the language a little and do a bit of interpretation. You will find that there is more truth than poetry in the matter of astrological compatibility.

Aries with Aries When you two get together, the sparks could fly far enough to start a forest fire! However, not all the friction is unpleasant. In the case of Aries, it takes one to know one, and with a little luck, you could do some marvelous and productive things together. Such a powerhouse team might have more difficulty in the romantic, love-marriage area, however, unless at least one of the partners has grown out of "Aries infancy." Even then, life could eventually get a little dull for both, and you two could part with the friendly words, "better luck next sign."

Aries with Taurus If you say, "Be patient with me; I'm not finished yet," you might have a shot at making it with patient, placid Taurus. However, the question is, would you want to? Taurus could provide excellent balance and ballast for sometimes lightweight Aries, but Aries might feel he/she is giving up too much freedom in return. Taureans demand loyalty in every respect, and prefer to spend a lot of time back at the ranch. Are you ready for this? In business, this team works well—one providing the initiative, the other the follow-through.

Aries with Gemini As you know, air fans fire, so air sign Gemini could really get you heated up—in a most positive way. However, the burning passion is likely to be short-lived, because neither of you likes to feel he/she is on a short leash. For pure fun and games, you could hardly find a better matchup, and you would find a million things to talk about. Unfortunately, a great deal of it is likely to generate "hot air," but if life-and-death matters are not involved, enjoy!

Aries with Cancer Since most Cancerians of either sex are often into mothering, you might find a great deal of comfort in this relationship. And for Cancer you could provide a much-needed shot of adrenalin. The fact that you are both strong cardinal signs is also on the plus side of the ledger. There is a negative, however, and that is the possibility that Cancer's water-sign downers would feel like "rain on your parade." When dealing with Cancer, remember that he/she is far from weak, so don't try any strong-arm tactics.

Aries with Leo   Here's another fire-fire relationship that could mean war—or the most beautiful of warmhearted friendships. Romantically, you might find yourself in power struggle, and the question would be whose will is going to prevail. Since you are both generous spirits, you might lavish each other with tokens of affection, and the whole thing could get rather costly. This works best when Leo's the boss and Aries knows it; there will be mutual respect for each other's territory.

Aries with Virgo   Practical Virgo could put landing wheels on some of your high-flying schemes, and the two of you could make some interesting things happen. However, you make nervous Virgo even more nervous, and you could even become cruelly dominating. Not that you would mean to be; you would just find it necessary to call a halt to Virgo's ceaseless fidgeting and busy work. You admire each other's smarts, so an after-class coffee relationship could be excellent. Just don't try living together.

Aries with Libra   This is truly a case of opposites attract. Libra is your polar opposite in the great wheel of the zodiac, which means you complement each other's needs. You are decisive, Libra is deliberate; you will act when Libra can't decide. Libra is willing to see all sides of a story, while you usually jump to conclusions. If you can develop respect for Libra, and not consider him/her too passive for you, this one could work very well for both people involved. Libra's heart is as pure as your own.

Aries with Scorpio   This could be the battle of the Titans or a truly magnificent relationship. If it works as challenge rather than conflict, you would never lack for stimulation—of all kinds. It all depends on the level you both have reached; for unevolved types of both signs, the whole thing could degenerate into petty bickering. In business, this relationship signals a power struggle, but you would both admire each other a great deal. This is one relationship you will have to "try on for size."

Aries with Sagittarius What a wonderful pair of "fellows" this is. If you team up, you will never lack for the best kind of companionship. If you resolve to learn some wisdom from Sagittarius, it could last a lifetime. You run the risk of being considered a bit childish by this older fire sign, and you could be a bit put off by his/her pontificating. In the long run, however, there is a lot of potential here, in every area of life. The parent-child bond could be very strong.

Aries with Capricorn Capricorn will seem old to you, no matter what your relative ages. Capricorn's overactive sense of responsibility may really put you off too. However, this sturdy sign could provide an excellent anchor for your occasional flights of fancy. You both admire the finer things in life, but Capricorn might strike you as a bit materialistic. Take time to get to know this sign, because you could learn from each other. You need to grow up and Capricorn needs to learn to play. It could prove interesting.

Aries with Aquarius This could be a "marriage made in heaven," regardless of what the nature of the relationship is. Aquarius doesn't seem as odd to you as this sign often does to others; you are practically there yourself. Intelligent Aquarius sees the real you under that sometimes rough exterior. You both require freedom, and are broad-minded enough to give it to each other. One cautionary note: you may find Aquarius a bit cold at times, and it is important to remember that his/her heart does not bleed as much as yours does.

Aries with Pisces You are strong where Pisces is weak; Pisces offers you the strength of deep spiritual-ity. There is a relationship here, but not the ordinary kind. You can really help misty Pisces cope with life, and stimulate this sign's wonderful sense of humor. If you accept the fact that life will be a game of follow the leader, marriage is possible. However, watch out for the tendency of some Pisceans to lean on others too much. Your shoulders could look temptingly broad.

15

The Aries Sex Role Dilemma

One of the most important ways in which the twelve signs of the zodiac are divided is into "masculine" signs and "feminine" signs, and there are six of each. The reason is simple: As one sign follows the other in the zodiac, they alternate energies, much like the Yin/Yang principle of eastern philosophy. The universe is made up of opposites that complement each other: light and dark, hot and cold, black and white, hard and soft. One is not better than the other; rather, each is essential to the existence of its opposite. In other words, you can't have one without the other.

The six fire and air signs are "masculine," since fire and air are connected with *active, assertive, outgoing* energy.

Aries	Gemini
Leo	Libra
Sagittarius	Aquarius

The six water and earth signs are "feminine," because water and earth represent *reactive, inner-directed, receptive* energy.

Taurus	Cancer
Virgo	Scorpio
Capricorn	Pices

To put it simply, *the masculine fire and air signs are positive, while the earth and water signs are negative*. To remain neutral and avoid placing a higher value on one or the other kind of energy (or sign) it is useful to think of a battery with positive and negative poles. Without both, it simply doesn't work.

Though the masculine/feminine division of the signs has nothing whatever to do with human physical sexuality or sexual preference, it has very important implications for human behavior. Bluntly put, women born into male signs can be more "masculine"-achieving-competitive than men born into female signs. On the other hand, men born in female signs can be more "feminine"-nurturing-cooperative than women born into male signs. Both men and women born into signs that match their own sex may overemphasize the behavior and attitudes connected with that gender. The ideal person, psychologically and metaphysically speaking, has a healthy mix of both masculine and feminine attitudes. Without at least some of both, we cannot be whole people, able to encompass and understand the total range of human emotions, desires, drives, and goals. Since none of us is perfect, just about everyone could stand a bit more gender blending. Your astrological sign offers some excellent clues about how you can accomplish that.

Since Aries is a masculine sign, the men born under it tend to be "puries"—all-male, very macho, more tough than tender. Aries women, on the other hand, are often better buddies than sweethearts, but go far in the world of business and competition. The Aries sex-role dilemma is clear:More than many, Aries men need to develop compassion and other female virtues: Aries women must make a special effort to get in touch with their feminine cores. Keep this in mind as you read the following Aries portraits and you will better understand the why of your Aries behavior.

16

The Aries Female

A Shakespearean Heroine

The plays of Shakespeare are filled with typical Aries women. Like Portia in the *Merchant of Venice* who takes on masculine disguise and skillfully defends her lover in court. Viola in *Twelfth Night* dresses up like a boy to get where she wants to go. The famous "Kiss Me Kate" of the *Taming of the Shrew*, refuses to be docile for her man. A latter day Aries-type heroine is Scarlett O'Hara, who toughs it out and refuses to give up—but also loses her man.

Aries women can cope with the world, but sometimes the men in their lives can't cope with them. A lot of Aries girls grow up thinking that daddy is a lot better role model to follow than mommy, who gives in all the time. The Aries female not only wants to do everything well, she wants to do it better than anybody else—male or female. And often she can. Though Aries women are some of the most delightful, refreshing people in the zodiac, they can be their own worst enemies.

As a child, the Aries girl is typically a tomboy—markedly so, even now when fewer girls tend toward stereotypical female behavior. If she doesn't literally run with the boys, she is the best runner among the girls. Aries children of either sex are a bit hard for parents to handle, but the Aries girl who refuses to be "little-girlish" may present particular problems. Especially for the feminine-sign mother who can't understand why her Aries daughter doesn't like dressing up and looking pretty. And why she insists on "doing it herself" before mommy thinks she's ready. Daddy may secretly admire her guts, but he too may be a bit put off by her dislike of being cuddled and coddled.

As a young woman, the Aries female really begins to "feel her oats" and enjoy her independence. Her quest for action—the thing that is most important to her—may make for a hyperactive sex life and possibly an unhappy love life. Aries women have a hard time understanding why they displease someone else and hate to be crowded. The male who tries to crowd an Aries woman will find that she can walk away faster than any sign in the zodiac. However, in her heart of hearts, she is looking for the perfect lover and, with idealistic Aries, that becomes a mighty tough act for anyone to live up to. She is "romantic" in the oldest sense of the word, hung up on finding someone who is brave, loyal, strong, true—and as warmhearted and generous as she really is, underneath.

Many Aries women seek and choose a full career over simply working until they marry, often in some kind of independent or active field. During their mate-seeking years, this compounds their problem, because they are constantly comparing the performance of the men they meet with their own—and usually find it wanting. Even though it may be unconscious, the Aries woman can't help competing with every man she meets. The scenario for some is to latch on to a guy who can't cope as well as she can, and to attempt to take care of him and run the show. It's usually bad news, because either she sours on the relationship because he seems weak or he begins to resent her success.

As a mate, the Aries woman usually begins to get in touch with her own feminine nature. It's been there all along, of course, but typically the Aries woman does not respect that softer part of herself. By the time she marries—and most eventually do—she has learned that it's okay to say "I need you" and that no one can be 100 percent independent all the time. For some, this knowledge comes only after having achieved some kind of satisfaction in their own endeavors in the outside world. Aries women make great wives because their ebullience and energy rarely lets down, nor do *they* get down in a crisis. Positive and upbeat, the Aries wife is more than willing to take on part of the load, quicker to combine work and family than some other signs. Her sex drive—like her mind and body—will remain young and healthy for a long time. In sex, as in every other activity they share, the Aries woman will be inventive and innovative.

As a mother, the Aries woman performs best when her children are old enough to play with. Infants and dependent toddlers she will find a bit of a drag, and seek all kinds of ways to cut the time and energy she must expend on their care. It's not that she doesn't adore them, it's just that they tend to try her patience by needing her too much. Later on she's usually great about letting her kids try their own wings; it's rare for an Aries mother to overprotect her children. Naturally, she will be better able to understand a fire-sign or air-sign child than one born into the water or earth element. In fact, the Aries woman must consciously avoid playing favorites and make a special effort with her daughters regardless of sign. It's all too easy for the Aries mother to show a preference for the child who is quicker and brighter than his/her siblings. Patience is one of the greatest feminine virtues, and the Aries mother must push herself to attain it before she pushes her children farther than they are ready to go.

17

The Aries Male

The Great Pretender

Underneath the generally rough and realistic exterior of the all-male Aries man beats a heart of pure gold and an active fantasy life few will admit to. Aries is a young sign, and the Aries male really does tend to see the world through the eyes of the child for whom everything is black and white and most people are good. Or the adolescent who looks up to good conquering heroes who worship and thereby conquer women. In the mind (or subconscious) of many an Aries male he is "Sir Galahad" and his motto is "Faint heart ne'er won fair lady." Idealistic to a fault, he is a little naive and therefore easily hurt and disillusioned. It's amazing how quickly Aries men will empty their pockets and hearts when they hear a "sob story" from a male *or* female. Though the manner may be gruff, the instinct to save and protect is real.

Rather than "macho," the Aries male is "manly," in the old-fashioned sense of the word. He learned it at his father's knee, who most likely was the strong one in the household. The way daddy took care of mommy, the Aries male wants to take care of his women too. However, he's a little uncomfortable with the kind of intimacy a close relationship demands: Mushiness really puts him off, and he's not able to distinguish it from a real expression of love.

As a child, many an Aries male was labeled "that fresh kid." Aries is brash and bold, and these characteristics are strongest when Aries is young. The Aries boy is constantly testing limits; he'll be the first one to see if they really mean it when they say "Keep off the grass." The parents of the Aries boy may be a little dismayed by his report card, too. He's all physical energy and finds it hard to sit still and listen to the teacher. He'd rather be out there doing something dangerous; the Aries boy has a strong daredevil streak in his makeup. However, it's likely to cause more mental anguish for his parents than physical pain for himself, because Aries is unbelievably agile. In spite of his faults, the Aries boy is usually a delight to his family. Generosity begins early, and his "me-first" tendency is nicely balanced by a genuine desire to help and protect his siblings.

As a young man, the Aries male is a ball of fire. His mental and physical energy are likely to jet propel him up the career ladder—if he forces himself to stick with one thing long enough before going on to the next. He is highly competitive, which can be a blessing or a curse. When he starts competing with his boss, he may be in big trouble. In typical Aries fashion, the Aries male generally believes he can do everything better, and a childish "I'm better than you are" attitude could cause him to come a cropper. His love life will usually be more tempestuous than his work life, however, because the young Aries male will be constantly dashing around on his white charger looking for damsels in distress. Since many young women these days aren't looking for a knight, he often has the wind taken out of his sails. Some Aries men have such a one-dimensional image of women as weak that they are considered insufferable male chauvinists. The women the Aries male is most likely to fall for are soft types—sometimes even "cute," in the less positive sense of the word. However, if Aries' choice is still tough at the core (like a Cancer female), she will eventually rebel and look for someone who's going to give her strengths equal time.

Still, the one who is wooed by Aries can look forward to a wonderful whirl of earthly delights, with an adoring male on her arm all the way. Aries men have a lot less trouble with the external factors of a relationship than they do with the more critical internal ones.

As a mate, the Aries male may suffer from his idealistic view of the woman he marries. As life becomes realistic and he sees her more often without makeup than with, he may feel a bit deflated that his romantic bubble has burst. He may also get a few shocks when she won't let him run the whole show. However, if he has at least matured to the point where he really wants an equal partner, he will continue to play the gallant, still courting his woman throughout the marriage. The Aries man can really be loyal, too. For him, a fling is only a fling, but his wife is the woman he loves. However, some Aries men do not have as much staying power as others, and may get bored with a marriage that doesn't provide sufficient stimulation. Aries men can walk away fairly easily unless they get what they want.

As a father, the Aries male may prove tough to deal with. Though he will love to romp and play with his children, he may expect too much of them in every area of life. His sons will be expected to be little men, with all the emotional repression that implies. His daughters will be loved and adored, but here too he may try to push them into a sterotype of his ideal woman. The Aries man must learn to say "Let them be." On the positive side, he will be indulgent with his children's "childishness," not coming down too hard on them for normal pranks and peccadillos.

18

Aries Help Wanted

Selecting a Career/Your On-the-Job Style

A vitally important aspect of your successful Aries game plan is making sure you land in the right job or career—i.e., the one that best suits your native talents and tendencies. It is more than a truism that people perform better doing what comes naturally. There are some natural careers for Aries, and they all have one common denominator: challenging limits. It is not possible to list *all* the specific jobs an Aries should do well at, but there are some Aries images that provide useful guidelines. Though you may not literally end up *doing* any of these things, conjure up an idea of what it takes to do the following jobs, and you'll have a better handle on what kind of inner resources Aries people have available to them for career success.

Veterinary surgeon
Athletic coach
Commodities trader
Salesman (of anything)
Explorer
Physiotherapist
Landscape architect
Jockey/gymnast
Courtroom litigator
Law enforcer
Investigative reporter
Public relations person

Equally important to finding the best job slot for you is understanding how your Aries sun sign affects your modus operandi on the job. And your potential for moving up. Every sun sign has certain success skills that can smooth and widen the career path, as well as blind spots that can cause roadblocks. The more you know about both, the better off you will be. Many Aries people appear to be born supervisors, and many are. The ability to lead others and to set an example of upbeat energy are invaluable assets of your sign. However, if Aries isn't careful, this talent for being the boss can turn into just plain belligerence, which turns everyone off, from the bottom to the top.

Another of Aries' two-edged swords is the sign's start-up quality; no one can get things going faster than an Aries with an idea. The problem comes when there are too many start-ups and not enough finishes. Though it sounds like a drag, you Aries people have to learn to concentrate your energy, and do a sustained piece of work. Sure, some of it is boring, but unless you demonstrate at least a *willingness* to see things through to the end, you are going to sell yourself short. The Aries who does a good enough job to move higher up the ladder can be a bit more self-indulgent; he/she can stick to having brilliant ideas and hire somebody else to deal with the nitty gritty.

A wonderful Aries quality that Aries may undervalue as a success skill is his/her excellent sense of humor and sense of play. Many a dull work environment is brightened by the presence of an Aries, who is able to "whistle while he/she works." In a manager, the ability to make one's employees look upon their work as creative play is usually highly valued—at least by enlightened employers—because it generally creates more productive employees.

In spite of the fact that Aries is highly competitive and eager to be the best, Aries also has a strong sense of honor—a good old-fashioned virtue that can be an enormous plus in the business world. It is very rare to see a genuine Aries who's into back-stabbing and other forms of unfair competition. And most people know how to appreciate the fact and respond to it positively. The point is, you don't have to be afraid of an Aries and therefore can freely exchange ideas and information. If Aries "borrows" anything, he/she will almost always give you the credit.

Most Aries thrive on crisis; unfortunately some like it so much they go out of their way to create it. The last-minute rush has the excitement and challenge that Aries thrive on. While Aries is quite capable of planning ahead, he/she will sometimes unconsciously delay doing something that looks easy. It's much more fun to show how quickly and deftly you can polish it off at the eleventh hour. For best success, get your kicks some other way.

19

How "Pure" an Aries Are You?

Your Moon Sign ... Your Rising Sign

No one is a pure Aries—or pure anything, for that matter—when it comes to astrological signs. As you will learn when you read "Defining Terms," there are many other factors in a horoscope that add up to the total person that is *you*. Yes, there are twelve basic personality types according to the zodiac, but within those broad groups there are almost infinite variations.

Though you are an Aries at the core and can count on the portrait of your sun sign to define you in essence, the two other horoscopic factors that count most are in your personality profile: your moon sign and your rising sign. Many people know their moon sign; anyone can quickly determine it via an ephemeris. If you know your birth time at least within one hour, you can use the table in this book to find out what your rising sign is.

The Moon—Your "Dark Side"
Almost more than your sun sign, your moon sign indicates what makes you run. Most of the time, you do not know it yourself, because the moon is your subconscious, your "dark side" not because it is bad, but because it is hidden. When the meaning of your moon sign is added to your Aries sun sign, it is a fuller

picture and a better indicator of your probable personality. Here's how an Aries sun sign mixes with each of the moon signs.

Aries sun sign/Aries moon sign With both sun and moon in Aries, you are a "double rebel" and may find yourself constantly warring with systems and all types of authority figures. Your mental agility is phenomenal, but you could be hazardously impulsive. Watch out for a tendency to exaggerate everything out of proportion—including yourself and your ego.

Aries sun sign/Taurus moon sign This combination makes for a more well-balanced Aries, with good practical sense as well as drive. Here is a person who can plan ahead and get things done much more easily than the "typical" Aries. However, this mix often makes for a rather dogmatic person who is always right and very obstinate.

Aries sun sign/Gemini moon sign It's easy to get lost with this sun/moon combination because there are so many ways to go that you run the risk of not going anywhere if you don't force yourself to settle on something. However, you should be one of the great wits of the world, with a lightning mind and a tongue to match. Don't simply talk about doing things; get out there and do them.

Aries sun sign/Cancer moon sign Intuition, imagination and memory are all strong with this combination. There is both the drive and ambition to get where you want to go. However, you could be ultrasensitive and subject to fits of peevishness when somebody or something rubs you the wrong way. You are the "stay-at-home" kind of Aries who doesn't mind just sitting still sometimes.

Aries sun sign/Leo moon sign Though you may have to watch out for a tendency to be rather vain, you have a terrific combination going for you. The moon in

Leo emphasizes all your warm Aries qualities, like a good heart and generous nature. And you've got plenty of force to put your ideas across. You are very naive, so don't let people flatter you into getting what they want.

Aries sun sign/Virgo moon sign No one can argue with your logic, but they can do without your waspishness when you get too exacting about things. Ease up a little. You've got excellent equipment for a scientific or literary career and are much more discriminating than the "typical" Aries. Choose your friends carefully, but don't be too hard on them when they don't live up to your standards.

Aries sun sign/Libra moon sign The moon in the sign of Libra takes off your Aries rough edges, and makes you more of a diplomat. However, Aries' independent streak is blunted with this combination, and you may find yourself with an internal dilemma: the conscious desire to go it alone, and the subconscious need to depend on others. You are a better follower than the usual Aries "leader."

Aries sun sign/Scorpio moon sign Jealous, dogmatic, combative, you could cause a lot of unhappiness by giving into your "warlike" instincts all the time. You have the capacity for self-control via your Scorpio moon, and you should try to cultivate it. Let your warmhearted, good-spirited Aries sun sign shine through for happiness.

Aries sun sign/Sagittarius moon sign This is a combination of extremes, and you should make sure that those you go to are positive ones. In general, they should be, because your nature is to be very sincere and straightforward. You do tend to run off at the mouth, however, and some of your enthusiasms are rather short-lived. You are an excellent teacher.

Aries sun sign/Capricorn moon sign This is a good combination for worldly success, but you could be overly ambitious. Let your good traits temper your tendency to be tactless and run rough-shod over others. In some Aries with this combination, selfishness may be quite marked; you'll have to learn to give a little in order to find happiness in a relationship.

Aries sun sign/Aquarius moon sign You have an extremely original mind, but you could present your ideas in such an erratic, hasty manner that people won't take you seriously. Calm down a bit. Your imagination is excellent and you should get along with people very well. Many people with this combination are the true humanitarians of the world and greatly loved by those that are humane too.

Aries sun sign/Pisces moon sign You are rather quiet for an Aries, and a lot more introspective than many of your sign. However, you can easily find yourself in a blue funk if you are not careful. Moodiness is likely to get you into all sorts of petty quarrels; you must make a conscious effort to use the positive, upbeat optimism that is natural to Aries.

Your Rising Sign—Know Your Cover
The third of the "big three" astrological factors is your rising sign, which you can think of as an *overlay* to your sun sign. Although it does not carry the psychological weight your moon sign does, your rising sign is also "unconscious" because it is a mode of external behavior that comes so naturally to you you may not be aware of it. In a sense, your rising sign is your "cover." It can never totally obscure the "real you" of your sun sign, but it can temporarily mask that sign, especially when people first meet you. Here's what happens to Aries when you lay each rising sign over "typical" Aries behavior.

Aries with Aries rising You are extremely extroverted. Slow down, and give others a chance to get a word in.

Aries with Taurus rising You are a real charmer with a big smile for everyone. Live up to the sweetness you project by your manner.

Aries with Gemini rising You are a real glad-hander, eager to meet and interrogate as many people as you can. Just don't ask too many personal questions.

Aries with Cancer rising You are a very sincere type, and people immediately trust you. Don't tell everyone your troubles.

Aries with Leo rising You come on very strong. Your outlook is refreshing, but you could try to steal everyone's show.

Aries with Virgo rising Don't look everyone over with a microscope; keep your observations to yourself. No one's perfect.

Aries with Libra rising You can be tactful, gracious and genuinely interested in what everyone has to say—when you want to.

Aries with Scorpio rising You run the risk of being overly assertive and more reserved than an Aries usually is. Loosen and lighten up.

Aries with Sagittarius rising You are the natural-born organizer. Just don't organize everyone out of their minds.

Aries with Capricorn rising You could come off as a bit sarcastic, even cold. However, you speak with the voice of authority.

Aries with Aquarius rising You may be considered a little on the "kooky" side. Keep some of your more original opinions to yourself.

Aries with Pisces Rising You could be the type everyone immediately falls for. Just don't get too cute, which is possible with this combination.

20

Find Your Rising Sign

It is easier than many people think to find out your rising sign. One reason is that it is based on "universal" or "sidereal" time—the measure used in space travel. To ascertain your rising sign, look through the following chart and locate the birthdate nearest your birth date; look across and locate the time nearest your birth time. Remember that if daylight saving time was in effect at your birth, you must subtract one hour from the time stated on your birth certificate. In the section for your date and time, you will find an abbreviation for the sign that was rising when you were born. For instance, if your birthdate is June 12 at 9:30 a.m., your rising sign is Leo; if you were born on the same date at 9:30 p.m., your rising sign is Capricorn.

You will notice that the *year* you were born does not affect your rising sign. However, the geographical latitude does. These tables are calculated for the middle latitudes of the United States. If you were born far to the south, it is wise to look at the sign that *follows* your rising sign as well. If you were born far to the north, check out the *previous* sign.

Rising Signs—A.M. Births

	1 AM	2 AM	3 AM	4 AM	5 AM	6 AM	7 AM	8 AM	9 AM	10 AM	11 AM	12 NOON
Jan 1	Lib	Sc	Sc	Sc	Sag	Sag	Cap	Cap	Aq	Aq	Pis	Ar
Jan 9	Lib	Sc	Sc	Sag	Sag	Sag	Cap	Cap	Aq	Pis	Ar	Tau
Jan 17	Sc	Sc	Sc	Sag	Sag	Cap	Cap	Aq	Aq	Pis	Ar	Tau
Jan 25	Sc	Sc	Sag	Sag	Sag	Cap	Cap	Aq	Pis	Ar	Tau	Tau
Feb 2	Sc	Sc	Sag	Sag	Cap	Cap	Aq	Pis	Pis	Ar	Tau	Gem
Feb 10	Sc	Sag	Sag	Sag	Cap	Cap	Aq	Pis	Ar	Tau	Tau	Gem
Feb 18	Sc	Sag	Sag	Cap	Cap	Aq	Pis	Pis	Ar	Tau	Gem	Gem
Feb 26	Sag	Sag	Sag	Cap	Aq	Aq	Pis	Ar	Tau	Tau	Gem	Gem
Mar 6	Sag	Sag	Cap	Cap	Aq	Pis	Pis	Ar	Tau	Gem	Gem	Can
Mar 14	Sag	Cap	Cap	Aq	Aq	Pis	Ar	Tau	Tau	Gem	Gem	Can
Mar 22	Sag	Cap	Cap	Aq	Pis	Ar	Ar	Tau	Gem	Gem	Can	Can
Mar 30	Cap	Cap	Aq	Pis	Pis	Ar	Tau	Tau	Gem	Can	Can	Leo
Apr 7	Cap	Cap	Aq	Pis	Ar	Ar	Tau	Gem	Gem	Can	Can	Leo
Apr 14	Cap	Aq	Aq	Pis	Ar	Tau	Tau	Gem	Gem	Can	Can	Leo
Apr 22	Cap	Aq	Pis	Ar	Ar	Tau	Gem	Gem	Gem	Can	Leo	Leo
Apr 30	Aq	Aq	Pis	Ar	Tau	Tau	Gem	Can	Can	Can	Leo	Leo
May 8	Aq	Pis	Ar	Ar	Tau	Gem	Gem	Can	Can	Leo	Leo	Leo
May 16	Aq	Pis	Ar	Tau	Gem	Gem	Can	Can	Can	Leo	Leo	Vir
May 24	Pis	Ar	Ar	Tau	Gem	Gem	Can	Can	Leo	Leo	Leo	Vir
June 1	Pis	Ar	Tau	Gem	Gem	Can	Can	Can	Leo	Leo	Vir	Vir
June 9	Ar	Ar	Tau	Gem	Gem	Can	Can	Leo	Leo	Leo	Vir	Vir
June 17	Ar	Tau	Gem	Gem	Can	Can	Can	Leo	Leo	Vir	Vir	Vir
June 25	Tau	Tau	Gem	Gem	Can	Can	Leo	Leo	Leo	Vir	Vir	Lib
July 3	Tau	Gem	Gem	Can	Can	Can	Leo	Leo	Vir	Vir	Vir	Lib
July 11	Tau	Gem	Gem	Can	Can	Leo	Leo	Leo	Vir	Vir	Lib	Lib
July 18	Gem	Gem	Can	Can	Can	Leo	Leo	Vir	Vir	Vir	Lib	Lib
July 26	Gem	Gem	Can	Can	Leo	Leo	Vir	Vir	Vir	Lib	Lib	Lib
Aug 3	Gem	Can	Can	Can	Leo	Leo	Vir	Vir	Vir	Lib	Lib	Sc
Aug 11	Gem	Can	Can	Leo	Leo	Leo	Vir	Vir	Lib	Lib	Lib	Sc
Aug 18	Can	Can	Can	Leo	Leo	Vir	Vir	Vir	Lib	Lib	Sc	Sc
Aug 27	Can	Can	Leo	Leo	Leo	Vir	Vir	Lib	Lib	Lib	Sc	Sc
Sept 4	Can	Can	Leo	Leo	Leo	Vir	Vir	Vir	Lib	Lib	Sc	Sc
Sept 12	Can	Leo	Leo	Leo	Vir	Vir	Lib	Lib	Lib	Sc	Sc	Sag
Sept 20	Leo	Leo	Leo	Vir	Vir	Vir	Lib	Lib	Sc	Sc	Sc	Sag
Sept 28	Leo	Leo	Leo	Vir	Vir	Lib	Lib	Lib	Sc	Sc	Sag	Sag
Oct 6	Leo	Leo	Vir	Vir	Vir	Lib	Lib	Sc	Sc	Sc	Sag	Sag
Oct 14	Leo	Vir	Vir	Vir	Lib	Lib	Lib	Sc	Sc	Sag	Sag	Cap
Oct 22	Leo	Vir	Vir	Lib	Lib	Lib	Sc	Sc	Sc	Sag	Sag	Cap
Oct 30	Vir	Vir	Vir	Lib	Lib	Sc	Sc	Sc	Sag	Sag	Cap	Cap
Nov 7	Vir	Vir	Lib	Lib	Lib	Sc	Sc	Sc	Sag	Sag	Cap	Cap
Nov 15	Vir	Vir	Lib	Lib	Sc	Sc	Sc	Sag	Sag	Cap	Cap	Aq
Nov 23	Vir	Lib	Lib	Lib	Sc	Sc	Sag	Sag	Sag	Cap	Cap	Aq
Dec 1	Vir	Lib	Lib	Sc	Sc	Sc	Sag	Sag	Cap	Cap	Aq	Aq
Dec 9	Lib	Lib	Lib	Sc	Sc	Sag	Sag	Sag	Cap	Cap	Aq	Pis
Dec 18	Lib	Lib	Sc	Sc	Sc	Sag	Sag	Cap	Cap	Aq	Aq	Pis
Dec 28	Lib	Lib	Sc	Sc	Sag	Sag	Sag	Cap	Aq	Aq	Pis	Ar

Rising Signs—P.M. Births

	1 PM	2 PM	3 PM	4 PM	5 PM	6 PM	7 PM	8 PM	9 PM	10 PM	11 PM	12 MIDNIGHT
Jan 1	Tau	Gem	Gem	Can	Can	Can	Leo	Leo	Vir	Vir	Vir	Lib
Jan 9	Tau	Gem	Gem	Can	Can	Leo	Leo	Leo	Vir	Vir	Vir	Lib
Jan 17	Gem	Gem	Can	Can	Can	Leo	Leo	Vir	Vir	Vir	Lib	Lib
Jan 25	Gem	Gem	Can	Can	Leo	Leo	Leo	Vir	Vir	Lib	Lib	Lib
Feb 2	Gem	Can	Can	Can	Leo	Leo	Vir	Vir	Vir	Lib	Lib	Sc
Feb 10	Gem	Can	Can	Leo	Leo	Leo	Vir	Vir	Lib	Lib	Lib	Sc
Feb 18	Can	Can	Can	Leo	Leo	Vir	Vir	Vir	Lib	Lib	Sc	Sc
Feb 26	Can	Can	Leo	Leo	Leo	Vir	Vir	Lib	Lib	Lib	Sc	Sc
Mar 6	Can	Leo	Leo	Leo	Vir	Vir	Vir	Lib	Lib	Sc	Sc	Sc
Mar 14	Can	Leo	Leo	Vir	Vir	Vir	Lib	Lib	Lib	Sc	Sc	Sag
Mar 22	Leo	Leo	Leo	Vir	Vir	Lib	Lib	Lib	Sc	Sc	Sc	Sag
Mar 30	Leo	Leo	Vir	Vir	Vir	Lib	Lib	Sc	Sc	Sc	Sag	Sag
Apr 7	Leo	Leo	Vir	Vir	Lib	Lib	Lib	Sc	Sc	Sc	Sag	Sag
Apr 14	Leo	Vir	Vir	Vir	Lib	Lib	Sc	Sc	Sc	Sag	Sag	Sag
Apr 22	Leo	Vir	Vir	Lib	Lib	Lib	Sc	Sc	Sc	Sag	Sag	Cap
Apr 30	Vir	Vir	Vir	Lib	Lib	Sc	Sc	Sc	Sag	Sag	Cap	Cap
May 8	Vir	Vir	Lib	Lib	Lib	Sc	Sc	Sag	Sag	Sag	Cap	Cap
May 16	Vir	Vir	Lib	Lib	Sc	Sc	Sc	Sag	Sag	Cap	Cap	Aq
May 24	Vir	Lib	Lib	Lib	Sc	Sc	Sag	Sag	Sag	Cap	Cap	Aq
June 1	Vir	Lib	Lib	Sc	Sc	Sc	Sag	Sag	Cap	Cap	Aq	Aq
June 9	Lib	Lib	Lib	Sc	Sc	Sag	Sag	Sag	Cap	Cap	Aq	Pis
June 17	Lib	Lib	Sc	Sc	Sc	Sag	Sag	Cap	Cap	Aq	Aq	Pis
June 25	Lib	Lib	Sc	Sc	Sag	Sag	Sag	Cap	Cap	Aq	Pis	Ar
July 3	Lib	Sc	Sc	Sc	Sag	Sag	Cap	Cap	Aq	Aq	Pis	Ar
July 11	Lib	Sc	Sc	Sag	Sag	Sag	Cap	Cap	Aq	Pis	Ar	Tau
July 18	Sc	Sc	Sc	Sag	Sag	Cap	Cap	Aq	Aq	Pis	Ar	Tau
July 26	Sc	Sc	Sag	Sag	Sag	Cap	Cap	Aq	Pis	Ar	Tau	Tau
Aug 3	Sc	Sc	Sag	Sag	Cap	Cap	Aq	Aq	Pis	Ar	Tau	Gem
Aug 11	Sc	Sag	Sag	Sag	Cap	Cap	Aq	Pis	Ar	Tau	Tau	Gem
Aug 18	Sc	Sag	Sag	Cap	Cap	Aq	Pis	Pis	Ar	Tau	Gem	Gem
Aug 27	Sag	Sag	Sag	Cap	Cap	Aq	Pis	Ar	Tau	Tau	Gem	Gem
Sept 4	Sag	Sag	Cap	Cap	Aq	Pis	Pis	Ar	Tau	Gem	Gem	Can
Sept 12	Sag	Sag	Cap	Aq	Aq	Pis	Ar	Tau	Tau	Gem	Gem	Can
Sept 20	Sag	Cap	Cap	Aq	Pis	Pis	Ar	Tau	Gem	Gem	Can	Can
Sept 28	Cap	Cap	Aq	Aq	Pis	Ar	Tau	Tau	Gem	Gem	Can	Can
Oct 6	Cap	Cap	Aq	Pis	Ar	Ar	Tau	Gem	Gem	Can	Can	Leo
Oct 14	Cap	Aq	Aq	Pis	Ar	Tau	Tau	Gem	Gem	Can	Can	Leo
Oct 22	Cap	Aq	Pis	Ar	Ar	Tau	Gem	Gem	Can	Can	Leo	Leo
Oct 30	Aq	Aq	Pis	Ar	Tau	Tau	Gem	Can	Can	Can	Leo	Leo
Nov 7	Aq	Aq	Pis	Ar	Tau	Tau	Gem	Can	Can	Leo	Leo	Leo
Nov 15	Aq	Pis	Ar	Tau	Gem	Gem	Can	Can	Can	Leo	Leo	Vir
Nov 23	Pis	Ar	Ar	Tau	Gem	Gem	Can	Can	Leo	Leo	Leo	Vir
Dec 1	Pis	Ar	Tau	Gem	Gem	Can	Can	Can	Leo	Leo	Vir	Vir
Dec 9	Ar	Tau	Tau	Gem	Gem	Can	Can	Leo	Leo	Leo	Vir	Vir
Dec 18	Ar	Tau	Gem	Gem	Can	Can	Can	Leo	Leo	Vir	Vir	Vir
Dec 28	Tau	Tau	Gem	Gem	Can	Can	Leo	Leo	Vir	Vir	Vir	Lib

21

Aries Astro-Outlook for 1986

It looks like a rather uncommon year coming up for you, Aries. For one thing, you'll be slowing down your usual breakneck pace and taking a closer look at who you really are. And when you take this time out, many of you will be giving some serious thought to your career goals and ambitions. For some, they could undergo a real change. The answer for more than a few Aries people will be continued education and/or job training—a must if you are going to bring your accomplishments in line with your ambitions. Others will find great satisfaction in investigating the whys and wherefores of the occult, in one form or another. A real mind-stretching experience for Aries this year will be coming into contact with people from backgrounds very different from your own. There's nothing like it to broaden your horizons.

Some Aries—particularly those born near the end of March—will find themselves undergoing a personal transformation. Not only will you grow in the process, you'll also be able to shake off a lot of hang-ups that have held you back in the past. A major and beneficial change will be in the way you handle your money, both making it, and making it grow, not to mention keeping up with bills. What's also rather uncharacteristic for you, Aries, is that you'll probably want more time to yourself in 1986. That does not preclude the possibility, however, that you will be drawn to a sensitive, empathetic individual—one who intuitively understands your outlook on life. Speaking of intuition, your own will be very strong and accurate this year, helping you to understand a romantic partner in greater depth. Your most receptive time for love and romance is March—particularly after the 9th when Venus enters the sign of Aries. The most significant months for making enterprising steps that will assure your future are January and October. To fill in the spaces, and get a lot more detail, read your day-by-day forecasts for 1986 in the pages ahead.

22

Fifteen Months of Day-by-Day Predictions

OCTOBER 1985

Tuesday, October 1 (Moon in Taurus) You may feel a bit under pressure today, but you are up to it and will emerge the winner. Suddenly the bits and pieces fall into place, and you've got the whole story. Use your new knowledge effectively and you will be able to cement a relationship that is valuable to you. Finances may look good too. The lucky number is 8.

Wednesday, October 2 (Moon in Taurus) Who owes what to whom may be the topic of the day. If you are feeling strapped it may be because of some recent self-indulgences of yours. Remember that you can't always live in "fat city." When you straighten out your books, you can straighten out your financial life—and keep it that way.

Thursday, October 3 (Moon Taurus to Gemini 8:26 a.m.) A relationship that's been a bit on the limp side recently suddenly regains vigor, and you wonder why you two haven't seen more of each other lately. You also manage to cut through some money and tax problems by some new accounting procedures. All in all you are rather satisfied with the day's events. Try your luck with number 1.

Friday October 4 (Moon in Gemini) The day finds you pulled in two very different directions; there is a way out, however. Be firm but kind with someone who insists on doing things the old way; convince him/her that an unorthodox procedure will get the job done a lot faster, and make you a lot freer. Don't be afraid to be a little selfish this time. A Cancer may be in the picture.

Saturday, October 5 (Moon Gemini to Cancer 8:42 p.m.) Today you find out that learning can really be fun—especially when the teacher is such a lively and interesting person. You are in the mood to display your own good sense of humor to which others respond. A slight worry you've had of late is put to rest by some information that comes your way from a distance. It's nice to be relieved.

Sunday, October 6 (Moon in Cancer) Someone close to you may do some complaining today, and you have to admit it is legitimate. Give in and agree that you will do things a new way so that everyone will derive more comfort and satisfaction from home surroundings. As you are the good guy others are appreciative and show it in tangible ways.

Monday, October 7 (Moon in Cancer) A slight uneasiness you feel early in the day about the fact that you are facing opposition simply vanishes into thin air when you recognize the fact that it is a healthy challenge. It gives you a chance to express your views quite dramatically and impress the other side. Matters of property and what belongs to whom figure in the picture.

Tuesday, October 8 (Moon Cancer to Leo 6:38 a.m.) Someone who's been digging in his/her heels suddenly agrees to do it your way. The agreement is agreeable to everyone, and a spirit of cooperation colors the day. With harmony restored on the domestic front you are able to enjoy a pleasant interlude with a child or young person. Taurus or Scorpio may be prominent in today's scenario.

Wednesday, October 9 (Moon in Leo) You are in a very generous mood today and have a friendly word for everyone. Don't spread yourself too thin, however, or you may find yourself losing emotional balance. It's nice to feel loved, but there are those who will make you buy it. Don't let yourself be deceived in your ingenuous Aries way; look at things realistically.

Thursday, October 10 (Moon Leo to Virgo 1:24 p.m.) You are able to throw your weight around quite effectively today, even if part of it is pure bluff. So what? You get what you want and are able to show others how intense you can be when you want to. As you successfully meet a challenge, those who may not have been on your side suddenly swing over. Good work. The lucky number is 8.

Friday, October 11 (Moon in Virgo) This is a day in which you must read all the fine print if you are not going to miss anything. Don't be slipshod when it comes to checking out all the details of a deal that may seem too good to be true. Keep your eye on the ball in health matters as well; if you've been meaning to make an appointment, do so now. Don't overindulge in sweets today.

Saturday, October 12 (Moon Virgo to Libra 2:38 p.m.) Today you resolve to toss out a situation that has been draining you for some time and replace it with more than is fairer to you. You don't lose anything in this transaction; someone you've been supporting realizes he/she can't expect it any longer. Enjoy the feeling of greater freedom; you deserve it.

Sunday, October 13 (Moon in Libra) Today's a day to keep a low profile and do some stock-taking. Consider the possibility of teaming up with someone whose skills and ideas complement yours. Your intuition is quite reliable now, so whatever feelings you have about the situation are likely to be correct. Don't get over-ambitious and plunge into a new project; there's plenty that needs finishing and you are better off concentrating on those things.

Monday, October 14 (Moon Libra to Scorpio 2:50 p.m.) It's a day to bust loose and try something new; yesterday you were a little confined. The best way to broaden your perspective is to latch on to some new people who appear on the scene. Several of them could be rather important to your future success, so listen carefully. If you are involved in a legal matter, you may get a decision in your favor.

Tuesday, October 15 (Moon in Scorpio) You may have to go back to square one today and start all over on something you thought was all neatly tied up. Don't despair; your second effort will be a much better one. You may be attracted to the glamorous today, and it could take one of several forms. One possibility is a "mysterious stranger" who seems to have all the answers. Be a bit cautious in revealing yourself.

Wednesday, October 16 (Moon Scorpio to Sagittarius 2:25 p.m.) You would rather pay attention to a member of the opposite sex who claims you are irresistible, but money matters make it difficult. A decision is at hand and you must make sure it is the right one in terms of its leading to your future economic security. Later on you will have time to deal with things that are far more attractive and interesting.

Thursday, October 17 (Moon in Sagittarius) The future is very much on the mind of someone close to you, and he/she indicates a discussion would be helpful. If you do get involved, be sure to be encouraging, and to help the person discern his/her own motives. As you play the role of counselor you get a lot of satisfaction out of it and yourself. Begin to think in terms of long-range plans and ultimate values.

Friday, October 18 (Moon Sagittarius to Capricorn 3:37 p.m.) Things have been a little vague lately in an area that concerns you very much; today the light dawns, and you are glad to be able to see clearly what is happening. Today you are the one to receive encouragement from someone whose opinion you respect; act on some suggestions this person makes to you because they are sound. Some good news is on the way from someone at a distance.

Saturday, October 19 (Moon in Capricorn) It's nice to hear someone say, "You were right all along," but don't get smug about it. Your prestige is rising in several quarters, and one of them may be your own community. Someone whose support you need in order to attain your goal tells you definitely where you stand—and it is on good solid ground. The lucky number today is 8.

Sunday, October 20 (Moon Capricorn to Aquarius 8:04 p.m.) A cycle is nearly completed, and you can feel it in the air. Now your direction is clear, and you know not only what to do but when to do it as well. It is a good feeling to know you can go forward on your own now with every expectation of exceeding. You are not wrong.

Monday, October 21 (Moon in Aquarius) Today you learn the meaning of the phrase "creative selfishness." You realize that you will be far more effective if you look out for your own interests as well as those of others. You can do it without guilt, too. On the romantic side, a wish comes true and you feel as if you have come down with "love fever." Enjoy the sensation and your own ability to attract.

Tuesday, October 22 (Moon in Aquarius) Yesterday you weren't quite sure, but today you know. Someone really cares. A demonstration of loyalty reassures you and makes you feel emotionally on more solid ground.

You will be called upon to play teacher today for someone who needs to brush up on something you know very well. You are delighted, because you learn something in the process.

Wednesday, October 23 (Moon Aquarius to Pisces 3:35 a.m.) A feeling of uneasiness mars the early part of the day; something is bothering you because it is so murky. The key is to look behind what you see and find out the real story. When you do, you will realize your fears were unfounded and that you really are in no danger at all. Celebrate and enjoy an evening that feels like a holiday.

Thursday, October 24 (Moon in Pisces) Sometimes you have no patience with people who seem to take the long way around things. This time you should listen carefully and restrain your instinct to walk away. There is more here than meets the eye, and what you hear can help you make a lot of progress more quickly in the end. Later on, give someone a ring who needs cheering up. The lucky number today is 4.

Friday, October 25 (Moon Pisces to Aries 2:09 p.m.) As the moon moves into your sign, you get a fresh burst of energy; but be sure to put it to use in the right directions. Even if it means a clash with someone, take the initiative. You two will eventually discover that your disagreement really was quite stimulating. Some changes are necessary, and now is the time to make them. You are very able to hit the bullseye today.

Saturday, October 26 (Moon in Aries) If you hold out for what you want today, you will get it—even though it does not seem that way at first. When you are declared the winner, be gracious about it and don't preen your feathers too much. Someone you love will present you with a charming token of affection, though in reality it benefits everyone around you.

Sunday, October 27 (Moon in Aries) Today you take care of yourself by taking care of someone else. The subject is an emotional dilemma which can only be solved by being direct and up-front. It makes you realize that you've been trying to avoid someone who brings up too many old memories. If you face the thing head on it will be better for both of you.

Monday, October 28 (Full Moon 1:59 p.m., Moon Aries to Taurus 2:11 a.m.) This may be a rather frustrating full moon for you; there is something that just seems to keep getting away from you. Don't despair, because the situation is going to boomerang in your favor before long. Just relax and strengthen your side of the story with as many of the facts as you can gather. The lucky number today is 8.

Tuesday, October 29 (Moon in Taurus) It feels good to bring something to a successful conclusion, and you have a right to feel proud of yourself. As your morale improves, you realize that things are brighter than you thought all the way around—including finances. You may feel like going on a spending spree; just keep it within bounds. A Libra may be there to help you spend.

Wednesday, October 30 (Moon Taurus to Gemini 2:35 p.m.) A tough job is placed in front of you, but you are up to it. In fact, it can mean a whole new start and a chance to erase a mistake of the past. Enjoy the help and stimulating company provided by a member of the opposite sex. He/she could be very good for your self-esteem.

Thursday, October 31 (Moon in Gemini) Things get off to a slow start today, but pick up quickly when you discover you've got to make a short hop of a side trip. It proves not only interesting, but positively enjoyable as well as a source of real pleasure. Know that your hunches are telling you what to do—and that they are right.

NOVEMBER 1985

Friday, November 1 (Moon in Gemini Someone in your circle of relatives makes a rather final announcement, and it may be a bit upsetting. Do not become involved and the situation will soon become clear. Sometimes people speak in haste, and no one knows that better than you. Try to keep your mind on the things that need doing—and make sure you yourself are communicating clearly.

Saturday, November 2 (Moon Gemini to Cancer 3:12 a.m.) Matters of the heart are very much at the top of your mind today; you want to know where you really stand with someone very special. You can find out, if you make it known that you are ready for a discussion. Be prepared to make some adjustments, however, because things cannot be exactly as you would have them. A Leo may be in the picture.

Sunday, November 3 (Moon in Cancer) Yesterday's revelations make you feel very secure today, and ready and eager to break bread with those who mean most to you. As a relatively uneventful day passes, you have a flash of intuition. It was there all along, but you just couldn't find the answer. Now you have it and should be able to fix that which you thought was unfixable.

Monday, November 4 (Moon Cancer to Leo 3:12 a.m.) Your curiosity has been piqued and you are determined to carry your inquiry through to a profitable conclusion. The more you learn, the more you realize you can turn the information to profit. As you deal with some really sharp and interesting people, you realize that you've been missing this kind of stimulation. Resolve to keep in touch.

Tuesday, November 5 (Moon to Leo) Your head and your heart may be at war today; realize that you can keep your eye on your objectives while still enjoying a romantic adventure. They are not mutually exclusive. The only thing to remember, however, is that it is important to protect yourself in the emotional clinches if you want to come unscathed. The lucky number is 4 today.

Wednesday, November 6 (Moon Leo to Virgo 9:14 p.m.) There's nothing like words of love and praise from a child or young person to raise your morale and your self-esteem. Enjoy it thoroughly because you have done a lot to deserve it. Your mind may be on adding some variety to your life; nothing will do the trick like travel. Think about it seriously.

Thursday, November 7 (Moon in Virgo) Today you may find yourself thoroughly dissatisfied with your working conditions—wherever you work. If it is at home, you may become acutely aware that some changes are necessary and that others will have to adjust. Don't be afraid to lay down some rules. Meanwhile don't forget your health and diet resolutions; renew them with a Libra or a Scorpio friend.

Friday, November 8 (Moon in Virgo) Again you are determined to make things work better—for you. If you go at it in the right way, you will impress the people who need to be impressed with how serious you are about this. Even those who seemed to be indifferent to your wants and needs will now come around. As a result, you will find yourself a lot happier and more contented doing what you do.

Saturday, November 9 (Moon Virgo to Libra 1:14 a.m.) If you act on impulse, you will be playing right into the hands of someone who would just love to see you stumble and make a mistake. Focus on the technical aspects of the thing and get them thoroughly under your belt before you take any action. You may have to get to see someone in a rather secretive manner, but it is worth your while in the long run.

Sunday, November 10 (Moon in Libra) Life is always trying to balance your needs against someone elses' today that issue becomes critical. It is necessary to be very clear with each other about rights and responsibilities. You are not the only one who feels shortchanged. At times you can be a little selfish; today it will be possible for you to think in terms of the "other" more than yourself. Good going.

Monday, November 11 (Moon Libra to Scorpio 1:53 a.m.) You harbor an interest in the occult, though sometimes you don't reveal it. Today one of your hunches proves so absolutely correct that you wonder seriously about the possibility of developing psychic powers. Look into the subject, because—no matter what happens—you will find it an absorbing study. The lucky number today is 1.

Tuesday, November 12 (Moon in Scorpio) You've been realizing of late that you need to know a lot more about how to improve things in the financial area; today is an excellent day to start your education. Seek out some friends who seem to do it better than you, and find out what their secrets are. It could be as simple as paying more attention than you do. Don't let a romantic interest distract you from more important matters.

Wednesday, November 13 (Moon Scorpio to Sagittarius 1:12 a.m.) Today it's okay to give in to your impulse to play—or at least get out from under the restrictions that have been placed on you lately. Don't just fritter your time away, however; do some serious thinking about some serious pleasure—like a trip or a vacation. You will be spurred on by getting news from someone you've been out of touch with for a while.

Thursday, November 14 (Moon in Sagittarius) Suddenly something that seemed an impossible tangle gets cleared up practically by itself. Well—with a little help from one of your friends. Say thanks for the help, but learn something in the process. If you look beyond the surface of anything, there usually are hidden clues. It's a good thing for simple Aries to keep in mind. The lucky number today is 4.

Friday, November 15 (Moon Sagittarius to Capricorn 1:10 a.m.) You don't like to deal with certain things, so you put them off. Today you can put one of them off no longer, and you meet the challenge with such ease that it surprises you. As the accolades come in from everyone, those that mean the most to you are from a member of the opposite sex. Whether you like it or not, you're involved.

Saturday, November 16 (Moon in Capricorn) It may come as a surprise when someone you consider very important to you comes through with an unexpected gift that says, "I love you." You may have thought it was the furthest thing from his/her mind. It's nice to know that this someone cares, because it makes it easier for you to make a necessary adjustment that isn't totally to your liking.

Sunday, November 17 (Moon Capricorn to Aquarius 3:54 a.m.) You start the day in an uncharacteristically spiritual frame of mind. It is as if you have undergone some kind of transformation and know something you've never known before. Though the interlude is brief, it is very instructive, and lets you take the rest of the day's events in stride. They are not momentous, but your experience has made you feel very loving toward those around you. And they seem to understand why.

Monday, November 18 (Moon in Aquarius) The week begins with you feeling sure of yourself and able to cope with the world. You are rewarded for your positive frame of mind when things that have seemed nebulous now become clear as crystal, and you know just what needs to be done. Now your efforts bring results instead of mere promises, and you are gratified. It's nice to know where you stand—especially when it is on firm ground.

Tuesday, November 19 (Moon Aquarius to Pisces 10:04 a.m.) Your recent successes have brought a relief from the strains of the recent past. Now it seems as if everything is coming together—including you with other people. Your popularity is on the rise and everyone seems eager to help you on your way to bigger and better things. You can be said to have charisma at this time, and you are wise to make the most of it.

Wednesday, November 20 (Moon in Pisces) The things that have been happening to you lately have given you new self-confidence; you are ready and able to throw away those old, restricting security blankets you've been wrapping yourself in. As you strip away old burdens, you feel much lighter. Enjoy the feeling, because you have earned this right to be independent—and creative as never before.

Thursday, November 21 (Moon Pisces to Aries 8:00 p.m.) You are on the brink of a really fresh start, and it makes you feel exhilarated. Don't get so carried away that you forget to notice what is going on right under your nose. If you feel you need help in coping with this unexpected obstacle, seek the help of someone who has been very helpful in the past. His/her advice—and help—will be invaluable to you.

Friday, November 22 (Moon in Aries) You are very conscious of your image today, which is good. However, don't let it go to your head. The rush of good things that have been happening to you may have made you a bit overconfident. One thing to watch very carefully for is overindulgence—in food, drink, or anything. You can have lots of great times without going over the line. The lucky number is 3.

Saturday, November 23 (Moon in Aries) Once again you may feel as if you can have the world at your feet, but you come down to earth enough to realize the most constructive way of using this energy is in the work at hand. It's nice to be able to trust your own judgment, however, and to be secure in the knowledge that you are loved. You may encounter more opposition than you expect from a Taurus, Leo or Scorpio.

Sunday, November 24 (Moon Aries to Taurus 8:37 a.m.) What started out as a rather annoying exchange yesterday turns into a stimulating clash of ideas today. You are at your most self-confident, and very formidable opponent. It's all in fun, however, and both you and your adversaries enjoy the whole affair. Why not put some of your very good thoughts down on paper. You may surprise yourself with how eloquent you can be.

Monday, November 25 (Moon in Taurus) With the moon transiting your second house of personal possessions and values, your mind may be very much on what you have rather than what you are. It is gratifying to see that the financial picture is bright, but don't let yourself get carried away with this aspect of your life. Rejoice with someone else who tells you some excellent news about him/herself.

Tuesday, November 26 (Moon Taurus to Gemini 9:02 p.m.) A while back you made some inquiries out of pure curiosity. Today you get some answers and they are surprisingly interesting. It could set you thinking about how you might add some variety to your life—and some extra cash as well. You feel like talking over the possibilities with some people who share your sense of adventure. The lucky number is 7.

Wednesday, November 27 (Full Moon 7:58 a.m., Moon in Gemini) What started as a glimmer of an idea yesterday today blossoms fully, and you are able to see how you can transform a casual interest into a profitable enterprise. Meanwhile, something that you have considered unfair to you changes in your favor, and you wonder why you put up with it so long. A short trip could be on the agenda.

Thursday, November 28 (Moon in Gemini) You are still in a mood to try new things, and you get the opportunity today. It's fun to experiment and test new waters, and even more fun to do it with someone else who is interesting. Your personal appeal is running high today, so if you want to make that new conquest you can. Just remember the return to reality may be rough.

Friday, November 29 (Moon Gemini to Cancer 8:59 a.m.) People around you may be particularly restless today, and it may be your job to calm them down. Be as encouraging as you can to someone who comes to you with what seems an insurmountable problem; you know it is really not so serious. Try to be as truthful as possible without bursting the other person's bubble of self-importance. In your lighter moments, try your luck with number 1.

Saturday, November 30 (Moon in Cancer) This proves to be an emotionally fulfilling day in which you are surrounded by people who believe in you. You find you really begin to believe in yourself and your instincts when a hunch pays off. Feel free to talk about your hopes and aspirations with people you trust, and do the same for them. The evening is particularly pleasant, but take care not to overeat, because you will be in the mood for rich and sweet foods.

DECEMBER 1985

Sunday, December 1 (Moon Cancer to Leo 8:04 p.m.) As the family gathers today, you realize some new thinking is needed in the area of home surroundings. Things could stand some improving, but you are not the only one who should have the responsibility. Be frank and open about it; a constructive approach will help resolve the dilemma. Leo or an Aquarian could prove a good companion today."

Monday, December 2 (Moon in Leo) You feel very ready for a challenge today, and one comes your way right at the start. You enjoy the feeling of being able to be creative about a problem and you relish the excitement of the discovery of a new technique. If you've got a hunch about something, chances are you are correct and should follow through. Don't listen to what others may say to discourage you.

Tuesday, December 3 (Moon in Leo) Today's one of those days you just feel like "goofing off" and enjoying yourself. To do so completely would be a little unrealistic, but it is a good idea to do some pleasure-seeking when there is time. You will be rewarded by a member of the opposite sex who finds you attractive and has no problem telling you so. Keep the big picture in mind, but do enjoy yourself.

Wednesday, December 4 (Moon Leo to Virgo 4:38 a.m.) It's back to business today, and you get the job done with a vengeance. You know you're on the right track when you get super cooperation from others who have the same goals in mind. Though part of what you must do is a bit tedious, stick with it, and your persistence will pay off. For another kind of payoff, try number 4.

Thursday, December 5 (Moon in Virgo) Sometimes it pays to be a specialist, and today you discover you really are, in your own particular way. The shortcut way of doing things that you come up with is very impressive to others. In another sphere, you need some help yourself, and you can count on an old friend who has been there for you before. An answer will come to you from long distance—whether via the phone or a letter.

Friday, December 6 (Moon Virgo to Libra 9:44 a.m.) Nobody likes to adjust, but you may have to in order to avoid a loud conflict right under your own roof. It's not possible to please 100 percent of the people

100 percent of the time, and you find that out now. Give in with grace, however, and you will avoid a lot of hurt feelings. Throw yourself into your work for best results; and try your luck with number 6.

Saturday, December 7 (Moon in Libra) There are those who disagree with you today and they let you know it loud and clear. Your best course is to keep a low profile and wait until the storm blows over; it is within you to be patient, though it is difficult. In other matters, clear your mind of any self-deception. In order to understand a situation you may have to read between the lines.

Sunday, December 8 (Moon Libra to Scorpio 1:05 p.m.) Harmony returns to the home scene and the less said about yesterday the better. Now you—and your partner—can turn your thoughts to more important matters and see where you can blend ideas from both of you into one happy whole. The best way to go about it is to set up some rules and regulations you both agree are fair—on both sides.

Monday, December 9 (Moon in Scorpio) It is wise to be very wary of one who tries to get you in on a deal you can't refuse. You can, and you had better if you want to avoid taking another's burdens upon yourself. Take a clue, however, from what you learn, and do some investigating on your own. There's more here than meets the eye, and it could be that you turn up something valuable after all. The lucky number today is 9.

Tuesday, December 10 (Moon Scorpio to Sagittarius 1:11 p.m.) Your discovery of yesterday bears more looking into today, but don't let the search make you stray from other interesting matters that present themselves. The key to getting your points across in a frank discussion is to show how intensely you feel about a situation; people are more willing to listen when they know you really care.

Wednesday, December 11 (Moon in Sagittarius) It began to dawn on you yesterday that you really do have something to say; continue to make your views known today. When more people know about you, the more potential success is yours. A family matter gets settled without too big a hassle, and it is a relief to be able to put it to rest. Travel is very much on your mind and should be.

Thursday, December 12 (Moon Sagittarius to Capricorn 1:03 p.m.) You keep on getting bright ideas these days, but remember that not all of them will pay off equally. Your luck is still running strong, however, so there's no harm in reaching beyond what you now have. If you reach too far, however, you could find yourself out on a limb. Stick with safer things like these travel plans that are taking more shape.

Friday, December 13 (Moon in Capricorn) Whether or not it's luck is a moot point, but today you make a break-through and get some real recognition for your special abilities. If you are honest with yourself, you will realize you really didn't work that hard on it; just imagine what would happen if you did. Things are heating up in your personal sphere as well, and you are less mild-mannered than of late. Luck comes with the number 4.

Saturday, December 14 (Moon Capricorn to Aquarius 1:34 p.m.) Someone asks for you today to do something very special, and the change of scene is quite stimulating. In addition, you make some great contacts for future projects. Some people you work along with have quite different ideas about how to do things, but it definitely broadens your perspective. A letter brings another request you are not sure you can fulfill.

Sunday, December 15 (Moon in Aquarius) You start off the day knowing it will be a pleasant one, and you are not wrong. A get-together with friends is both full of fun and instructive too; you get to observe how some people create harmony where there might be discord. Tuck the lesson away for the future. Don't forget to remember someone who deserves a gift.

Monday, December 16 (Moon Aquarius to Pisces 6:21 p.m.) You may hear some talk that is music to your ears today, but you should be aware that the person who speaks them may not be able to follow through. At least at this time. You are the one who must be realistic and gently point out that there are some holes in the plan. Things are not always the way people want to see them.

Tuesday, December 17 (Moon in Pisces) Though you may feel it, remember that you are really not hemmed in permanently; this is only temporary. As the weight of responsibility becomes a bit uncomfortable, remember that greater rewards are right around the corner. Dig in and define your intentions to yourself so that you will have a clear goal in mind; things will go a lot easier if you do.

Wednesday, December 18 (Moon in Pisces) You are amazed! Something you thought was truly a lost cause has life again, and you get a second chance to do things right. Grab it, and make a vow that you won't let things get away from you this time. Another Aries and/or a Libra may figure prominently in the scheme of things and be of great help. You really don't need much, however.

Thursday, December 19 (Moon Pisces to Aries 2:55 a.m.) A feeling of vitality returns and you are ready to go out and beat the world. Perhaps because you are on the alert for opportunity, someone interesting who crosses your path definitely catches your eye. He/she may be the clue to a whole new start in a whole new direction. Don't be overly hasty, however; time is definitely on your side.

Friday, December 20 (Moon in Aries) This is the perfect day to be the Aries pioneer you are; you need not fear trying something new because your reflexes are excellent and your judgment right on target. As you win your way, you remember what it feels like to be able to swing others over to your side. Keep the feeling in mind on less vital days; it will keep you going. The lucky number today is 2.

Saturday, December 21 (Moon Aries to Taurus 3:09 p.m.) You've always liked to tell stories, and today you get the chance to hold others enthralled as you do so. You needn't exaggerate too much; you'll get an audience anyway. As you find yourself the center of attraction, don't be insensitive to some less forward people who are in the crowd. Draw them out and let them share your limelight.

Sunday, December 22 (Moon in Taurus) Today's a day to get all your ducks in a row, financially speaking. You've been letting things slip a little lately, so you and your partner should do some tightening up of the ship. Not that your financial position is bad; in fact, when you sit down to do an accounting, you may find you are better off than you think. Don't blow it all on impulsive spending; you know where that has gotten you in the past.

Monday, December 23 (Moon in Taurus) A goal you set a while back is now plainly in sight; you can stay in the driver's seat and go directly towards it, if you maintain self-control. The key is to figure out which things are most important to you, and eliminate those that are marginal. You will build up capital much more quickly that way—and learn some lessons about "living smart" as well. Ask as many questions as you can think of; the more information you have the better off you will be.

Tuesday, December 24 (Moon Taurus to Gemini 3:46 a.m.) An early holiday gift proves exciting, because it is so unexpected. You love the combination of luxury and practicality. A family reunion is on the agenda, and it turns out to be a particularly harmonious get-together where some old rifts are settled. Your sense of humor is the key, and everyone appreciates the way you handle the situation.

Wednesday, December 25 (Moon in Gemini) It is vital to take it easy today, in spite of the holiday atmosphere. Or perhaps because of it. You could easily overdo and feel rather tense and irritable, which would spoil your fun—and everyone else's. Let small mishaps roll off your back, and resolve to keep the spirit of the season at the top of your mind. Communicate with relatives who are waiting to hear from you.

Thursday, December 26 (Moon Gemini to Cancer 3:41 p.m.) In spite of your attempts to play it cool yesterday, today you may feel rather strung out. Take a positive approach by getting back on that program of diet and exercise; it is more vital than ever at this time of year. You are very gratified when someone who does not often express pleasure with you comes across with a nice compliment about how you are handling things.

Friday, December 27 (Full Moon 2:46 a.m., Moon in Cancer) Serenity returns in full measure today, and you and someone special exchange ideas about your basic values. It feels good to be back on firm ground again, and you are able to complete a project that's been hanging over your head for a while. You are delighted when others tell you you've done a good job; self-confidence is returning.

Saturday, December 28 (Moon in Cancer) You will want to return to home base early today, and stay there for the evening. You are feeling very content right where you are, but you may accept the invitation of some friends who say they'd like to come over. As you enjoy an evening of quiet domesticity, you feel closer than ever to someone; and you both agree you've been taking each other for granted a bit too much lately. Do better next year.

Sunday, December 29 (Moon Cancer to Leo 1:51 a.m.) A young person may seek you out today to talk about matters of great importance—like where to live and how to live. Be your Aries self and answer honestly, remembering what it feels like to want your independence so badly. Be receptive and encouraging, and give some sound advice about how to get your feet wet without totally going under. Meanwhile, a hunch of your own pays off.

Monday, December 30 (Moon in Leo) You feel like playing today and should try to round up some compatible company to play with. The holiday spirit is in the air, and you've got a real dose of it. Someone really wants you to come to a very special event, and says it won't be the same without you. You are flattered, but shouldn't be carried away by the compliment. Keep on an even keel emotionally.

Tuesday, December 31 (Moon Leo to Virgo 10:06 a.m.) The year ends on a note of responsibility, as you realize you are very serious about the resolutions you are making, and intend to keep them for everyone's good. Everyone is feeling rather open and lighthearted today, and you are there in the middle of everything with your excellent sense of humor. A pleasant day ends with a lovely night which turns out to be the most romantic of the year.

JANUARY 1986

Wednesday, January 1 (Moon in Virgo) Something that happens today gives you confidence and makes you look at the year ahead with a sense that all kinds of good things can happen. Somehow you just know you are going to succeed. Also on the positive side you get rid of an unnecessary burden, and it lightens your spirits. Good as you feel, you mustn't neglect a job that needs doing.

Thursday, January 2 (Moon Virgo to Libra 3:45 p.m.) Today you plunge into postholiday activity ready to make good on something you neglected to follow through on before. Be glad of this second chance to do it right. You may find there are an awful lot of people depending on you, but you will also get a lot of cooperation from others. Your greatest helper may be a Taurus or possibly a Scorpio. Take a lesson in persistence.

Friday, January 3 (Moon in Libra) Though you are sometimes a bit biased, today you find it easy to be objective. You will have to be in order to sort out what belongs to whom and who has a right to what. Partnerships of all kinds are emphasized—and that could include your marriage or live-in arrangement. Maintain a steady course, and take a tip from an Aquarian. Some kind of luck comes through being in the right place at the right time.

Saturday, January 4 (Moon Libra to Scorpio 7:44 p.m.) You can have a ball today, but you may have to let somebody else take the lead in making plans. Don't worry, you'll be popular wherever you go. The waiting game you play today will pay off tomorrow. Keep the big picture in mind.

Sunday, January 5 (Moon in Scorpio) Don't be fooled by surface indications now; there's a lot more here than meets the eye. Remember that still waters run deep, and that you may have to be subtle to find out what is really going on. Be persistent and you could strike pay dirt. Romp a little with a Scorpio or a Leo.

Monday, January 6 (Moon Scorpio to Sagittarius 9:47 p.m.) You tend to be a little too trusting of others; don't be a patsy now. You could have a straight-from-the-shoulder talk with a member of the opposite sex—with good results. Some very basic problems are at issue now; keep a cool head and you'll come out on top. Your spirits get a boost when you find you have an enthusiastic new friend. Your lucky number today is 5.

Tuesday, January 7 (Moon in Sagittarius) Money may be burning a hole in your pocket today, and you may be very tempted to make an impulsive and extensive purchase. Listen to what someone else has to say about it; it's possible the two of you will agree that it could make life easier or lovelier. Take advantage of your expansive mood to plan ahead—possibly for travel. Your highest values may be tested now. Keep on the straight and narrow.

Wednesday, January 8 (Moon Sagittarius to Capricorn 10:42 p.m.) A goal comes within sight now and you should go for it. Reach beyond your current expectations and try to grab the brass ring. You have a good chance of snagging it. Be willing to toss out some old things and/or ideas. You need to clear the decks. A Virgo or a Pisces could be very helpful in your efforts to streamline things.

Thursday, January 9 (Moon in Capricorn) You're still on a roll today, and you find that the way to succeed in business is to prove how trustworthy you can be. Show them that their confidence is well placed when they place it in you. No matter what your sphere of influence, your influence will be much stronger now. It's a great time to get involved in extracurricular activities. A Cancer or a Capricorn could prove to be a good running mate. The lucky number today is 8.

Friday, January 10 (Moon in Capricorn) You round out the week by rounding out a project you've been involved in, and you feel you can sit back and relax. Great—but don't consider yourself finished too soon. Make sure you pick up all the pieces so you won't trip over one later. Another Aries—or possibly a Libra—may ask you to go out and play. Have a ball!

Saturday, January 11 (Moon Capricorn to Aquarius 12:01 a.m.) You should be feeling positively terrific today and you should take advantage of it by using your powers of persuasion on someone who has been difficult to convince. You will find that you suddenly get a green light which has only been a red one before. For some it's an excellent day to let romantic run wild. Some of you could also be lucky with the number one.

Sunday, January 12 (Moon in Aquarius) Trust the first thought that comes to you today—it is likely to be a very valid one. It is also likely to help you solve a dilemma that's been bugging you of late. Instead of jumping feet first into an argument, be receptive and sit back and listen. You can get a lot more by turning on the charm than by turning on your competitive spirit. Remember, you are among friends. Keep it friendly.

Monday, January 13 (Moon Aquarius to Pisces 3:39 a.m.) If your mind is a bit fuzzy today, make an attempt to gather together your rather scattered forces. Force yourself to concentrate and not to give a once-over-lightly treatment to certain procedures. Something you hear blows your mind, and you realize that a lot has been going on behind the scenes. Some of you may get extra responsibility heaped on your shoulders, but grin and bear it. There's light at the end of the tunnel.

Tuesday, January 14 (Moon in Pisces) Don't let this day be a downer in terms of your feelings. Remember that you will get back exactly what you put in. Put a smile on your face for the whole human race—and you'll get through the day beautifully. Whatever happens, don't be tempted into an indiscretion. Someone may be looking to trip you up now. You can lighten the atmosphere by trying your luck with number 4.

Wednesday, January 15 (Moon Pisces to Aries 11:03 a.m.) The moon moves into your sign today, Aries, and you should feel an immediate lift. However, you still need to protect your interests—don't let your guard down. Your sense are very sharp and it's easy to pick up signals from those around you. For some those signals may project romance. Are you ready?

Thursday, January 16 (Moon in Aries) Your Aries independence may be particularly apparent today, however, others around you make you realize you do not have to go it alone. You've got lots of support from those who love you—and they want to show it. Make a personal appearance and you will be a smash. Jot down those thoughts—they could be great ones today.

Friday, January 17 (Moon Aries to Taurus 10:14 p.m.) No matter how you try to wish it away, you can't avoid the need to be practical now. It's essential to be realistic and not to fool yourself about people or situations. Nothing is going to happen unless you make it happen. You are still in a high cycle, however, so you should be able to handle matters just swimmingly. A sympathetic person—possibly a Pisces—may help you understand what is really happening.

Saturday, January 18 (Moon in Taurus) You won't feel good when you are pulled in two opposite directions today. It is a difficult choice you have to make; but even you are aware that relief is in sight. Here's a tip: Take the route that is popular with more people, even if it is not necssarily a personal preference. There's plenty of time to pamper yourself later on. You could easily pick a winner today; don't be too afraid to gamble.

Sunday, January 19 (Moon in Taurus) You see? It pays not to be petty. Today someone—possibly a relative—makes a major concession to you, and it lightens your load considerably. It's an excellent time to take some of your hidden talents out of hiding; get involved in something where you can shine. Stay alert!

Monday, January 20 (Moon Taurus to Gemini 11:12 a.m.) You're off and running on a fresh start period. Don't dwell on a previous error, but make up for lost time. A sparkling member of the opposite sex may say something surprising today; trust the fact that he/she is sincere. Don't hesitate to ask some hard questions. The lucky number today is 1.

Tuesday, January 21 (Moon in Gemini) You've got so much energy now, you could find that your mind is running away with you. It's great to feel stimulated, but be sure you sort things out before you go off on a tangent. Some hard difficult exercise would be excellent therapy. Some terrific financial news comes your way—it could take a rather unusual form. Don't trust yourself to appraise something; get a professional involved.

Wednesday, January 22 (Moon Gemini to Cancer 11:14 p.m.) You are full of high spirits today, and you should know it is possible to go too far in one direction or another. Show others how inventive and clever you are, but don't try to beat everybody out. It's a day to live and let live equally. Your current popularity is great for the ego—but the socializing involved could be disastrous to your body image. Make moderation your word for the day. The possibility for a short trip comes up, take it.

Thursday, January 23 (Moon in Cancer) Today you may feel as if someone is trying to invade your territorial rights; react appropriately. In this or another matter, however, you will have to be aware of subtle nuances. That is not always your specialty, so you might want to ask for help from a more sensitive and/or perceptive person. Things are changing fast now, and you'll have to stay alert to keep in step. Try your luck with number 4 today.

Friday, January 24 (Moon in Cancer) If you feel someone has been taking you for granted lately, come out and say it. A frank approach is the right one today, as long as you don't overdo and get brutal. Your self-esteem is important, but so is the other person's. Be sure you maintain a balance. Some of you may find an opportunity to increase your assets fall in your laps today; examine it carefully. For the most part, it's best to sit close to home base today. You'll feel most comfortable there.

Saturday, January 25 (Moon Cancer to Leo 8:47 a.m.) You should be grateful that someone you love asks you to do something for him/her today; it signals that you've got a lot of emotional security available. Don't risk it by breaking promises or not coming through. Today you are able to reestablish your authority in an area where it has been a bit shaky lately. Stand up for your rights. In everything you come across today, be aware that renegotiation is possible. The lucky number today is 6.

Sunday, January 26 (Moon in Leo) This full moon is possibly the best of the year for Aries. It falls right in the area of your chart that highlights romance, change, travel, and a variety of experiences. However, there is a possibility of getting carried away by someone or something if you do not exercise a bit of discipline. For some it's the ideal time to pin down travel or vacation plans. For others, a matter that has been covered in darkness now has full light shed on it. Children and young people could easily play dominant roles today.

Monday, January 27 (Moon Leo to Virgo 3:51 p.m.) The full moon is still making you feel like blossoming out all over. It's a fabulous day to show your style and prove how creative you can be. You are visible in the best sense of the word—so visible a member of the opposite sex is drawn to you. Make careful mental notes of any tips that come your way today regarding money and how to make it. They could prove valuable later on. The lucky number today is 8.

Tuesday, January 28 (Moon in Virgo) Whatever your work is, you will have great satisfaction doing it today. The reason is that you are able to get something out of the way that has been like an albatross around your neck of late. Among the other good things that happen today is a favor that is returned to you by someone you helped in the past. Some may even collect an old debt. Don't be surprised to hear from someone who's been out of touch for a long time. It could be a relative.

Wednesday, January 29 (Moon Virgo to Libra 9:10 p.m.) Make a special effort to open up to someone today; he/she has been wanting to get to know you for a while. It could be a beautiful realtionship—even a romantic one. Don't be afraid to make an executive decision today—even if you aren't an executive. You are likely to be right, and to be rewarded as well. The lucky number is 1.

Thursday, January 30 (Moon in Libra) You may find yourself smack between a rock and a hard place today. You will not find it comfortable to make either choice, but you must make one of them. A key to today's activity is to stick with agreements you have made. It is not a time to slough off responsibility. On the positive side, someone could offer you a very sweet deal. Don't be afraid to take it.

Friday, January 31 (Moon in Libra) Unlike yesterday, today you can sit back and play a waiting game. By letting others show their hands, and by listening to opposite points of view, you'll get a much clearer picture of what is really going on. Try to conserve your energy today in every sense of the word. You may receive a slight shock now, but it will be a pleasant one.

FEBRUARY 1986

Saturday, February 1 (Moon Libra to Scorpio 1:19 a.m.) Some Aries may do a bit of eavesdropping today, but they may not like what they hear. If it is a critical remark, take it with good grace and try to improve the area of your life that is being criticized. A mystery is solved when you turn up a missing piece of information. Emotions are running rather deep today and someone in your circle may tell you just how much he/she cares about you. Respond in kind.

Sunday, February 2 (Moon in Scorpio) You can break out of that cage because you are not really a victim of circumstances. By acting in your characteristic Aries style, you will find that independence is there for the taking. Listen to someone who tells you about alternatives that do exist; it is true that you could use a lot of help from your friends. Some Aries will have a very heartwarming experience today; it could occur right around home base. You might want to stay close to it today.

Monday, February 3 (Moon Scorpio to Sagittarius 4:31 a.m.) You may take a look in the mirror today and decide that something's got to be done about the shape you are in. For many it will mean that this is *D*-day, *D* for diet. It is an excellent time to undertake any kind of self-improvement program. Some will have their horizons broadened by making an exciting new contact. It could be with a whole new social circle. Don't come on too strong, and don't get too competitive. You are among friends.

Tuesday, February 4 (Moon in Sagittarius) Today you step back and look at some events of the recent past; now they make sense. With this clearer focus on things, you will be able to leap right over some kind of barrier that's holding you back. Isn't it nice to know your own mind? And your own strength? You can start rebuilding with confidence now.

Wednesday, February 5 (Moon Sagittarius to Capricorn 7:02 a.m.) Change is generally not threatening to you, which is a good thing. It is a particularly good thing now as there are definite changes in the air. If you keep your eye on the main chance and your finger on the pulse on the situation, you will come through beautifully. For some, a heart-to-heart talk is on the agenda, and it is definitely called for. Thrash things out once and for all. An opportunity for travel may fall in your lap.

Thursday, February 6 (Moon in Capricorn) You could easily get in an argument today, and it could easily be with an authority figure in your life. Don't let your hot temper run away with you, but rather try to reason things out calmly. It's possible you may have to adjust to what is expected of you; do it with a smile. Some Aries may receive a gift or some other token of affection today; realize that it is genuine. If you feel inclined to speculate, the lucky number today is 6.

Friday, February 7 (Moon Capricorn to Aquarius 7:35 a.m.) Don't depend on anyone else; if you do, you may be disappointed—particularly about a promise that has been made to you. Go it alone, because it is time to take charge of your own destiny in a fairly important matter. The clue to handling this day is to avoid self-deception at all costs. Someone who appears to be well meaning may be quite the opposite; realize this and avoid disappointment.

Saturday, February 8 (Moon in Aquarius) Aries in sales capacities could have an absolutely super day. No matter what you do, you will be able to apply friendly persuasion quite successfully today. Some will be asking for extra responsibility—and getting it. Along with some tangible rewards. Get out and mix and mingle today because social activity is likely to be particularly pleasant. All in all, it's a day to enjoy.

Sunday, February 9 (Moon Aquarius to Pisces 11:32 a.m.) Once again it's opportunity day. Keep an eye out for personal advantage in any form; you have every possibility of getting what you aim for. Don't let a muddleheaded person distort your view of things. Realize that you are the realistic one. Try your luck with number 9 today.

Monday, February 10 (Moon in Pisces) Don't mince any words today; you've got to be absolutely direct and let others know you have the courage of your convictions. Those who are seeking leadership may very well be cast in that role today. For others, a previously dark situation becomes much lighter and brighter. A Leo or an Aquarian could be an excellent person to team up with today. Resolve to keep a secret you hear.

Tuesday, February 11 (Moon Pisces to Aries 6:21 p.m.) Your Aries sense of fairness may be offended today. There's little you can do except stay above the battle. It may mean disillusionment about a particular person you thought could be trusted. Don't let it spoil your day or interfere with your plans. Just be glad your own integrity is intact. Spice up your day by doing something amusing. A Cancer or a Leo could be good buddy to do it with.

Wednesday, February 12 (Moon in Aries) The moon is on your side now, and you should take full advantage of it. You should be feeling a sense of your own potential and sizing up the odds that face you. You could easily overcome them now. Some will focus their newfound strength on keeping resolutions about diet, exercise, and nutrition. Many will find themselves particularly popular now; enjoy the burst of social activity. Just take care not to overindulge.

Thursday, February 13 (Moon in Aries) You are able to revive something today and give it new life. What appeared to be a losing proposition could now be very profitable for you. It's a relief to cut through a mass of red tape and get right to the heart of a matter. With your new greater understanding of a situation, you can easily turn it around. With your moon cycle continuing high, it's time to get going.

Friday, February 14 (Moon Aries to Taurus 5:38 a.m.) Happy Valentine Day, Aries! This may be the happiest you've had in years. For some it will be love that comes along; for others it might be money. There's even a possibility you may find something you thought was lost or stolen. If the stakes aren't too high, try your luck with number 5.

Saturday, February 15 (Moon in Taurus) It is not wise to be your Aries blunt self today; at all costs, try a diplomatic approach. This applies particularly where members of the opposite sex are concerned. There may be some adjusting that has to be done—on both sides. Be sure to do your bit. Financially you could be feeling a lot more secure. You may also find new things to admire in an old friend—possibly a Taurus.

Sunday, February 16 (Moon Taurus to Gemini 5:17 p.m.) Take some time out from this day of rest to consider your values. Do you really have a sharp clear focus on what is most important to you? Realize that you can make some recent gains permanent ones if you make a greater attempt to understand someone or something who appears to be standing in your way. A key to happiness now is to replace resentment with love; you will be surprised what that can do for you.

Monday, February 17 (Moon in Gemini) For some the pressure is really on. Accept the challenge someone tosses in your lap, and know the pleasure of meeting it. Later on, think about rewarding yourself—perhaps with a short pleasure trip. Some kind of an agreement must be made at this time; be sure each side is clear on exactly what the other expects. A Cancer or a Capricorn could come your way today and make it a more profitable one.

Tuesday, February 18 (Moon in Gemini) Prepare to bask in the glow of a compliment today. It may come from an unexpected source; you never know who is watching! This or some other occurrence puts you in an extremely good humor—so good you are able to race through what might have been a tedious task. Stay flexible for best results. You might try your luck today with number 9.

Wednesday, February 19 (Moon Gemini to Cancer 7:39 a.m.) It certainly is not like Aries to take a back seat to anyone. If you've been doing that, today's the day to turn things around. It may take a bit of courage and a lot of determination, but once you take the initiative you're on your way. Help can come from someone close by; an unexpected message comes from someone far off. It could be a day full of surprises.

Thursday, February 20 (Moon in Cancer) You may have a touch of the moody blues today and you will just have to shake yourself out of it. One way is by deciding on a definite course, even though you are pulled in two directions. Keep you and yours uppermost in your mind, and you will see the secure road quite clearly. Long-range matters count a lot. Talk it over with a bright Aquarian who knows how to pick the odds.

Friday, February 21 (Moon Cancer to Libra 3:25 p.m.) Some may receive an unexpected and last-minute invitation today. Even if you've got to scurry about to get ready, you will find it well worthwhile; don't be a stay-at-home. It's a good time to take time out and look ahead to see where you may expand and where you may have to pull in your horns. The important thing is to look beyond the immediate.

Saturday, February 22 (Moon in Leo) For many Aries, the emphasis today is on love and romance. If you are in a relationship it will intensify; if you're out of one you may meet someone new. Whatever your situation, today you should be able to express your feelings in a quite dramatic demonstrative manner. Don't worry if you don't get feedback right away. It will come. Your lucky number today is 4.

Sunday, February 23 (Moon Leo to Virgo 11:58 p.m.) You may be amazed that something you want comes your way today almost as if by magic. If you think about it, you will realize that you planted the seeds a while back. Congratulations! Some of you may have an absolute inspiration or brainstorm today; be sure to jot your ideas down on paper. Children or young people may provide pleasure today—or challenge your wits. Be ready to deal with it. There will be no lack of variety to spice up your life today.

Monday, February 24 (Moon in Virgo) This full moon may find you with lots of obligations to deal with. In fact, you may be feeling that life is a bit of a drag today. Stick with the necessaries and get them out of the way as soon as possible. In the course of it—earlier on—you'll have the pleasure of reaching a greater understanding of someone close to you who's been restless and moody of late. The two of you end the day in harmony. Your lucky number today is 6.

Tuesday, February 25 (Moon in Virgo) Don't waste time brooding today, and don't try to make yourself feel better by fooling yourself. You must see people and issues as they really are. The sure cure today is to put on your practical hat and get down to basic issues—in other words, get the job done. You may find some pleasure in doing old things a new way or coming up with ingenious techniques. A Pisces will be very prominent in the picture.

Wednesday, February 26 (Moon Virgo to Libra 4:07 a.m.) Your spirits should be much lighter now and you may be able to see what seems like a setback as a kind of blessing in disguise. Someone gives you breathing room, and you enjoy it. In a legal or contractual matter, don't let some small details escape your attention. They could crop up later and cause some annoyance. The lucky number today is 8.

Thursday, February 27 (Moon in Libra) People around you may seem particularly cooperative today; it could be your much improved state of mind. Whatever happens, however, turns out that much better because of teamwork. Your most important partnership may need a bit of work now—be willing to negotiate, adjust, and make peace. Don't be afraid to reach beyond your current expectations; there's lots more that's available to you.

Friday, February 28 (Moon Libra to Scorpio 7:06 a.m.) As a fire sign, Aries tends to be future-oriented. That works in your favor as you have to make a break from the past—a situation, a person, or an attitude. In the course of it, you not only get to the heart of the matter, you earn the respect of someone very important to you. Some Aries may find that someone who has seemed indifferent now takes a second look and is suddenly enthusiastic. It could mean a whole new start—particularly in business or career.

MARCH 1986

Saturday, March 1 (Moon Scorpio) You could be an easy mark today; don't let someone sell you a bill of goods about something that is not really worth the price. Take inventory of what you have before you invest in more. This could apply to non-material as well as material possessions. The best course is to let someone else—possibly a professional—assess the value of what you have. On all fronts, stay alert today—something or someone could sneak up on you. Have fun with a Cancer or a Capricorn.

Sunday, March 2 (Moon Scorpio to Sagittarius 9:51 a.m.) What you need is a change of routine, and many of you will get that today. Go along with the idea, even though you are not wild about it. What happens is beneficial to you in the long run. Make a point of relaxing, but don't let down your guard about keeping your body healthy and fit. Your lucky number is 3.

Monday, March 3 (Moon in Sagittarius) Someone gives you a chance to prove yourself today; don't knock it. It is a rare opportunity. Some of you who have been looking for a new location—for home, business, or whatever—may find the ideal one today. Actual travel, or simply journies of the mind, are also featured on this day. Recontact someone you've been thinking about lately. He/she is waiting to hear from you. The lucky number today could be 4.

Tuesday, March 4 (Moon Sagittarius to Capricorn 12:56 p.m.) Someone switches over to your side today; it's great to have him/her on your team. Together you may find a solution that has been rather elusive of late. There is also a possibility that an interesting new person may wander onto the scene today; strike up a conversation, because you could learn something. The signs that could possibly punctuate your day are Gemini, Virgo, and Sagittarius. Take advantage of your expansive mood.

Wednesday, March 5 (Moon in Capricorn) Your sense of security should be much greater than it has been in the recent past. For some, harmony will be restored where chaos has reigned. If you maintain a steady course today you should be able to see solid results of your efforts. In fact, someone may reward you with an unexpected gift. For fun, try your luck with the number 6 today.

Thursday, March 6 (Moon Capricorn to Aquarius 4:42 p.m.) Don't take anything at face value today; know that current conditions are subject to change. The most important thing is to protect your own interests by keeping your options open. You have plenty of them. The wisest course is to keep your eyes open and your mouth shut. Those who are looking for it could easily find romance today—in a very unexpected form.

Friday, March 7 (Moon in Aquarius) Influences converge to make this a power play day for Aries. Those really in love should find it blossoms even further today. All should experience a special popularity, and play the opportunities it brings to the hilt. Keep your eye on a Capricorn who could play a significant role.

Saturday, March 8 (Moon Aquarius to Pisces 7:48 p.m.) If you've been involved in a losing proposition, today's the day to leave it behind you. Break free by asserting your independence—it is one of your best assets. Some of you may be flirting with fame and enjoying the limelight. It's a splendid day to reassess your circle.

Sunday, March 9 (Moon in Pisces) Your spirits should continue to rise today, and you should be able to cast off any down feelings you had of late. For some, that may mean retreating from the scene to concentrate and count your blessings. Others may literally make a fresh start, and even see tangible results of their efforts. You could get involved in a secret meeting; steer clear of plotting and planning that strikes a false note. The lucky number today is 1.

Monday, March 10 (Moon in Pisces) An emotional bruise you suffered of late is now totally healed. You start out the work week full of vigor and determination. Keep it that way. Some of you will receive a very desirable invitation; it should bring a great feeling of satisfaction. The focus today is on food and love. Don't overindulge in either area.

Tuesday, March 11 (Moon Pisces to Aries 5:03 a.m.) It's an excellent day in all respects. With the moon in your sign, you will be in the right place at the right time. Make it a point to rise above a petty quarrel that erupts in your immediate circle; you can rise above it. Trust your first impressions today, because they are likely to be valid. Be a good buddy and help someone who needs you. It's a day to learn by teaching.

Wednesday, March 12 (Moon in Aries) Don't be afraid to take the plunge today, because your judgment and intuition are still exceedingly sharp. Use your mental clarity to check out all details and scan the small print. Don't sell yourself short when someone offers you an opportunity to show your stuff. Good people to mingle today are Taurus and Scorpio.

Thursday, March 13 (Moon Aries to Taurus 3:04 p.m.) Your special spark ignites a member of the opposite sex, and you could wind up with a new romance. For others, this top-notch day simply brings a second emotional wind—and the energy to make necessary changes. Make sure you get your ideas across to the right person. The lucky number today is 5.

Friday, March 14 (Moon in Taurus) You must take advantage of the moon influence by getting your financial house in order. Some may pay bills, others may find money that's owed coming in. Your current living arrangement deserves some attention too; isn't there something you can do to promote harmony? Think it over. You may find yourself dealing with some other strong-minded individual—but you can hold your own.

Saturday, March 15 (Moon in Taurus) Spend part of this day in clearing the decks for action—getting rid of what you do not need. That includes material possessions as well as unnecessary expenses. It is possible to run things on a much leaner basis. You can show someone important that you do really matter now—it could mean a rude awakening for the other.

Sunday, March 16 (Moon Taurus to Gemini 3:23 a.m.) You could be positively bubbling over with optimism today; it might make you tough to deal with. Understand that others are not quite as stimulating as you, and do something nice like taking a pleasure trip to break the routine. On another front, be selective about whom you deal with. The lucky number could be 8.

Monday, March 17 (Moon in Gemini) Some of you will get involved in a friendly argument today and be able to show your snappy conversational style. Be sure to keep it friendly! Someone has something to celebrate, and it could be you. However—no matter who the party is—take care not to overdo it. Another Aries or a Libra could be an excellent companion today.

Tuesday, March 18 (Moon Gemini to Cancer 4:04 p.m.) It might be wise to steer clear of someone whose ideas are directly opposed to your own. There is the possibility of a direct confrontation. However, if you are ready for a new approach, meet the situation head-on. Some will get right to the heart of the matter—others will get closer to a very special person. It's not a good day for strenuous exercise.

Wednesday, March 19 (Moon in Cancer) You may feel a bit tied down today, but realize that the security requires your staying put for now. Some may get involved in an important transaction—possibly involving real estate. A new home is in your future, and today the future may arrive. Someone older can help a great deal. The lucky number today is 2.

Thursday, March 20 (Moon in Cancer) Today you are able to move about a lot more freely and to diversify your activities. Some will entertain; others will be entertained. Enjoy this open-minded day and resolve not to get bogged down in routine again. A flaky friend—possibly a Sagittarian—could lead you astray. Go, if it's not too far.

Friday, March 21 (Moon Cancer to Leo 2:38 a.m.) Your heart could easily rule your head today and you could experience runaway emotions. One of those may be love. Some of you will have illusions shattered, but in the long run you are wiser, if a bit sadder. No matter what the scenario, you should feel alert, vital, and alive. If you're inclined to speculate, try your luck with number 4.

Saturday, March 22 (Moon in Leo) Once again, your feelings are uppermost. That means that on the positive side you can trust your intuition. On the negative side, you must take care not to let "romantic notions" cloud your vision. Do some sharing of interests with an interesting person; your best bet is to keep it on the intellectual side. The lucky number today is 5.

Sunday, March 23 (Moon Leo to Virgo 3:39 a.m.) Be prepared to get back what you give out. If it's a token of affection, you are in luck because it will be returned. For many a relationship is becoming more serious than originally anticipated. Are you ready for it? The best people to mingle with today are those who are young in heart—regardless of their age.

Monday, March 24 (Moon in Virgo) Life settles down and practical matters surface—deal with them. It's important to take nothing for granted now, and to be sure what you see is real. That may take some getting behind the scenes. You could be unsettled by a nervous person today—possibly a Pisces or a Virgo. Keep your cool.

Tuesday, March 25 (Moon Virgo to Libra 1:22 p.m.)
Someone may nag you about your responsibilities today; some of his/her complaining is justified. Recognize this and correct where you must correct. On the other hand, your chances of fulfillment multiply now. Some may feel overburdened with cares—mainly of those who depend on you. Realize it is temporary, and accept your role.

Wednesday, March 26 (Moon in Libra) Life is a bit "looser" today, and you breathe a sigh of relief. As you reach out, someone confides his/her problems. Be sympathetic, but don't get involved. Some will achieve satisfaction by finishing off a long-term project. Relax and enjoy!

Thursday, March 27 (Moon Libra to Scorpio 3:05 p.m.) That love that has been just around the corner comes into view now—and it is mutual. If this is not your scenario, you will receive a wonderful compliment that warms your heart considerably. Try to find an outlet for your creative energies because you could create something of lasting value. Realize you have the opportunity to take charge of your own destiny. The lucky number could be 1 today.

Friday, March 28 (Moon in Scorpio) Don't be satisfied with half-baked answers. Demand that others be as straightforward as you are. What seems like a mystery is really not that complicated and can be solved easily. Someone close to you may be in financial difficulties; listen and do what you can. A Cancer or a Capricorn could have a brilliant suggestion.

Saturday, March 29 (Moon Scorpio to Sagittarius 4:20 p.m.) Don't turn a deaf ear to someone who is trying to tell you something; what you learn could benefit you tremendously. Indifference is the enemy now—force yourself to get involved. What seems like an idle hunch could pay off. Someone is dying to hear from you and you know who it is. Don't let him/her wait any longer. The longer number today could be 3.

Sunday, March 30 (Moon in Sagittarius) Today you open up and communicate, and it helps to clear the air. By resolving this current dilemma, you feel much more secure. Some will have their thoughts on travel, and it is an excellent time to plan. Others may be struggling with some important values, you can get a clear sharp focus now. A deep-thinking Scorpio could help a lot.

Monday, March 31 (Moon Sagittarius to Capricorn 6:25 p.m.) Sometimes you tend to gloss things over; try to be more analytical. There is something you must take apart in order to understand it—and it could involve some personal detective work. Your wit and sense of humor are particularly sharp today; take advantage of it. The lucky number today is 5.

APRIL 1986

Tuesday, April 1 (Moon in Capricorn) You are highly visible to higher-ups today. Be sure your performance can stand the spotlight. Many will be in a party mood, and may find the occasion to celebrate. Your best bets for fun and games are a Sagittarian or a Gemini. Don't overlook a valuable contact you make today.

Wednesday, April 2 (Moon Capricorn to Aquarius 10:11 p.m.) If you're smart, you'll realize you're in a much stronger position than you thought. It's definitely a day you can throw your weight around with excellent results. Just be sure you know what you're talking about and have all the facts at hand. Some will have to be careful not to give away something for nothing.

Thursday, April 3 (Moon in Aquarius) If you can't face the changes you may have to face the music. Be willing to bend with circumstances—and possibly with people. For some a wish is fulfilled, and it's almost as if a dream has come true. For others the positive energy flow will result in your being in the right place at the right moment. For all, it's not simply business as usual today. Try your luck with number 5.

Friday, April 4 (Moon in Aquarius) This is one of those days when you should feel lucky; it should help you pick a winner in anything you do. You yourself could be the winner of a contest. For some, the money picture looks brighter than in the recent past. Others may get satisfaction when someone makes a major concession; and lightens the atmosphere for everyone. If you try a little tenderness, you will be rewarded.

Saturday, April 5 (Moon Aquarius to Pisces 4:03 a.m.) Some frustrations of the recent past are eased today and you should find it a lot easier to communicate with those who have been difficult to reach. Though you are rarely a timid soul, Aries, you've had a lot of doubts and fears—and now they are proved false. Isn't it a great feeling?

Sunday, April 6 (Moon in Pisces) Some of you will have to deal with a minor crisis today; you do beautifully and respond well under the pressure. For others the pressure will be a member of the opposite sex who is demanding equal time. Have you been spreading yourself too thin lately? Take a tip about money and how to earn it from a solid citizen—perhaps a Capricorn.

Monday, April 7 (Moon Pisces to Aries 12:12 p.m.) The picture is beginning to brighten as the moon is beginning to move into your own sign, Aries. This month that event coincides with the new moon—and this should be an excellent next few days. Today you feel the first of it when a burden is removed and you can say good-bye to something or someone that has been a drag. You will want to express your feelings freely, and you should feel confident in doing so.

Tuesday, April 8 (Moon in Aries) Sudden and unusual circumstances turn the tide in your favor—and you reap the benefits. All of you should rise and shine today with your personal charisma at a high. Trust that little voice that tells you what to do, because it should be right on target. Don't hesitate to be direct with others, especially where love is concerned.

Wednesday, April 9 (Moon Aries to Taurus 10:36 p.m.) Something that already looked good looks even better today, and the long-range prospects are positively fantastic! Those of you who don't experience this are looking in the wrong direction. At the very least, you will enjoy extreme cooperation from others today; the green light is flashing for progress. It's a great time to make a deal—particularly in real estate.

Thursday, April 10 (Moon in Taurus) You should still be feeling clear-headed and optimistic now. Use your mental sharpness in the areas of money and possessions. You may find that you are a lot better off than you thought. Some will receive very flattering comments today and be complimented on their appearance; let yourself be seen! The lucky number today is 3.

Friday, April 11 (Moon in Taurus) You feel a powerful pull toward someone else; the involvement is much more intense than you originally anticipated. If you protect your own interests and keep your wits about you, you could wind up with an excellent new relationship. Just use your logic as much as you use your feelings. Some may be asked to go back to square one and start over again on a project. Be patient.

Saturday, April 12 (Moon Taurus to Gemini 10:51 a.m.) This is no time to be long-winded or to beat around the bush; speak up for what you want clearly and concisely. Then, be sure to get the answer in writing. Some could be invited on a short trip today and should accept. A canny person could spot a bargain for you—buy it!

Sunday, April 13 (Moon in Gemini) This should be a busy day with lots of pleasant activity. Don't get so involved in it that you neglect a request from someone who loves you—and who deserves some consideration. Though you may be tempted to go out on a limb, stick to a familiar course in purchases of all kinds. Be agreeable when someone asks you to make an adjustment.

Monday, April 14 (Moon Gemini to Cancer 11:42 p.m.) You could fool yourself all too easily today. Realize that you can't wish things away. Deal with what must be dealt with, although you should be able to streamline things so that they are less of a hassle. Some may have to insist on getting access to something called "confidential." It isn't really; you have the right of review. A message that comes in is both heartwarming and useful.

Tuesday, April 15 (Moon in Cancer) Whatever this day brings, be your honorable Aries self and refuse to compromise your principles. Even if you are not aware of it, your actions are noticed and your prestige will swing upward as a result. For some, the focus of this day should be on security and safety measures at home. Check things out and repair what needs repairing. For many, the lucky number today is 8.

Wednesday, April 16 (Moon in Cancer) Don't be disheartened by people who don't believe in what you can do; you can get what you want if you go after it with confidence. You may simply have to have faith in yourself. For some, an obstacle overcomes a stepping-stone towards progress. A *sympatico* person today could be a Libra or another Aries.

Thursday, April 17 (Moon Cancer to Leo 11:10 a.m.) Today you should feel a lot freer and enjoy being on a much longer leash. The money picture is brighter too, and you may even get the wherewithal to go ahead with a pet project. Someone thinks you are quite terrific, and makes no secret of it. Accept the compliment graciously and don't be falsely shy. It's no time for a faint heart.

Friday, April 18 (Moon in Leo) All of the advice of a mentor or teacher who has been quite right in the past; you are lucky to have this kind of backing. A hunch that comes to you out of the blue could be quite correct, and is worth following. This is an excellent playday, no matter what else you have to do. Leave some time for romping—possibly with a Leo or an Aquarian. The lucky number today is 2.

Saturday, April 19 (Moon Leo to Virgo 7:24 p.m.) This is a day for feeling good all over, and enjoying your popularity. You may even think there are too many demands on your leisure time; try to pace things accordingly. Some could fall madly in love—or at least believe they have. Realize that today's tempestuous affair could be tomorrow's forgotten incident. Keep it light with a Gemini or a Sagittarian.

Sunday, April 20 (Moon in Virgo) It's a day to lay back and slow down. You need some time to get a second wind. Focus attention on the basics today like diet, nutrition, proper rest, and exercise. Things needn't be somber, because an unexpected visit from a fascinating individual is highly possible on the agenda. Enjoy the exchange of ideas.

Monday, April 21 (Moon Virgo to Libra 11:50 p.m.) It's not a day to force issues; try diplomacy instead. You can be tactful if you try, Aries, and now it is worth the effort. Team up with someone who has the same problems you do or who is concerned with the same issues. Together you can make a lot of progress and alleviate the pressure. Be cautious in everything today, and stick close to home base if possible.

Tuesday, April 22 (Moon in Libra) Someone could get a bit testy today when you demand your rights; don't let it throw you. As long as you are aware of each side of the bargain, you can insist on your rights without being overbearing. Summon up your public relations ability and you can straighten things out.

Wednesday, April 23 (Moon in Libra) Realize that someone who is sincere could also be misinformed;

check things out for yourself. You are not generally a leaner, and that is a good thing now. In a certain situation you are going to have to go it alone and be realistic about what kind of support you can expect from others. A needy person asks for help and you should give it. But don't break the confidence.

Thursday, April 24 (Moon Libra to Scorpio 1:15 a.m.) At this full moon it is wise for you to avoid controversy. If you can, remain neutral and refuse to be drawn into the fray. Some of you may be asked to help financially; say no and stick to your guns—just because someone else is embarrassed you do not have to be. Don't take anything at face value, and reject anything that smacks of a superficial answer.

Friday, April 25 (Moon in Scorpio) Today you are able to come up for air and throw off gloom. Don't let anyone burst your bubble. Even if you are not wildly happy today, you will at least be more comfortable when a problem that wasn't yours in the first place is taken out of your hands. Many could find this day spiced up by a member of the opposite sex who does some flirting. Respond and enjoy.

Saturday, April 26 (Moon Scorpio to Sagittarius 1:16 a.m.) You may be inclined to do some heavy thinking now about a vacation, travel, or some other route to greater self-awareness. No matter what you do, be open to the possibility of making a new start. It could be as simple as opening up the lines of communication between you and someone you've been wanting to know. You may do some wheel spinning today, but you are not really losing time. It's the long-range view that counts.

Sunday, April 27 (Moon in Sagittarius) If something doesn't feel right today, trust your feelings and stay away from it. Some of you may find yourself at a fork in the road; let your conscience be your guide in choosing the direction you're going. And think in terms of what is comfortable for everyone. Some will find themselves interacting with a rather strong-willed person—possibly a Cancer or a Capricorn. Don't let him/her wear you down. Your lucky number today is 2.

Monday, April 28 (Moon Sagittarius to Capricorn 1:41 a.m.) With your great Aries sense of humor, you should be able to laugh at your own little foibles. Don't get hot under the collar instead. After all, the goof you made grew out of your attempt to do a lot of things at one time. Your face will be less red when someone in authority says, "Nice work." Some may receive actual rewards rather than simply promises now. Get out and get around with a Gemini or a Sagittarian.

Tuesday, April 29 (Moon in Capricorn) A face-off with a tough person—possibly a Scorpio—is indicated. Some will be unable to avoid it; but at least something constructive will come out of the controversy. All should do some serious thinking about where they are going professionally. You may want to remodel your ideas a bit and bring them in line with reality. The lucky number today is 4.

Wednesday, April 30 (Moon Capricorn to Aquarius 4:06 a.m.) Today you could experience a midweek peak; the moon position indicates an open road to romance, and even a fond desire being fulfilled. If your day is not that superlative, what you accomplish now will come in very handy later on. Get your thoughts on paper. The lucky number today should be 5.

MAY 1986

Thursday, May 1 (Moon in Aquarius) Refuse to be a patsy today; someone may try to give you the short end of a bargain. You deserve much better, and you should let him/her know it. A slight frustration because of a temporary delay should not spoil your excellent mood. You will be tempted to "snoop" and invade someone's privacy; don't do it. Not everyone is as open as you.

Friday, May 2 (Moon Aquarius to Pisces 9:30 a.m.) Love—or something equally wonderful—appears to be right around the corner; you have reason to be optimistic. Some may get a strong creative urge today and should use it wisely. For some, that means putting it down on paper; for others, that means putting your ideas into action immediately. You should be particularly aware of your own special style.

Saturday, May 3 (Moon in Pisces) Keep a low profile today—and guard a secret you hear. Your loyalty to others is one of your best characteristics and you should cherish it. In fact, this time you may be tangibly rewarded for your discretion. It's a day to concentrate on those many small things that need doing around your own home base; some will find the ideal solution to a space problem.

Sunday, May 4 (Moon Pisces to Aries 8:01 p.m.) Someone older—or at least wiser than you—will help you solve a current dilemma. Largely it's a matter of perceiving your own potential and not selling yourself short. A picky person might try to intrude on your day and spoil it; refuse to get rattled. Your lucky number today is 7.

Monday, May 5 (Moon in Aries) You should start out the week with a lot of energy—enough to carry you to victory! Doors seem to open now, and people seem to know exactly what you want before you even ask for it. Take advantage of your own resources and make this the most productive day you've had in a while. As far as love and romance are concerned, you could find them waiting for you. Try your luck with number 8 on this lovely day.

Tuesday, May 6 (Moon in Aries) Many of you will be highly visible today and should dress to take this into consideration. If you don't actually make a personal appearance, be prepared to make a stunning impression on everyone you come in contact with today. An opportunity to expand your horizons can come floating by; grab it. This is the kind of chance that doesn't come along every day. Trust your judgment.

Wednesday, May 7 (Moon Aries to Taurus 4:59 a.m.) An opportunity to play pioneer may come along today; the task or project may be a simple one, but it will show others just how independent and creative you can be. Someone important says, "You're okay," and sends your spirits soaring. If you've lost something, try looking for it today; you have every chance of finding it. A Leo or an Aquarian could prove to be an excellent companion now. Your lucky number today is 1.

Thursday, May 8 (Moon in Taurus) You could be uncharacteristically stubborn today. Don't let pride let you dig your heels in; you will be impeding your own progress. Admit you are not always right, and let it go at that. On the positive side, cash should be flowing more freely. A first impression is probably correct—let it guide you.

Friday, May 9 (Moon Taurus to Gemini 5:26 p.m.) Aren't you glad you said yes yesterday; now you can see that it was the right action. Prepare yourself to be jack of all trades today—and to show that new things don't daunt you. Some may be paying bills; others may be seriously considering higher education or travel. The lucky number today is 3.

Saturday, May 10 (Moon in Gemini) Keep your sense of humor handy today because you will most likely need it. Though some minor bickering does not really involve you, it could put a dent in your day. Rise above it and concentrate on your own concerns; there is something that needs redoing and you are going to have to bite the bullet and do it. The lucky number today is 4.

Sunday, May 11 (Moon in Gemini) It's a fine day for sharing, and you may find yourself doing just that with relatives or close friends. In a discussion, be sure to stand up for your principles; compare notes on them with someone you respect. Excellent opposite numbers today are Gemini, Virgo, and Sagittarius. The lucky number is 5.

Monday, May 12 (Moon Gemini to Cancer 6:18 a.m.) You are sensitive to the feelings of others today and willing to cooperate. That willingness makes others swing over to your side. Congratulations! It should prove to you that diplomacy works better than bullying. Some may be thinking in terms of long-range security and decide to tighten the belt in the short run. Not a bad idea. The lucky number today is 6.

Tuesday, May 13 (Moon in Cancer) Today you are the one who is in danger of being intimidated; realize that one who speaks very loudly carries no stick at all. Jealousy may be a factor, and you should recognize your own worth. Some of you may be forced to be realistic about practical matters—if you haven't used something recently, throw it out. You've got to streamline things.

Wednesday, May 14 (Moon Cancer to Leo 6:15 p.m.) This could be a high-pressure day and you may be feeling a bit weighed down with responsibility. Try to shake off your feeling of anxiety by telling yourself you really are in a very strong position. It is not necessary to drive yourself into the ground. On the positive side, interpersonal relationships look promising. Romance is near at hand. The lucky number today is 8.

Thursday, May 15 (Moon in Leo) You are in the mood for love, fun, and excitement—or perhaps all three. Some may find all three, but all at the very least will feel the pleasure of completing something and getting great satisfaction out of it. You may be singled out for recognition today; be prepared to accept it gracefully.

Friday, May 16 (Moon in Leo) It is important not to pull any punches today; be direct as you can be. That's the only way you will untangle a sticky problem and move things along. Realize you don't need any "security blankets." Some will be celebrating; just don't overdo.

Saturday, May 17 (Moon Leo to Virgo 3:45 a.m.) Though this may threaten to be a dull day, it doesn't have to be. Some dull routine chores can definitely be spiced up if you turn them into a challenge; try to figure out a new way of doing things. You can feel sure of yourself in a certain area where you act on a hunch. You are right on target. Something heartwarming happens in one of your relationships today.

Sunday, May 18 (Moon in Virgo) In a dispute that arises, be willing to give up the floor to someone else. If you listen you may learn something. Moderation should be the key word today; some may be tempted to break recent resolutions about health and diet. Stick to your course.

Monday, May 19 (Moon Virgo to Libra 9:41 a.m.) Someone who challenges you today could end up being one of your favorite people; try to see beyond the heat of the moment. Some may have to check out facts and read the fine print; be sure your sources are reliable. For moral support, seek out a Taurus who's willing to listen. The lucky number today is 4.

Tuesday, May 20 (Moon in Libra) Partnership is the uppermost issue today. An agreement may be up for scrutiny and someone may be accusing you of not holding up your end of the bargain. Don't react immediately; take time out to consider your options. No matter what happens, you should be easily able to patch it up. Use your PR ability.

Wednesday, May 21 (Moon Libra to Scorpio 12:02 p.m.) Once again you are better off stepping aside and letting someone else take the initiative. Your most productive role now is that of observer. Just make sure you don't miss a trick and that you file all the facts away in your memory data bank. Most of you will find greatest satisfaction at home today. The lucky number today is 6.

Thursday, May 22 (Moon in Scorpio) Those with an interest in the occult may be able to indulge that interest today. For all, mystery is the general tone of the day. Take an opportunity you get to acquire information; once you know what you are facing, you will feel much more secure. It's really quite simple.

Friday, May 23 (Moon Scorpio to Sagittarius 11:57 a.m.) This should be a very positive full moon for you. The emphasis is on everything creative—including love and romance. You will be tempted to act on impulse, but be sure to temper it with logic. You should be able to put the pressure on today—and accomplish a great deal. Show that you have the courage of your convictions.

Saturday, May 24 (Moon in Sagittarius) This is a day for new experiments. It could be as simple as trying a new dish or foreign cuisine. Some may be even adventurous and set out on a whole new course. Others will find that they are able to get rid of a problem that has been sandbagging them. It should be a nice, free feeling! Further your education in some way today.

Sunday, May 25 (Moon Sagittarius to Capricorn 11:15 a.m.) Your inner voice should be sounding loud and clear today; listen to it carefully. You may be forced to declare your intentions today, so be ready to do it. Once you've taken the plunge, the rest will be easy. Don't squelch your own lofty ideas; they really are stepping stones to progress.

Monday, May 26 (Moon in Capricorn) You will find supporters for your cause quite easily today. For some it will take quite tangible form, and the money picture will be brighter. What appears to be a casual conversation is actually a gold mine of information; record it carefully. Prestige is a cure for the day.

Tuesday, May 27 (Moon Capricorn to Aquarius 12 Noon) Don't commit yourself to any specific course of action now; keep your options open. It is not necessary to be a follower. You are very popular in your home circle right now; some may even be given a promotion or chosen as leader. If your work involves writing, it should be easy for you to be eloquent today. The lucky number is 3.

Wednesday, May 28 (Moon in Aquarius) Adventure, discovery and romance—all are distinct possibilities today. However, the daily routine needs some attention too, and you should not shirk it. Your powers of persuasion should be at a high, and you should be able to talk people over to your side. One of those people may be an Aquarian, a Scorpio or a Leo.

Thursday, May 29 (Moon Aquarius to Pisces 3:54 p.m.) Something that is quite obvious hits you between the eyes today, and you may berate yourself for not seeing it sooner. Don't waste time with remorse; move to correct things immediately. You will have reason to celebrate success in an affair of the heart. Everyone should look marvelous under this moon influence. The lucky number is 5.

Friday, May 30 (Moon in Pisces) Be receptive to someone who is trying to tell you something; there is potential advantage for you in the veiled message. Some will get a backstage view of a complicated situation and thereby understand it a lot better. Get some exercise to throw off those uneasy feelings you could experience today. The lucky number is 6.

Saturday, May 31 (Moon in Pisces to Aries 11:43 p.m.) You may not have been successful in cheering yourself up yesterday, and your brooding could continue in to today. Instead of dwelling on your loneliness, relish an opportunity for privacy. You will find answers within you. In fact, some of you are on the verge of a major discovery and should feel quite optimistic. Spend some time with a Pisces or another Aries.

JUNE 1986

Sunday, June 1 (Moon in Aries) As the moon moves into your sign, the sun begins to shine for you. No challenge should be too much for you now, and you should take advantage of this hot cycle. If you've been wanting to get something in writing, now's the time to do it. Direct talk and constructive action is the order of the day. The lucky number today is 5.

Monday, June 2 (Moon in Aries) This is no time to hide your light under a bushel; make yourself as visible as possible and show off your own special style. Some will have a serious talk today about a serious matter—possibly a change of residence or permanent alliance like marriage. No matter what your goal today, you gain most through diplomacy. Follow your intuition about where to be when.

Tuesday, June 3 (Moon Aries to Taurus 10:45 a.m.) You could really be a softie today and thereby be taken advantage of. Don't let your emotions run away with you. Things are still on the upswing, and you should be able to state your own terms today. For some, a new romance is a distinct possibility. The lucky number today is 7.

Wednesday, June 4 (Moon in Taurus) If things have been a bit rocky financially of late, today you should be back on steady ground. In fact, money that has been difficult to obtain should now flow rather freely. If that is not your scenario, you can expect greater rewards from greater responsibility you accept now. Go for it!

Thursday, June 5 (Moon Taurus to Gemini 11:26 p.m.) You may have to do some fast talking to convince others to go along with your plan. Skepticism is in the air. Your best course may be to lay back and wait. An exchange of genuine affection may be the brightest spot in this day for many. For others, recouping a loss will be the highlight.

Friday, June 6 (Moon in Gemini) Someone around you needs reassurance, and may make a rather unusual request; grant it if you can. This person has helped you when you've been in the same situation. It's a day for new experience and diversification of interest. A trip or a visit may prove a delightful surprise.

Saturday, June 7 (Moon in Gemini) Many are restless and seek new kinds of stimulation. Don't dissipate your energies, but use them in a creative way. No matter what your role in life, you could play "teacher" today—and get a great deal of satisfaction out of it. A good pal, possibly an Aquarian—gives you a great idea. Run with it. The lucky number today is 2.

Sunday, June 8 (Moon Gemini to Cancer 12:16 p.m.) Get out and get around on this sociable Sunday. If you must stick close to home, get in touch by phone—particularly with someone at a distance. Clear communication is a necessity. Some may feel there are too many demands on their time; be selective about what you do.

Monday, June 9 (Moon in Cancer) Don't feel you must apologize when someone confronts you; after all, your intentions were the best. Some will face off with a parent or other type of authority figure today; Be polite but firm. Some pieces of the puzzle are beginning to fall into place, and you should feel on more solid ground. The lucky number today is 4.

Tuesday, June 10 (Moon in Cancer) You will find you have lots more elbow room than you have had in the recent past. It should be a good feeling. Some may close out an important transaction today; others may start in on a long-range project. Know when the sale is made and it's time to step aside; don't be a pest.

Wednesday, June 11 (Moon Cancer to Leo 12:11 a.m.) You may be tempted to be extravagant today; curb the urge if your bank account won't stand it. On the other hand, the aspects are excellent for special purchases, particularly of luxury items. If that is not your story today, you will want to self-indulge in some other manner. Treat yourself, but take care of others.

Thursday, June 12 (Moon in Leo) What started out as a flirtation may now be turning into a serious involvement. Make sure you are not looking at things through rose-colored glasses. See people as they really are and not merely as you wish they would be. Even if this is the real thing, you will save yourself disillusionment later on. Some are highly popular now, and run the risk of burning themselves out. Conserve your energy.

Friday, June 13 (Moon Leo to Virgo 10:18 a.m.) You should take a promise seriously because it is made in all sincerity. It may be a member of the opposite sex who is reaching out to you. Challenges abound today, but so do opportunities to better your position. Keep your ears open when someone just seems to be rambling on; he/she has some excellent ideas. The lucky number today is 8.

Saturday, June 14 (Moon in Virgo) If a minor health problem has been bugging you, take care of it today. You may also have to take care of some rather tedious matters having to do with those who depend on you; do them in a spirit of love. On the bright side, someone indicates that he/she is really not indifferent—it was all in your mind. Some will find themselves with new allies. Others will be relieved of a responsibility and rejoice because of it.

Sunday, June 15 (Moon Virgo to Libra 5:38 p.m.) You are involved in a dilemma, but you don't have to sweat it. A simple answer is to choose a course that puts you in the best light. That means, where you can show off your originality and innovativeness. Get ready for some straight talk from someone close to you. It clears the air. The lucky number today is 1.

Monday, June 16 (Moon in Libra) Trust your intuition to tell you when to lie low today, and when to surface. That way you can stay out of a minor hassle that may arise. For many, the trouble spot is marriage or a live-in arrangement. Be prepared to be cooperative. A Cancer could provide an excellent shoulder for you to cry on.

Tuesday, June 17 (Moon Libra to Scorpio 9:36 p.m.) The air clears today—mainly because of your willingness to defer to the wishes of others. Remember that you did it freely and don't play the martyr. In fact, a light touch is your best asset today. Use your sense of humor and play a waiting game for best results. The lucky number is 3.

Wednesday, June 18 (Moon in Scorpio) Be firm and say no to someone who asks you for a financial favor. Generosity should start at home. Some will turn up an interesting fact today and thereby solve a mystery. Someone near you brags with little reason to do so; don't be too hard on him/her. Everyone needs reassurance once in a while.

Thursday, June 19 (Moon Scorpio to Sagittarius 10:36 p.m.) Realize that full commitment is necessary if you are to be successful in a serious project. Don't start something unless you are prepared to finish it. Emotions are running today, and you should be sensitive to the feelings of others. Don't trifle where romance is concerned. The lucky number today is 5.

Friday, June 20 (Moon in Sagittarius) Someone opens up to you today and confides his/her highest hopes and aspirations. It should inspire you to a broader view of things. Some may decide they are in a rut as far as life-style is concerned. Changes may have to be made. Someone who talks big is really rather small-minded.

Saturday, June 21 (Moon Sagittarius to Capricorn 10:00 p.m.) Some Aries people tend to be too literal-minded; practice the art of abstract thinking today. That may mean entering a discussion of higher values. The person you interact with is an excellent teacher. Some may be thinking about long-range travel plans—or doing something adverturous near home. It's a great day to experiment.

Sunday, June 22 (Moon in Capricorn) Last night's full moon lit up your career area. Today you may find yourself dealing with people in authority, and you must realize there will always be a boss. Hold your tongue when you are tempted to speak, and get all your ducks in a row. Then you will be able to present your ideas in a clear concise dramatic manner. You would do well to take a tip from the style of a Cancer or a Capricorn. You have the chance to observe.

Monday, June 23 (Moon Capricorn to Aquarius 9:50 p.m.) Today you are able to make a vivid impression on the right people; in fact, you are able to widen your audience. Many will feel appreciated today, and receive a tangible token of that appreciation. For some it could be loving words; for others, money or a promotion. The lucky number today is 9.

Tuesday, June 24 (Moon in Aquarius) Be willing to slough off somebody or someone that has become outmoded. Your broach with tradition will make you feel marvelous and free and independent. In case you have doubts, you will be reassured by someone who applauds your actions. By day's end, your morale should be soaring. Don't be afraid to give free reign to your hopes and aspirations today.

Wednesday, June 25 (Moon in Aquarius) You are able to wheel and deal successfully today, and your maneuvering should pay off handsomely. It is definitely a "green-light" day when you can go full speed ahead down the wide road to success. If nothing that dramatic happens, you will at least find people particularly cooperative now. Try your luck with number 2.

Thursday, June 26 (Moon Aquarius to Pisces 12:12 a.m.) Don't backslide on some resolutions you made recently. Keep the proper balance between work and play. And don't forget rest. Someone may ask you to join a special interest group, but you should consider whether or not you are spreading yourself too thin. Some of you will have a secret meeting which could involve romance. Don't give away some privileged information.

Friday, June 27 (Moon in Pisces) You will be drawn toward anything that smacks of showbiz today. Just make sure you don't create your own little drama in which you play the major role. It is possible to be deceived now. Be absolutely realistic about your chances and about the intentions of others. Some answers are to be found behind the scenes. The lucky number today is 4.

Saturday, June 28 (Moon Pisces to Aries 6:35 a.m.) Today reality is better than fantasy; the moon in your sign heightens the positive vibrations around you. In fact, you should have a special charisma today and should be able to get your point of view across in a very effective manner. Some will find the perfect outlet for creative expression—especially writing. Some people to pal with today are Gemini, Virgo, and Sagittarius. The lucky number today is 5.

Sunday, June 29 (Moon in Aries) Your strength and vitality are back in full force today. Someone may offer you a new deal, and you should be prepared to jump at it. This is one time it is not necessary to look before you leap. Some are really coming into their own and getting a much greater acceptance. You should value your originality and sense of humor as much as others do. Be prepared to make some kind of an adjustment at home.

Monday, June 30 (Moon Aries to Taurus 4:54 p.m.) An apparent loss boomerangs in your favor. It should shore up your natural optimism. To go about getting what you want, it is important to take the initiative. Your special appeal could create many converts. Take advantage of being in the right place at the right time. Try your luck with number 7, too.

JULY 1986

Tuesday, July 1 (Moon in Taurus) No matter what happens today refuse to be intimidated by someone who attempts to undermine your self-confidence. You are much nearer that goal than you think, and you should not lose heart now. For some, money will seem to fall from the sky and enable you to buy that prized possession you've been lusting after. Good luck! All of you should take a look around your home surroundings and decide how you can make them more beautiful.

Wednesday, July 2 (Moon in Taurus) Once again you must watch out for the danger that someone will attempt to take away your faith in yourself—or something more tangible. Don't give anything up. At the same time you are protecting yourself, keep your eye open for an opportunity to purchase for or bargain for a bargain. You can rest assured that it is a real one. A Pisces or a Virgo may figure big in your scheme of things today. The lucky number today is 7.

Thursday, July 3 (Moon Taurus to Gemini 5:32 a.m.) Something you say in jest today isn't as much of a joke as you think it is—you may have had a gold mine of an idea. It's a day to keep all your options open and your mind even more so; you can be receptive without being gullible. You may have to go on a short trip or run an errand you hadn't counted on, and you may be feeling rather put upon. Don't worry, your gesture will be appreciated by the right person or people.

Friday, July 4 (Moon in Gemini) If you have been feuding with someone of late, today the dispute is settled, and you both lay down your arms. Things end in a draw, and though you do not like to lose, you are glad the bad feelings are gone. It's a very sociable day all the way around, and any group you find yourself in will be very talky. Don't get carried away and make stories taller than they are; you do like to exaggerate. Have a great holiday! The lucky number today is 9.

Saturday, July 5 (Moon Gemini to Cancer 6:19 p.m.) You may have to show just how agreeable you can be when you are asked to change some long-standing plans. Be flexible, and don't grumble; show your independence in some other way. Some confusion gets cleared up when a telephone call comes through and you learn the real story. It should make you resolve not to jump to conclusions. The lucky number today is 1.

Sunday, July 6 (Moon in Cancer) Those around you could be a bit moody today and you should make allowances for it. You've got a hard choice to make, and it would be wise to resolve it by choosing the most conservative course. This is not a time for risk-taking. If you try, you can brighten life significantly for everyone around you today. Be a good sport!

Monday, July 7 (Moon in Cancer) This month's new moon occurs in the domestic sector of your chart. That means you may feel a burst of energy and an urge to do things to make home a nicer place to be. Even those who work will find their thoughts straying to home base today. Restlessness is very likely today as is awareness of your state of body. Take a look and decide if you should do something about it.

Tuesday, July 8 (Moon Cancer to Leo 5:56 a.m.) Right from the start this feels like a playday—and it is. You should find yourself much freer to move around both literally and figuratively. Most will try something new today, and the experience could lead to a new interest—or passion. That includes the romantic kind. No matter what your age, you feel young in heart. Luck could easily support your own efforts today. Use it wisely!

Wednesday, July 9 (Moon in Leo) Be prepared to cast off that old security blanket and move on ahead with confidence that you can go it alone. You should recognize the fact that you have been pampering yourself emotionally as of late. Be ready to turn over a new leaf in that department. Some will attract attention by what they say or write today; be prepared to back up your statements. The lucky number today is 5.

Thursday, July 10 (Moon Leo to Virgo 3:50 p.m.) Some seeds that you planted a while back come into full flower now. Be prepared to make your garden grow even more beautiful than this. Some may find themselves actually doing something of a nurturing nature today. Children, pets and all kinds of dependents are featured. Some get pleasant feedback from the area of love and affection—possibly even a gift. You could be lucky with number 6 today.

Friday, July 11 (Moon in Virgo) For most, life is lived on a rather basic level today. There is much that needs doing and needs coping with; don't quarrel with necessity. On the other hand, intrigue is in the air and you could meet or hear from someone rather fascinating. At the very least, you will hear some gossip that puts some spice into an otherwise full day.

Saturday, July 12 (Moon Virgo to Libra 11:40 p.m.) Don't let pride stand in your way when you realize you need the help of someone who has already helped you a good deal. Simply thank your good fortune. Many will find that something that once seemed an impossibility now can become a reality. Go for it! Some could find luck with the number 8 today.

Sunday, July 13 (Moon in Libra) If you find yourself more or less alone today, you shouldn't mind it a bit. In fact, you might find it a relief from the past few days' rather tense events. Don't impose your wishes on anyone else today; it's your turn to say "You first." Realize that today's change of pace is necessary and use the down time wisely.

Monday, July 14 (Moon in Libra) You can come out of your cocoon today—and possibly even get that wonderful second chance that rarely comes along. As you correct what needs correcting, take note of how easy it is to be cooperatively—and how much more satisfaction you derive out of your efforts. For some there is a heart-to-heart talk with someone whose emotions are entangled with yours.

Tuesday, July 15 (Moon Libra to Scorpio 4:58 a.m.) Don't try to hide anything today because those closest to you will quickly see that you are feeling even if you aren't saying. On the other hand, some of you might want to appear "mysterious" today for your own purposes; you should be able to do it. It is an excellent time to regain clarity as far your sense of direction is concerned. You might try your luck with number 2 today.

Wednesday, July 16 (Moon in Scorpio) Something stimulates your intellectual curiosity today, and you will be tempted to explore it further. It won't be easy, because this is a subject that requires deep digging; however, realize there is much to be gained. Some could actually have a financial windfall today, and feel like blowing all of it at once. Make yourself put a little aside. Those who work or dabble in the arts will find they have a lot of creative energy.

Thursday, July 17 (Moon Scorpio to Sagittarius 7:34 a.m.) You may find it necessary to go back to square one today and begin something all over again. Consider it rebuilding in order to have a stronger structure, and you will feel more encouraged as you work. This need not take material form. Some will engage in activities for their eyes only; others will find that someone who has talked bit does not have the resources to match. The lucky number today could be 4.

Friday, July 18 (Moon in Sagittarius) If yesterday you were under cover, today you are right out there in the bright lights of reality. Some may have to justify recent performance; others may be asked to put it in writing. It is an excellent day for anyone involved in a lawsuit, because there could be a decision in their favor. Your cycle is on the upswing.

Saturday, July 19 (Moon Sagittarius to Capricorn 8:10 a.m.) You may run into a couple of tough customers today. One is particularly stubborn, and it is a great victory for you when he/she grudgingly has to admit that you are right. Don't gloat too much. Take some time out to do planning with the one closest to you—possibly for a long-distance trip. The lucky number today is 6.

Sunday, July 20 (Moon in Capricorn) This is an excellent day to do that clean-up task you've been putting off for quite a while. That could mean literally domestic chores that need to be done, but on the other hand your sweeping the decks could be in the paper or financial area. In other words, get down to it and pay those bills, reconcile that checkbook, whatever. Some will get an excellent compliment today and be surprised that they are held in such high esteem. You never know who's on your side.

Monday, July 21 (Moon Capricorn to Aquarius 7:17 a.m.) This month's full moon falls directly in that sector of the chart which deals with your public image. For some, this could mean an actual step up the ladder now. For others, it could signify a run-in with an authority figure. Keep your cool. In another area of life, there is the possibility that you are becoming inextricably with someone. Make sure you know where you are going.

Tuesday, July 22 (Moon in Aquarius) Today some of you are likely to find out who your friends really are. In both cases, it will be a pleasant experience. It may be your side of the friendship that is tested however, and you may have to make a little effort to come through for someone else. You will not regret it. Your powers of persuasion are particularly high today.

Wednesday, July 23 (Moon Aquarius to Pisces 9:59 a.m.) Teamwork is the order of the day and it should be extraordinarily fulfilling. You should enjoy new involvements with people who share your interests. One may prove to be rather stubborn, but will end up appreciating how unusually creative you are. Just don't show off.

Thursday, July 24 (Moon in Pisces) This should be an excellent day for those who must think and talk on their feet—especially salespeople. For anyone, it is a day to know that you are right when you think that you are right. Trust your first impressions. An Aquarian could play a key role in your life today, and bring to it something that has not been there before. The lucky number is 2.

Friday, July 25 (Moon Pisces to Aries 3:02 p.m.) Here you go again! It's moon-in-Aries time, and your very best time of the month. Some will find an audience without seeking it; rest assured you will give your best performance. In general, your scale of operations will become broader and you will find yourself breaking new ground. For some, it's possible a secret admirer will reveal him/herself.

Saturday, July 26 (Moon in Aries) This should be an excellent weekend for any kind of independent or creative activity. Place that germ of an idea that's in the back of your head and do something to make it grow today. Circumstances are all in your favor, and you should make the most of it. This could be as simple as dressing up, going out, and showing everyone how special your style can be. The lucky number today is 4.

Sunday, July 27 (Moon in Aries) Yesterday's experience made you aware of how much you need that kind of outlet for your energy. You should be feeling positively renewed! Today another chance comes along to be creative and you are able to dump a lot of excess emotional baggage you've been dragging around. You may find that you are far happier than you've been in a while.

Monday, July 28 (Moon Aries to Taurus 12:11 a.m.) For some, it may be come-back-down-to-earth day. You find that the need to be practical strikes you right between the eyes; it's all very well and good to theorize, but now action has to be taken. This matter may be one of property and basic security needs. A lovely thing happens when a family member comes to the fore and offers a very strong shoulder to lean on.

Tuesday, July 29 (Moon in Taurus) Today you must concentrate on getting all your ducks in a row, which may include checking out some material to see if it conforms to regulations. You've got a funny feeling that some people you are dealing with are not giving you the whole story—or the straight story. It's possible to be both subtle and demanding at the same time—this is too important to goof up. Do your homework, and try your luck with number 7.

Wednesday, July 30 (Moon Taurus to Gemini 12:19 p.m.) The early part of the day brings some niggling problems with finance; your own or someone else's. The pace picks up later on and you should be feeling a lot freer and able to breathe a sigh of relief. For some, this is a day where a commitment will be demanded. If it is in your romantic life, try to stall until you can get some advice from a person who has been there before.

Thursday, July 31 (Moon in Gemini) Many of you will be exceedingly restless today; try to get rid of some of that excess physical or mental energy by testing the limits of your strength. For some, that could mean presenting an idea that's a bit farther out than expected. You may be surprised at the reception you get. All should demonstrate their versatility today and polish up their sense of humor for immediate use. Be willing to experiment. The lucky number today is 9.

AUGUST 1986

Friday, August 1 (Moon in Gemini) Don't get talked into saying yes to anything unless the terms have been fully and properly defined. Whatever you do, don't find yourself stuck later on with something you hadn't bargained for. Some run the risk of being gullible today; check out everything you hear. If the delay is frustrating, realize that it's all part of this game plan.

Saturday, August 2 (Moon Gemini to Cancer 1:04 a.m.) Home is where the heart is for many of you today. In fact, you may need the kind of TLC only those closest to you can give. Serious talks and intense emotional involvements are highlighted today; make sure you are ready. The lucky number today is 8.

Sunday, August 3 (Moon in Cancer) You are rarely paranoid, but you have been of late. Today you find out that someone who appeared to be indifferent lately actually has been caught up in a lot of other things. Today you find out that you are far from forgotten. It's possible to win a point today by sticking to your guns; however, don't let determination turn into aggressiveness. Have fun with another Aries.

Monday, August 4 (Moon Cancer to Leo 12:26 p.m.) This is an excellent time to try to get to the bottom of something. You may feel someone has been less than forthcoming about his/her feelings. Today you can make people open up. Some will find they are treading much more secure emotional ground than in their recent past. For others, replace emotional with financial. The lucky number is 1.

Tuesday, August 5 (Moon in Leo) Even if you feel a bit insecure today, be confident that you are on the right track. However, it might help to seek out the views of someone more experienced than you; a good buddy reappears on the scene and comes through for you once more. Try to think of some way in which you can show that you are always there, too. A Cancer or a Capricorn may play an important role in today's activities.

Wednesday, August 6 (Moon Leo to Virgo 9:44 p.m.) Don't settle for anything less than top quality today—in anything, including people. Sometimes you tend to be a little indiscriminate in your choice of friends. Children or young people deserve some attention today, and you may find yourself dealing with restlessness. Some will revive old ideas and aspirations; remember that practically nothing is impossible.

Thursday, August 7 (Moon in Virgo) Your usually sunny disposition may be a bit dimmed today. The reason is probably that you've got an awful lot of things to cope with. Try doing things one at a time, and change the pace when you can. Some tedious work you have to do will pay off later on. Honest! The lucky number today is 4.

Friday, August 8 (Moon Virgo to Libra 5:05 a.m.)
It's a relief when a change in routine takes place, and you can do more of what you like rather than what you must. However, don't neglect to make that call or write that letter someone is waiting for. The subject could be romance, but the same applies to friendship or family. Those who depend on you could be particularly demanding today.

Saturday, August 9 (Moon in Libra) For some, a major adjustment and/or change of place could be in the air. However this affects you, be sure to go slowly and walk on eggshells if you must. It's not the time for hasty action. Happy-go-lucky Aries would do well to pay attention to caloric and junk food intake. Limit it now.

Sunday, August 10 (Moon in Libra) This is a good day to let your motor idle. It does not mean doing nothing, but does mean reflecting on events and your own performance of the recent past. You may decide to make some revisions. You may be called on to be particularly diplomatic today; you can handle it. The lucky number today is 7.

Monday, August 11 (Moon Libra to Scorpio 10:36 a.m.) For many the week starts out with a heavier-than-usual workload. However, extra compensation could be there too. You could definitely cement a relationship today, whether it is in your personal life or your business circle. You will have little difficulty getting someone on your side. The lucky number today is 8.

Tuesday, August 12 (Moon in Scorpio) It would be easy for you to feel resentment at this time. In fact, someone may even give you cause to do so. Try to rise above the battle and do not react immediately. You will be able to get yours later on. Don't get discouraged if you cannot get information you need; just keep plugging away at it.

Wednesday, August 13 (Moon Scorpio to Sagittarius 2:17 p.m.) Once again, resentment or suspicion could be aroused. Try to keep a clear head and look at the situation realistically. If asked, stress your views in a direct manner and refuse to be intimidated. For some, the problem may be the finances of someone else—a close associate or partner. Another Aries may play a key role.

Thursday, August 14 (Moon in Sagittarius) The temptation may be for you to drown your sorrows in food or drink today; hold back. Things are really not that bad, and you may be getting bogged down in the nitty-gritties of the problem. Be philosophical about it instead, and take the large view. It might be a relief to confide your problem to someone close. The lucky number is 2.

Friday, August 15 (Moon Sagittiarus to Capricorn 4:22 p.m.) Today you have a lot more breathing room. Your spirits should definitely be lighter; if they are not, get around and socialize. Even if you do not enjoy your own company, others will. Realize that someone does have your best interest at heart, even though it is difficult to see that now. The lucky number is 3.

Saturday, August 16 (Moon in Capricorn) Someone throws you off your pins today by being even more frank and outspoken than you are. It is a refreshing change in the relationship. Some may get special commendation today and/or be recognized for an achievement. Nice going! Others should check some fine details carefully, because a small mistake could trip you up later on.

Sunday, August 17 (Moon Capricorn to Aquarius 5:44 p.m.) Some feelers you put out yesterday got a very positive response; today you find yourself in the company of a member of the opposite sex who found you so fascinating he/she is back for more. Enjoy the interlude, but take your particularly high spirits into consideration. Will they last later on? If you are out for fun, you will find it.

Monday, August 18 (Moon in Aquarius) A third party intervenes in a difficult situation, and you find you are able to resolve a dilemma. Show your thanks in some tangible way. For some, a wish actually comes true—even though it is not in the way you expected. Your popularity should be at a high.

Tuesday, August 19 (Moon Aquarius to Pisces 7:52 p.m.) If you play it right, this full moon could make a difference in your sphere of influence—either in business or in friendship. Try to arrange to be at the right place at the right time. Some may find themselves involved in a secret meeting and/or a "mission of mystery." Don't get involved if you suspect the slightest bit of intrigue. The lucky number is 7.

Wednesday, August 20 (Moon in Pisces) A touch of surprise could color your day. For some, it comes through finding out what is really going on behind a pleasant facade. The revelation may not be such a pleasant one. You should be feeling quite confident and willing to jump in and say "I'll do it." You'll be glad you did.

Thursday, August 21 (Moon in Pisces) What started out as a little hint yesterday could be a major discovery today—one you find very exhilerating. If nothing that dramatic occurred, you still should achieve satisfaction through some communication that comes your way today. All indications are that the right people are aware of you. The lucky number is 3.

Friday, August 22 (Moon Pisces to Aries 12:27 a.m.) This can be your day all the way! You should be calling the shots and letting others know just what you want. And you should get it. The emphasis today is on your own ability—that means independent action is prescribed. Don't worry, your judgment and timing should be fabulous. Don't face off with another fiery type—possibly a Leo.

Saturday, August 23 (Moon in Aries) A complainer in your circle threatens to bog down your day; don't let him/her do it. Follow your own instincts and you should continue on the right track. It's an excellent time to toss out things you don't need anymore—they are only cluttering up your life. Some of you will have a pleasant interlude "teaching" and you will learn a lot by it.

Sunday, August 24 (Moon Aries to Taurus 8:36 a.m.) Some could receive a very tempting offer today—possibly to travel. Accept it, that is if your personal coast is clear. Wear a smile and other bright things today in order to make the maximum effect. You are easily able to do it.

Monday, August 25 (Moon in Taurus) Be sure to count your change today, because you could easily be ripped off in some way or another. What you lose may not necessarily be money. The way to avoid the problem is to refuse to be a soft touch; everyone knows you are generous, and that's the problem. The lucky number today is 4.

Tuesday, August 26 (Moon Taurus to Gemini 8:00 p.m.) Once again, invest only in yourself. That is the most sure thing now. Some should be ready for a rather unpected change of pace or a totally new experience. If it means changing things, be flexible.

Wednesday, August 27 (Moon in Gemini) Today you should play "good guy" when someone makes a request of you. It is essential to restoring harmony. Many will feel like blowing a lot of money on something they desperately want. Are you sure it is not simply a self-indulgence? Take everybody into consideration.

Thursday, August 28 (Moon in Gemini) Signals could easily get mixed today, and there is a high possibility of confusion. Make sure you are definite in what you say and that you understand another's meaning correctly. If something does get fouled up, keep your sense of humor. It isn't really that important. Many will feel like indulging in extracurricular activities; don't scatter your energy.

Friday, August 29 (Moon Gemini to Cancer 8:40 a.m.) For some, this is a day of decisions. Something—and it could be something important—is coming down to the wire, and it is necessary for you to commit yourself. If you feel a bit uneasy, it may be that you do not have enough information. Insist upon it. The lucky number today is 8.

Saturday, August 30 (Moon in Cancer) The sky's clear today and you should feel you are on a much more secure footing. Everyone gets a bit shaky when their territorial rights are in danger. You should take comfort in the fact that you have many allies, and that you have people rooting for you. For some, an important assignment will be completed.

Sunday, August 31 (Moon Cancer to Leo 8:08 p.m.) Someone tosses you a challenge today and you should grab it immediately. Don't be held back by fears of breaking with the past. It is necessary now. Love could come along for some Aries people now; it will be your rather unusual ideas that attract the other person. However, it won't stay strictly mental.

SEPTEMBER 1986

Monday, September 1 (Moon in Leo) A surge of energy should propel you forward today. And, for some, major things could happen. In some cases, a gap is closed and you are able to make progress on several fronts. Be careful how you wield power today; you need not be overbearing.

Tuesday, September 2 (Moon in Leo) There is no doubt about what you want today—you can state your need in quite a dramatic fashion. Don't be overly dramatic, however, or you will put some less feisty types off by your show of power. You are in a strong enough position anyway. Those around you could be particularly complimentary today.

Wednesday, September 3 (Moon Leo to Virgo 5:05 a.m.) Many will have a chance to show off their special talents today. And find that others are surprised by your unique way of doing things. Let it give you confidence and encourage you to shake up the status quo a little bit. You need some spice in your life. A Leo or an Aquarian could provide it. The lucky number today is 1.

Thursday, September 4 (Moon in Virgo) You could be feeling a bit rocky today; but your condition is not serious. In fact, many of you will have to admit you have been overindulging yourself a bit. It's an excellent time to start a new course of study for any kind of personal regime. You can get a lot of basic things done today and feel a lot better for it.

Friday, September 5 (Moon Virgo to Libra 11:33 a.m.) Avoid people who tend to sap your strength; you need it all yourself. The leaners around you will simply have to go it alone. Try to pull yourself together and don't let anyone take advantage of your good nature. Better times are coming soon.

Saturday, September 6 (Moon in Libra) You are coming out of the woods, but you still should lie low and keep your eyes open. Sooner or later the puzzle pieces will fall into place. However, it is more than alright to have a quiet talk with someone who shares your concern—and possibly your resources. Be willing to play partners.

Sunday, September 7 (Moon Libra to Scorpio 4:12 p.m.) Although you are in no danger, you might do well to stick close to home base today. In a group discussion, do more listening than talking; if you keep your ears open, you will learn something very new and useful. Some may have to be particularly discreet, and hold their cards close to their chests. For others, the give-and-take scenario is necessary if you are to avoid disharmony. The lucky number today is 5.

Monday, September 8 (Moon in Scorpio) You have been thinking about doing a total overhaul; this is the ideal day to toss out the old and initiate something new. In another area, realize that someone may be playing games with you. Be pleasant, but not gullible. A Libra could be very helpful in giving you ideas about how to beautify your surroundings.

Tuesday, September 9 (Moon Scorpio to Sagittarius 7:40 p.m.) It would be very easy for you to go overboard today. That applies particularly in the area of your interpersonal relationship. There may be a special person who more than attracts you now. You could easily be mesmerized. A lot is going on behind the scenes, and you should recognize that fact and not be concerned about your confusion.

Wednesday, September 10 (Moon in Sagittarius) A thought you have had about travel could today turn into an obsession. Use this to make some clear, sensible plans. You can do it if you organize yourself. Some will have a chance to prove a major point, and gain prestige as a result. Others will find themselves concentrating on spiritual values today. Realize that it is an important activity.

Thursday, September 11 (Moon Sagittarius to Capricorn 10:28 p.m.) It may be difficult to zero in on small things today because your thinking tends to be "in the large." Don't get too "spacey." Any kind of back-and-forth between you and another individual today should be very productive. In fact, some will learn new tricks of the trade they can turn into profit.

Friday, September 12 (Moon in Capricorn) Someone may call in an old debt today, and you will be obliged to pay up. Actual money may not be involved, but your effort and attention are. Be sure to keep promises and resolutions; it is no time to play fast and loose with anything. In some cases, praise is due. The lucky number is 1.

Saturday September 13 (Moon in Capricorn) Keep your hopes and your goals in clear sight, and you will be able to realize them. Your potential is tremendous, even though it is difficult for you to get a handle on that now. Let your intuition serve as a guide in a tricky situation. The lucky number today is 2.

Sunday, September 14 (Moon Capricorn to Aquarius 1:07 a.m.) This is an excellent day for partying and socializing of all kinds. If you are entertaining, it will go splendidly. No matter what your particular scenario today, you will find yourself in a position to count your blessings. Enjoy a verbal exchange—possibly with a Gemini or a Sagittarian.

Monday, September 15 (Moon in Aquarius) Realize that something upsetting you here today is merely a rumor; don't let it throw you off balance. If you are uncertain, don't hesitate to revise something you've already done. Better to be safe than sorry. Trust in yourself and the fact that victory is at hand!

Tuesday, September 16 (Moon Aquarius to Pisces 4:27 a.m.) Play "private eye" today, and you will be amazed at what you find out. It is important to be analytical and to focus on areas that seem mysterious. It is really all quite simple, and you will find you have reason to celebrate when you untangle this. A Sagittarian could play a key role. The lucky number today is 5.

Wednesday, September 17 (Moon in Pisces) You are beginning to see light at the end of the tunnel. It gets even brighter when someone decides to cooperate with you. Some of you may have to be especially diplomatic today, and willing to compromise. Envy may threaten to spoil your day; don't let it.

Thursday, September 18 (Moon Pices to Aries 9:33 a.m.) This full moon should heighten your ability to deal with subtleties; it is not always your forte. Some may discover that they have been missing the forest because of the trees. It should come as a satisfying revelation. Watch out for someone who may have an ulterior motive when he/she offers to help you. Be self-protective.

Friday, September 19 (Moon in Aries) You can pull out all the stops with every expectation of success today; you won't get a chance like this for a while. Simply put, you should take the initiative. If your most intimate relationship is involved, it is even more important to make the first move. Some have their values tested. The lucky number is 8.

Saturday, September 20 (Moon Aries to Taurus 5:25 p.m.) The notion that "life is timing" is absolutely true in your case today. Don't jump the gun—and don't hold back. If you trust your intuition, you will know exactly when to strike. Some will reveal their hidden talents today and get a lot of excellent playback. Others receive credit that's long overdue. Be willing to give advice to one who seeks it.

Sunday, September 21 (Moon in Taurus) It would be very easy for you to be a softie today and to give where you should be taking. Or rather, where you have already given before. Insist on your needs, though it is not necessary to be petulant. For many, a family gathering could warm the heart. The lucky number today is 1.

Monday, September 22 (Moon in Taurus) Today you get what is coming to you—in the form of a favor returned. You should take pride in your willingness to do things for other people. You can make a hit today, almost anywhere you circulate. And you should follow your hunches about where to do that. A sincere compliment comes in and sort of brightens the day.

Tuesday, September 23 (Moon Taurus to Gemini 4:13 a.m.) Stay loose today and be willing to change plans on the spur of the moment; you can be very flexible when you want to. The emphasis of the day is on pleasure. That means, however, that you should keep an eye on your caloric intake and state of your body. Both could stand some attention. A Virgo or a Sagittarian could prove an unusually delightful playmate today.

Wednesday, September 24 (Moon in Gemini) Tell somebody that you are ready to move up today, and he/she will take you seriously. Asking for things at the right time is the right way to do it. For many, the puzzle will be solved and a small discomfort will be removed. Show that you can be nice without being a total patsy. The lucky number today is 4.

Thursday, September 25 (Moon Gemini to Cancer 4:44 p.m.) No matter what your status, a member of the opposite sex could prove to be a valuable ally today. And you may need it. Your mental circuitry could be a bit overloaded, and you could be experiencing a bit of confusion. Take any help that comes your way—and be sure to read the fine print. Some could find themselves on a short unexpected trip.

Friday, September 26 (Moon in Cancer) Listen carefully today when someone talks money; you could pick up some very valuable tips. And you could use them. For those who seem to have been on the losing end recently, there'll be a turn in the other direction. Check out security measures at home.

Saturday, September 27 (Moon in Cancer) You can get your way without walking all over someone else. Force an issue but don't beat it to death. Someone who watches quietly really knows what your true worth is.

And you will know it soon. For many, some fuzzy terms are finally defined and a matter can move forward.

Sunday, September 28 (Moon Cancer to Leo 5:39 a.m.) For the first time in a while, you wake to a day you feel you can master. It is good to have your vitality returned. Many are able to make significant changes and advance their cause in personal relationships. As a matter of fact, true intimacy is possible today. You are proved right on a major point and the power struggle ends. Don't gloat!

Monday, September 29 (Moon in Leo) Your vital powers are at a high today. For some, that means an absolutely charismatic appeal to others. If you are challenged, don't meet a challenge head on; it could be an unpleasant collision. Many will find that the most pleasant thing that happens today is having an unnecessary burden removed. Relax and enjoy it!

Tuesday, September 30 (Moon Leo to Virgo 1:57 p.m.) You are not necessarily a gambler, but today you are tempted to speculate. You may be simply taking a chance on life, and not risking a cent. Either way, you can't resist. Chances are you will be the winner because your faith in yourself is very strong. No matter what the day brings, have the courage of your convictions and be your independent self. You are an original!

OCTOBER 1986

Wednesday, October 1 (Moon in Virgo) This should be a rather orderly day during which your main concentration will be on rather mundane things. You should experience a sense of peace and rightness in the world. At some point, you will come into contact with someone—possibly one of your own circle—who surprises you by his/her wisdom and ability to understand your situation. Rejoice that you have such a sturdy ally. The lucky number is 9.

Thursday, October 2 (Moon Virgo to Libra 8:03 p.m.) A fascinating challenge presents itself and you are more than willing to volunteer. The issue may not be a monumental one, but it appeals to your sense of "adventure." An incident punctuates what could be an otherwise fairly routine day. For many of you, it is the way for you to stay out of trouble. Some will discover a unique and unexpected talent in the process.

Friday, October 3 (Moon in Libra) The new moon and solar eclipse influence that area of your life where you experienced your closest ties. The effect could be felt in your marriage, live-in arrangement, or business partnership. It is best to play the diplomat during this period and to defer to your opposite number. By being a shrewd observer, you could come out way ahead. At any rate, this is not a contest—both of you stand to win or lose. Your best course is to wait it out. Try your luck with number 2.

Saturday, October 4 (Moon Libra to Scorpio 11:35 p.m.) Something or someone has aroused your curiosity, and you must satisfy it. Don't be afraid to ask a lot of questions and dig for further information. You could be pleasantly surprised. Many will find that luck strikes from the blue today; actually, it is actually something that has been brewing for some time, and the moment happens to be right. Today enjoy yourself with a Gemini or a Sagittarian today.

Sunday, October 5 (Moon in Scorpio) There may be storm clouds on the horizon; the storm center appears to be in the area of money and who is responsible for it. Don't immediately assume your own innocence in the situation, but be willing to subject your own behavior to scrutiny. Arguing is not the solution, greater care is. You may discover that what you need is information, help, or advice from someone far more experienced in these matters. A Scorpio would be the ideal person to contact.

Monday, October 6 (Moon in Scorpio) You could start off the week full of determination to straighten someone or something out. It has occurred to you that someone could be playing you for a sucker. It is not a nice feeling, and you are not feeling very nice about it. Follow through, do not let the situation explode. Some will find that they are attracted to a most attractive person. Realize that though it is fascinating, you are treading on dangerous ground.

Tuesday, October 7 (Moon Scorpio to Sagittarius 1:48 a.m.) You could easily get carried away today—in any number of areas. Try to trim your sales a bit and make your objectives more realistic. You can be happy without having it all. Some may receive a gift or loving attention from someone they considered out of reach; it is a very heartwarming experience. The lucky number today is 6.

Wednesday, October 8 (Moon in Sagittarius) You may want to spend some time alone today; unusual as that feeling is for you, it is understandable. The answers you seek are only found within, and you need quiet time to get them together. This is no time to try shortcuts or get involved in flimsy schemes. Don't let anyone deceive you—especially yourself. A Pisces could be very prominent today.

Thursday, October 9 (Moon Sagittarius to Capricorn 3:52 a.m.) People in high places could take note of you today. Whatever your status in life, it could easily improve now. Some of you will say, "I can handle more," and take it on. Others will reap the rewards of recent hard work. You deserve it! The lucky number is 8.

Friday, October 10 (Moon in Capricorn) Even if you try to hide today, you will not be able to. Something you do or say catches fire, and there are those who want to know more about it and about you. You might as well relax and enjoy the notoriety. Some will want to get involved in a group project. On another level, this could simply be a day where you are obliged to take over the reins and manage—possibly more than you want to manage. The lucky number is 9.

Saturday, October 11 (Moon Capricorn to Aquarius 7:45 a.m.) Gone is that downer feeling you may have experienced yesterday; you are definitely out of the doldrums. What it means for most is a return of a sense of fun and the desire to play. For some, there could be all kinds of invitations and opportunities to mix and mingle. All should have the feeling that a new feeling is possible—and highly likely. Your lucky number today could be 1.

Sunday, October 12 (Moon in Aquarius) You may question someone's sincerity today—and that someone might even be you. You are uncertain about your own feelings, and how deep they really run. Are you simply having fun? Don't let it ruin your day; it has a lot more to offer. Many will make an important decision about a life direction. You may not realize its import now, but you will later on. At the very least, you will come out of your shell today.

Monday, October 13 (Moon Aquarius to Pisces 11:03 a.m.) You instinctively keep your guard up today when you encounter a couple of very bright people who have a lot of amusing things to say. A little voice tells you they could lack substance. Don't be overly suspicious, however, because you could enjoy this day more than you have many others in the recent past. Just don't give up something for nothing. Many will have to be flexible even though they do not wish to; a sense of humor will make everyone come smiling through. The lucky number today is 3.

Tuesday, October 14 (Moon in Pisces) If you have the feeling you are being talked about today, you are probably right. The aspects point to a behind-the-scenes meeting with important consequences for you. Realize that there's no way you can affect the situation at this point. Some will have to deal with a few little niggling details, and may not be happy about it at all. Others should remember obligations to people who are in some kind of bind. Do what you can.

Wednesday, October 15 (Moon Pisces to Aries 5:13 p.m.) Give your feelings free reign today; you have everything to gain. Some will find romance, or at least great affection returned. Others will simply feel more liberated than they have in a while. Good news could come in in connection with something you have been striving for. Discoveries of all kinds are indicated. Be ready to move quickly. The lucky number today is 5.

Thursday, October 16 (Moon in Aries) Almost in spite of yourself, you find your spirits soaring today. You could ask yourself, "What's so great?" If you tune into today's vibrations you will find the answer. Things are turning in your favor, even if the hints you get are subtle ones. Not so subtle could be an individual who makes it clear just how much he/she is attracted to you and supports your cause. Try to arrange for a personal appearance, because you will be a smash.

Friday, October 17 (Moon in Aries) This full moon occurs in your sign and offers you a very rare opportunity—the rarest of the year. You can wipe the slate clean, and eliminate a lot of excess baggage. That includes some debts that may be burdening you. The important thing is to be realistic about your own capabilities and that of others. Resolve to eliminate deception from your life. You might even find love.

Saturday, October 18 (Moon Aries to Taurus 1:35 a.m.) Today for most of you it's money that's on your mind—or the things that money can buy. Don't let it obsess you. Instead, make an inventory of all your valuables; you may find that you have overlooked some very important personal assets, though they may not be in tangible form. For some of you, a relationship is growing stronger and the responsibilities connected with it greater; it is important to know this going in. The lucky number today is 8.

Sunday, October 19 (Moon in Taurus) It is a day for closeness and family ties. Though you may not be celebrating anything in particular, it is a day you will want to celebrate life—and all its bounties. Among them may be good food and good drink; don't overdo. Some may find that a personal passion or a hobby is turning into more than that. Have you thought about how you can turn this into cash?

Monday, October 20 (Moon Taurus to Gemini 12:15 p.m.) Some of you may feel like shaking loose from a connection that is getting a bit too connected for your taste; make sure you do it with grace. Independence marks this day, as do new starts. Enjoy your energy, but realize that it is not endless. Take a second chance when it comes your way.

Tuesday, October 21 (Moon in Gemini) Make that decision and get on with your life; you've been hesitating too long. Remember that there is no choice so final that it cannot be reversed or revised later on. Most should be getting good moral support from those around them. Keep this in mind as you go through your day: Follow that instinct you have about someone or something because it is quite likely to be the right one. A Leo or an Aquarian may be in the picture and very prominent.

Wednesday, October 22 (Moon in Gemini) Your emotions may not be on even keel today. Along with your mood swings, there may be the tendency to overdo or underdo what needs doing. Try to sort things out and keep them on the track. Some may be tempted by a fad diet or get-thin-quick scheme; it's only a mood of the moment.

Thursday, October 23 (Moon Gemini to Cancer 12:37 a.m.) For the most part, you are a fast talker; you may have to employ that skill today in order to get out of a touchy spot. Ad lib the best you can, and resolve to tie up loose ends later. For some, basic security is an issue—home or property could be involved. Take the safest and the straightest course. The lucky number today is 4.

Friday, October 24 (Moon in Cancer) Someone is sending you a message, and you must try to decode it. There is a lot more here than meets the eye—or the ear. For many, this scenario will involve a member of the opposite sex—or at least one who is a "passionate friend." Others will enjoy the healthy change of pace and a general picking up of the tempo all around. Good companions today could be a Gemini or a Sagittarian. The lucky number is 5.

Saturday, October 25 (Moon Cancer to Leo 1:02 p.m.) Something may loom large and threaten to overwhelm you today; do not lose heart. The opposition is only temporary, and, what's more, someone may be simply attempting to intimidate you. Realize how strong your position is. On the positive side, favorable recognition could come your way; however, you will have to live with the label "stubborn."

Sunday, Octoer 26 (Moon in Leo) If you do not enjoy the spotlight, you will not enjoy yourself today. However it happens, you will end up the center of attention and the object of all eyes. Some of you will have their opinions sought; others will be asked advice. Either way, prepare yourself for a day that is far from run of the mill. The lucky number is 7.

Monday, October 27 (Moon Leo to Virgo 11:20 p.m.) You start out the week on a high note—in a strong position that could get stronger. Do not be afraid to make an executive decision today. It will be the right one if you say it is. Confidence is your best asset now, and you could even make great strides because of it. Leave your doubts behind you.

Tuesday, October 28 (Moon in Virgo)   You are definitely on a roll; good things continue to happen today. Even if nothing that spectacular happens, you will have the chance to show off some special skills or talents. Whether you like it or not, people will be drawn to you to confide their hopes and aspirations. Try to listen with a sympathetic ear. You can even learn something.

Wednesday, October 29 (Moon in Virgo)   Today you are the one who gets help from an unexpected quarter; it could be the beginning of a wonderful friendship—or a romance. Some are beginning to realize their tremendous potential and learning not to be "afraid of the dark" anymore. In a face-off, you may get the chance to prove a major point. The lucky number is 1.

Thursday, October 30 (Moon Virgo to Libra 6:04 a.m.) After a few days, on the high road, you may feel like lying low. Wise course to take. Take some time to focus on what belongs on your side of the fence and avoid what is more likely someone's elses. It's an excellent time to review a partnership or an agreement—possibly even your own marriage. The lucky number today is 2.

Friday, October 31 (Moon in Libra)   You may be amazed when a former "enemy" now speaks out for you and comes over to your side. Could it be that you had him/her wrong all the time? You may have to keep your sense of humor handy today, and to laugh off a practical joke someone else thinks is not *funny*—but you do not. Have fun with a Gemini or a Sagittarian and try your luck with number 3.

NOVEMBER 1986

Saturday, November 1 (Moon Libra to Scorpio 9:19 a.m.)   Someone may nag you today, but you should be fair enough to recognize your fault in this matter. A willingness to cooperate can easily smooth over the waters. Don't get flustered when someone throws technical language at you—possibly legal mumbo-jumbo. It is really much simpler than that. The best thing you could do today is throw out something that is no longer usable.

Sunday, November 2 (Moon in Scorpio) You run the risk of being at the mercy of your hotheaded temperament today. At all costs, try to practice objectivity and refuse to get riled. Finances may be under discussion, they are always difficult. On the bright side, you could receive a delightful invitation to a very special meal. Here, too, exercise moderation.

Monday, November 3 (Moon Scorpio to Sagittarius 10:19 a.m.) It is wise to avoid getting locked into some plans with someone whose finances are a bit shaky. You wouldn't want to be disappointed when those plans fall through. The best course for most today is to keep all the options open; in other words, hang loose. Some should realize that a recent new contact could be enormously significant to the overall scheme of things. Search your mind, and put your finger on who that person is. It could be a Gemini or a Sagittarian.

Tuesday, November 4 (Moon in Sagittarius) This is not an everyday day. If you keep tuned in to your deeper feelings, you will arrive at a very important insight. Possibly even a spiritual one. At the very least, a current situation will be clarified and your understanding will be a relief. If taxis, travel, or insurance is an issue in your life, do something about it today.

Wednesday, November 5 (Moon Sagittarius to Capricorn 10:49 a.m.) Don't let yourself in for a letdown by being too optimistic about a new relationship. Be as analytical as you can, and do some checking up as well. There's no harm in finding out as much as you can about a person. A message or a visit will be a high-point today for many of you. Enjoy the reunion! The lucky number is 5.

Thursday, November 6 (Moon in Capricorn) A pleasant surprise is in store for many today; it could have to do with the tables being turned. Aren't you sorry you wasted all that time worrying? Family matters of every kind are spotlighted today. In fact, there could be a showdown about the household budget. For those of you less troubled, a great bargain may suddenly turn up. Buy it!

Friday, November 7 (Moon Capricorn to Aquarius 12:29 p.m.) Don't trust your memory today; put instructions down in writing. Especially if they are someone higher up. Changes of all kinds are a definite possibility, and you may have to turn on a dime. Don't fool yourself about anything or anyone; be as realistic as possible. The lucky number today is 7.

Saturday, November 8 (Moon in Aquarius) Whatever your objectives, you should be able to sweet-talk just about anyone into what you want today. Along with persuasion, use a little discretion as well. Sure, you want what you want; however, there is another side to this story. It should be an extremely sociable Saturday. If you are not being entertained, why not do some entertaining yourself? The lucky number is 8.

Sunday, November 9 (Moon Aquarius to Pisces 4:30 p.m.) No matter how independent an Aries you are, today you will want to slip into the comfortable cocoon of love and warmth from those around you. Some may be feeling a bit battered; others may be experiencing a delay in plans. Try to look beyond the here and now and see how really great your potential is and how small the present problems are. In company, you tend to have a "cutting edge"; temper it.

Monday, November 10 (Moon in Pisces) So that's what it was all about! Something that seemed just one big jumble now becomes clear as a bell. It's a relief to have things out in the open where you can see and untangle them. Romance is highly possible for many; a spirited exchange of thoughts is in the cards for others. All should have the opportunity to go back to square one and correct a previous mistake.

Tuesday, November 11 (Moon Pisces to Aries 11:14 p.m.) It's possible you have been neglecting someone who desperately needs a call or visit. Just think of how you would feel if you were confined in that way. If this is not your lot, you could still experience loneliness. Realize that it is all in your mind and that you really do have a lot of support. Some will hear a "voice from the past."

Wednesday, November 12 (Moon in Aries) As the moon swings into your sign, you swing into high gear. In fact, some of you might feel like taking on the whole world today; while you are in a strong position, that is not quite the case. Be satisfied with small progress and a minor coup—and you will make your day. Some will be looking at themselves with a critical eye and saying, "I need working on." Get to work. The lucky number today is 3.

Thursday, November 13 (Moon in Aries) You should be able to write your own program today—and put it into effect. However, don't think you can skim over the details. It is important to check your sources and be sure of your facts. It is an excellent day for throwing out the old and bringing in the new. Some may find themselves tangling with a Taurus or a Scorpio; realize that they have more staying power than you.

Friday, November 14 (Moon Aries to Taurus 8:24 a.m.) There is a shake-up today, and when things shake down you are in a better position. Some may be uncomfortable with the changes, but understand that they are in your interest. Though you are not known for your tact, there is little you can do today to offend.

In fact, you may be unusually popular with your peers. A thought comes, and you should put it in writing. The lucky number today is 5.

Saturday, November 15 (Moon in Taurus) This should be a mellow day with you in an uncharacteristically cooperative mood. Isn't it great when things hum in harmony all around? Some may even find that the money picture is brighter and that good news comes in concerning a deal or an investment. The lucky number is 6.

Sunday, November 16 (Moon Taurus to Gemini 7:26 p.m.) This full moon could bring many of you a feeling of completion and contentment. If the circumstances of your life are such that this is not the case, you should at least find some small satisfaction with a victory you have today. Be careful to get things in writing and not to gloss over reality as it is. Don't let wishing replace doing.

Monday, November 17 (Moon in Gemini) Today could turn into a bit of a hassle if you let it; your best course is to take a deep breath and resolve not to get confused or irritated. Don't overlook someone who really is trying to help; and don't let your pride not to take this person up on his/her offer. Some will find there is a sociable quality to today that is very pleasant—if you are in the mood for a lot of chatter. When evening comes, relax and enjoy it. It may be one during which you say, "I want to be alone." The lucky number today is 8.

Tuesday, November 18 (Moon in Gemini) You may have to play private eye today and ferret out some information someone does not want to give up. Be subtle, but reject any superficial responses you get. Some will get a great kick out of successfully winding up an assignment or project; others may get the chance to display some fancy mental footwork—and gain confidence because of it. You may be involved with a Libra or another Aries today, and either one is an excellent companion. The lucky number is 9.

Wednesday, November 19 (Moon Gemini to Cancer 7:46 a.m.) Don't try to be a hero today and do it all yourself; you will end up exhausted, both mentally and physically. However, indicate that you are willing to head up a task force, then do as much delegating as you can. Some will find a pleasant member of the opposite sex an excellent companion today, and he/she may even show the way out of a current dilemma. Don't be surprised if the advice you get is to be independent. Your lucky number today could be 1.

Thursday, November 20 (Moon in Cancer) Someone around you will need TLC today, and you should give as much of it as you can. If it makes you feel like a martyr, realize that this person has given to you a great deal of the same kind of love and affection. Some of you will find that their home is the center of social activity; others may find they need to pay some attention to that home. Fix it up now for future security. The lucky number is 2.

Friday, November 21 (Moon Cancer to Leo 8:25 p.m.) This is a day to try a new way of doing an old job—or finding a new solution to a long-standing problem. You may be surprised to discover that your best weapon has been with you always, and that is your excellent sense of humor. Some loose ends will have to be tied up today and some arrangements completed before you can feel comfortable. Don't hesitate to define your territorial rights if someone tries to "invade" your property. Realize that you've got more on the ball than he/she has.

Saturday, November 22 (Moon in Leo) This could be a day for high drama; don't let it degenerate into shoddy melodrama. Intensity is in the air, and many could find themselves in a face-off situation. Change may come even if you do not seek it; do not fight the inevitable. For many, the day will be brightened considerably by children or romance. In the later area, be as discriminating as you can.

Sunday, November 23 (Moon in Leo) Today is far more relaxed and should be a "sunny Sunday," no matter what the weather. It is an excellent time to devote some attention to a personal pastime, possibly a creative one. Those who write will find that the words flow today. For some, a clash of ideas is indicated, but it should be a stimulating session rather than an unpleasant encounter. There is a strong element of luck underlying this day. You may make a winning choice.

Monday, November 24 (Moon Leo to Virgo 7:46 a.m.) It is heartening to discover that someone is truly loyal and stands up for you in spite of opposing views. On the other hand, you may discover it is necessary to make an adjustment that does not totally suit your way of doing things. Be a good sport! Some will find they are focusing a lot on home decorations and remodeling. It is an excellent time to beautify your surroundings. The lucky number today is 6.

Tuesday, November 25 (Moon in Virgo) You won't be satisfied with mediocre performance today—including your own. As you strive for perfection, realize that everyone is human—including you. However, you are to be congratulated for your high standards. Some of you will have people relying on their judgment today and thus should make any pronouncement with great care. A dig-in-and-work day—but the lucky number is 7.

Wednesday, November 26 (Moon Virgo to Libra 3:59 p.m.) No matter what your holiday plans, and no matter what preparations you must make for them, you'll also have to deal with other responsibilities today. The pressure is on, but you can handle it if you realize there is light at the end of the tunnel. A lot of it. That could mean financial reward as well. For some, excellent news comes in connection with a career opportunity.

Thursday, November 27 (Moon in Libra) This should be a particularly harmonious holiday for Aries. The moon position indicates a willingness to balance personal needs against the needs of others. There's a lot of love around you today and you should return it in great abundance. A conversation you get into today is more than simply idle talk; if you listen carefully, you will pick up some clues that could help you enormously. The subject may be investment. The lucky number today is 9.

Friday, November 28 (Moon Libra to Scorpio 8:13 p.m.) Once again there is a give-and-take quality to the day which should affect all your actions and feelings. In fact, some should take the initiative and reach out to someone where there has been some hard feelings. You can successfully mend some fences. In everything, it is wise to go slowly and attain a low profile now. If you are inclined to speculate, the lucky number today is 1.

Saturday, November 29 (Moon in Scorpio) Some of you may be down, but realize that you are not out. Far from it. What appears to be a setback will almost miraculously turn into a victory later on. If you are in the mood for studying, you might dabble in occult subjects. Your mind will be very open to them now. For some, a hunch proves accurate and you should not hesitate to follow it. Listen carefully to a secret you hear today; someone may be trying to manipulate you.

Sunday, November 30 (Moon Scorpio to Sagittarius 9:08 p.m.) You will feel loved and needed today because someone close to you opens up and tells you how he/she feels. It's great to be that important in the life of another. Those who are not so blessed should better their chances of being loved by cooperating with someone who really wants to strike up relationship. All would be wise to keep their plans flexible because changes are likely. Another Aries or a Sagittarian may be an ideal playmate today.

DECEMBER 1986

Monday, Dec. 1 (Moon in Sagittarius) You may be tempted to go out on a limb today, but you are far better off sticking with the straight and narrow; what is familiar will in the long run be far more comfortable than what is not. Make it a point to get in touch with someone you haven't chatted with in a while, and resolve that you won't let it go so long the next time. Your family will be a source of comfort now.

Tuesday, December 2 (Moon Sagittarius to Capricorn 8:26 p.m.) Many of you will be feeling a touch on the heavy side today—in the physical sense, that it. Now's the time to decide what your ideal weight is, do something about getting there and remaining there. It may be an interesting invitation that makes you particularly aware of your body image; good! Now maybe you will really do something about it. Your lucky number is 3.

Wednesday, December 3 (Moon in Capricorn) Don't mince words with a superior about just what your ambitions are; people like people who want to go places. In another area, you may experience some confusion, but realize you are putting together the parts of a puzzle—and that you will soon have it completed. Check all the fine print today if you don't want any foul-ups.

Thursday, December 4 (Moon Capricorn to Aquarius 8:23 p.m.) Today somebody helps you solve that riddle, and you will be much more comfortable with your doubts resolved. Your prestige is on the line today, so take every opportunity to look good. There will be a chance to express yourself in a particularly forceful and unique manner; don't blow it by getting too carried away. The lucky number is 5.

Friday, December 5 (Moon in Aquarius) Somebody wants you to give an evaluation of a purchase he/she wants to make; if you really don't know much about it, say so. This is no time to fake it. You will be in the mood for fun and games—and possibly a rather daring business or career maneuver. It's okay to give it a try, but make sure you've got a fallback position if things don't work.

Saturday, December 6 (Moon Aquarius to Pisces 10:48 p.m.) Somebody's been holding out on you, but today the information you've been wanting comes through. Be very careful when analyzing it so that you don't get the wrong message. Now's the time to get rid of some stuff that you really have no more use for and that is simply taking up space. For some, there will be a romantic encounter that could be of an underground nature.

Sunday, December 7 (Moon in Pisces) One of your relationships is getting a lot stronger, and it feels very good. It also feels good to be around family and friends today, and for some there will be a real reunion. Some Aries people will feel like doing something dramatic; you could find yourself getting rather emotional in the process. Have a good cry. It's okay! The lucky number is 8.

Monday, December 8 (Moon in Pisces) You start out the week by finishing up a big job and getting lots of praise for it. It should bolster up your slightly shaky confidence and make you realize you will be out of the woods soon. A love situation is getting rather serious, and you should be aware of it. Have some fun with another Aries, a Leo, or a Libra.

Tuesday, December 9 (Moon Pisces to Aries 4:49 a.m.) Now the moon swings into your sign, and you should feel a return of initiative and energy. Whatever it is you want, go for it in a direct manner. It's best to show your Aries independence now and to let your true personality shine. Just follow your instincts, because they should be working quite well. The lucky number is 1.

Wednesday, December 10 (Moon in Aries) Many of you will walk through a door that's been previously closed; in some cases it means being let into a privileged group that's been pretty tight up to now. At this high in your cycle, you should find yourself in the right place at the right time—in every respect. Some will get treated to an excellent meal, but should watch themselves. Keep the word "moderation" in mind today.

Thursday, December 11 (Moon Aries to Taurus 2:10 p.m.) You could easily have multiple invitations today, but take care not to scatter yourself all over the place. By standing in just one spot you could have everything come to you, the vibes of timing and luck are so good today. You'll have an excellent opportunity to show off your great sense of humor—as well as your willingness to learn. The lucky number is 3.

Friday, December 12 (Moon in Taurus) Keep your ears wide open today for ideas about how to increase your income potential. Don't miss a trick. Some will be preoccupied with personal possessions, and in some cases the lost will be found. Pay some attention to paying bills and getting other financial things in order if you are to feel your best. An apparent setback will boomerang in your favor.

Saturday, December 13 (Moon in Taurus) Something arrives in the mail today that could call for a special appearance, and possibly an opportunity for a hearing on a certain matter. Your cycle is high, and you can count on a positive judgment. It is important, however, to explain your side in a precise, direct manner—although without stepping on any toes. Your lucky number is 5.

Sunday, December 14 (Moon Taurus to Gemini 1:41 a.m.) A short trip could mean a get-together with relatives—or the completion of an assignment. On the home front, a concession may be necessary, as well as a touch of diplomacy. Wouldn't you rather have harmony restored? Some Aries will be full of bright ideas, but should be selective about which ones to act on.

Monday, December 15 (Moon to Gemini) Realize that everything is subject to change today, including your best-laid plans. Keep your options open, and do not let someone else's indecisiveness get on your nerves. You are the one who may have to supply the alternatives—and the decisions. A Pisces or a Virgo could figure prominently. The lucky number is 7.

Tuesday, December 16 (Moon Gemini to Cancer 2:09 p.m.) During this full-moon period you should feel particularly romantic, and may even experience the deepening of a relationship. It may mean your taking on more responsibility. In some cases, a message comes in that clears up a mystery, much to your relief. A nice boost comes when you realize someone has your best interests at heart after all.

Wednesday, December 17 (Moon in Cancer) Some kind of burden is removed now, and you will feel as if the green light is finally flashing for progress. It's good to see a long-range plan come into view, and to feel that you no longer are adrift. Some Aries will be completing an agreement that has to do with property or some other tangible asset. This should result in a secure feeling.

Thursday, December 18 (Moon in Cancer) You will feel good when you get the chance to rectify a past mistake and to patch something up again so it's practically brand-new. Resolve to keep people around you informed; it may be necessary to call a "conference". It's possible to get to the heart of things and to make a whole new start, if necessary. The lucky number is 1 today.

Friday, December 19 (Moon Cancer to Leo 2:44 a.m.) Emotional involvement colors much of this day. In some cases, it will be made very clear that someone really does care, and is willing to go to the mat to help you solve your problems. Respond in kind! Other Aries will find children are especially important in the day's scenario, but the indications are all pleasurable. Some will feel like speculating, or taking some other kind of flyer.

Saturday, December 20 (Moon in Leo) Show that you are a gracious winner when you come out on top; there is no point in gloating. Contests of all kinds are indicated today, and you should find yourself in a very strong position, no matter what the odds. Many Aries people are very popular now, and may find themselves invited to a rather unusual event. Accept, because there is adventure in the air. Holiday plans will get firmed up via a call, possibly long distance.

Sunday, December 21 (Moon Leo to Virgo 2:30 p.m.) If you've got to tear something down in order to rebuild it properly, be willing to do so. It could even be a relationship, and there may be a break with the "old order." Your inventiveness and creativity are at a high, and you should take full advantage of it. A young person shows that he/she really wants to be on your team; it could be a Taurus or a Scorpio. The lucky number is 4.

Monday, December 22 (Moon in Virgo) You will plunge into the work week willing to grapple with detail, and ready to make some productive changes in your methods of doing things. Some may pick up an error in the "fine print," and may get praised for it. Someone of the opposite sex may show that he/she really is interested in your welfare; don't hesitate to use this to your advantage. A Gemini or a Virgo could play a key role.

Tuesday, December 23 (Moon in Virgo) Avoid any kind of extremes today; it's important to maintain a steady pace—and nerves to match. Some will have diet and nutrition on their minds, and will be doing something to improve things. Others will receive a surprise gift—which could be simply some kind words and an expression of affection. Show your gratitude. Your lucky number today is 6.

Wednesday, December 24 (Moon Virgo to Libra 12:05 a.m.) This is a lovely day to start the holidays; your more spiritual side should be in focus, and you should be feeling quite open-hearted toward others. Cooperative efforts are both easy and productive today, and you may find that you put a relationship on a whole new footing. It is a result of your being more giving toward others. A Pisces or a Virgo could be your opposite number.

Thursday, December 25 (Moon in Libra) Today you back up very generous thoughts with actions; your family feeling is quite strong, and you will benefit through a kind of reunion that happens now. You are also very much in the mood for all pleasurable things, and you should have your share of them today. Even better, some Aries people will discover the money situation is brighter than they thought.

Friday, December 26 (Moon Libra to Scorpio 7:06 a.m.) In spite of the holiday atmosphere, there is some kind of problem that requires you to dig deep for information today; you'll strike gold if you persist. Your powers of concentration should also be at a peak, so you will be able to finish what you start. You and someone close may have to talk about money; keep it on a civil basis.

Saturday, December 27 (Moon in Scorpio) Go only for what is quality now; your ability to be selective may determine your future security. If someone gives you easy answers, insist on more than a superficial explanation; you deserve more. Some Aries people may discover that something they own/have is more valuable than they had thought. Once again, resolve to hang onto it tightly.

Sunday, December 28 (Moon Scorpio to Sagittarius 8:20 a.m.) Don't feel you have to go it alone now; discuss things openly with those whose support you can count on. The important thing is to ask for help when you want it; you need have no fear about receiving it. Shared experiences of all kinds are important now; sometimes hearing more than one answer can clarify how you should go. The lucky number is 2.

Monday, December 29 (Moon in Sagittarius) Suddenly you may feel as if opportunities are coming in through the windows! Don't let a multiplicity of choices confuse you or throw you; however, you should be ready to deal with a change in the status quo. Many Aries people will be thinking about travel, and should start to make plans. Team up with a Gemini or a Sagittarian.

Tuesday, December 30 (Moon Sagittarius to Capricorn 7:54 a.m.) Ask for an accounting from someone today, and you will get it. In the course of the day, someone will make a rather unorthodox suggestion, and you should listen carefully. It could open the door to some big things, and you are adventurous enough to try it. Also, you should feel you are on much more solid ground now than recently.

Wednesday, December 31 (Moon in Capricorn) You should end the year on a fine note, full of vigor and optimism about the year to come. Your celebration is likely to be a rather quiet one, but you can count on feeling good tomorrow. Some Aries may be thinking about business even though the main event is the holiday. Good for you; and a good way to start out a prosperous year to come.

About This Series

This is one of a series of
Twelve Day-by-Day Astrological Guides
for the signs in 1986
by Sydney Omarr

About the Author

Born on August 5, 1926, in Philadelphia, Omarr was the only astrologer ever given full-time duty in the U.S. Army as an astrologer. He also is regarded as the most erudite astrologer of our time and the best-known, through his syndicated column (300 newspapers), and his radio and television programs (he is Merv Griffin's "resident astrologer"). Omarr has been called the most "knowledgeable astrologer since Evangeline Adams." His forecasts of Nixon's downfall, the end of World War II in mid-August of 1945, the assassination of John F. Kennedy, Roosevelt's election to a fourth term and his death in office ... these and many others ... are on record and quoted enough to be considered "legendary."

COUPON

PROF. LALLEMEND
Dept SO-8 • POB 252
BROOKLYN, N.Y. 11204

516 Fifth Ave., N.Y., N.Y. 10036

Dear Reader,

You do not have to 'merely believe' Professor Lallemend, the renowned astrologer, because he will **PROVE** to you how he can help you make your life better!

Just fill out this form and mail it. Professor Lallemend will prepare **YOUR HOROSCOPE** and predict—without charge **TWO ESSENTIAL EVENTS IN YOUR LIFE**. You will be thoroughly convinced by the precision of the forecast and will also learn how you can gain success and inner contentment, as well as avoiding everything which can be an obstacle in the path of your happiness. You will receive his advice absolutely free of charge. All you have to do is, answer the questions below, and mail the coupon TODAY.

Please send me free of charge and without any obligation on my part my horoscope and two predictions in an unmarked envelope.

My Birthdate ....

Time .... Place ....

Please let me know as well, my lucky numbers. I enclose here a number between 0 and 9 which suddenly comes to my mind:

_____

NAME......................

ADD. ....

....

CITY ....

STATE .... ZIP ....

How well do you know yourself?

This horoscope gives you answers to these questions based on your exact time and place of birth...

How do others see you?
What is your greatest strength?
What are your life purposes?
What drives motivate you?
How do you think?
Are you a loving person?
How competitive are you?
What are your ideals?
How religious are you?
Can you take responsibility?
How creative are you?
How do you handle money?
How do you express yourself?
What career is best for you?
How will you be remembered?
Who are your real friends?
What are you hiding?

Many people are out of touch with their real selves. Some can't get ahead professionally because they are doing the wrong kind of work. Others lack self-confidence because they're trying to be someone they're not. Others are unsuccessful in love because they use the wrong approach with the wrong people. Astrology has helped hundreds of people with problems like these by showing them their real selves.

You are a unique individual. Since the world began, there has never been anyone exactly like you. Sun-sign astrology, the kind you see in newspapers and magazines, is all right as far as it goes. But it treats you as if you were just the same as millions of others who have the same Sun sign because their birthdays are close to yours. A true astrological reading of your character and personality has to be one of a kind, unlike any other. It has to be based on exact date, time, longitude and latitude of your birth. Only a big IBM computer like the one that Para Research uses can handle the trillions of possibilities.

A Unique Document Your Astral Portrait includes your complete chart with planetary positions and house cusps calculated to the nearest minute of arc, all planetary aspects with orbs and intensities, plus text explaining the meaning of:

★ Your particular combination of Sun and Moon signs.
★ Your Ascendant sign and the house position of its ruling planet. (Many computer horoscopes omit this because it requires exact birth data.)
★ The planets influencing all twelve houses in your chart.
★ Your planetary aspects.

Others Tell Us "I found the Astral Portrait to be the best horoscope I've ever read."—E.D., Los Angeles, CA
"I could not put it down until I'd read every word. It is like you've been looking over my shoulder since I arrived in this world!"—B.N.L., Redding, CA
"I recommend the Astral Portrait. It even surpasses many of the readings done by professional astrologers."
—J.B.
Bristol,
CT

Low Price There is no substitute for a personal conference with an astrologer, but a good astrologer charges $50 and up for a complete chart reading. Some who have rich clients get $200 and more. Your Astral Portrait is an analysis of your character written by some of the world's foremost astrologers, and you can have it not for $200 or $50 but for only $22. This is possible because the text of your Astral Portrait is already written. You pay only for the cost of putting your birth information into the computer, compiling one copy, checking it and sending it to you within two weeks.

Permanence Ordinarily, you leave an astrologer's office with only a memory. Your Astral Portrait is a thirty-five-page, fifteen-thousand-word, permanently bound book that you can read again and again for years.

Money-Back Guarantee Our guarantee is unconditional. That means you can return your Astral Portrait at any time for any reason and get a full refund of the purchase price. That means we take all the risk, not you!

You Hold the Key The secrets of your inner character and personality, your real self, are locked in the memory of the computer. You alone hold the key: your time and place of birth. Fill in the coupon below and send it to the address shown with $22. Don't put it off. Do it now while you're thinking of it. Your Astral Portrait is waiting for you.

© 1977 Para Research, Inc.

Para Research, Dept. BT, P.O. Box 61, Gloucester, Massachusetts 01930 I want to read about my real self. Please send me my Astral Portrait. I understand that if I am not completely satisfied, I can return it for a full refund. ☐ I enclose $22 plus 1.50 for shipping and handling. ☐ Charge $23.50 to my Master Card account. ☐ Charge $23.50 to my VISA account.

Card number		Good through Mo.	Day	Yr.
Mr/Ms		Birthdate Mo.	Day	Yr.
Address		Birthtime (within an hour)		AM/PM
City		Birthplace City		
State	Zip	State	County	

Know in advance the changes in your life

Wouldn't it be useful to know when important events in your life are going to happen? How would you respond? What will you experience emotionally, intellectually and psychologically? And how will these experiences affect your life.

Your transits can provide valuable clues to various trends or stages of personal growth. This is especially true for the slower moving outer planets—Jupiter through Pluto. The transits for these planets are long lasting and profound in their psychological consequences. Many occur only once in a lifetime. The Astral Forecast is all about the outer planets.

This horoscope provides a reliable tool for astrological forecasting. The Astral Forecast will show you how the outer transits affect your sense of timing, that is, the times that are appropriate for you to take certain kinds of actions and inappropriate for others. This horoscope includes every significant transit to your outer planets that occurs in a twelve-month period. You can use your Astral Forecast to better understand how the outer planets affect such important life issues as career, child rearing, love, marriage and more.

For example, when Jupiter is in the first house, this transit represents a major growth cycle in your life. This is the best time for you to explore who you really are as an individual. Under this transit, you will feel more secure about yourself and the impression you make on others. Therefore, understanding yourself and your influence on others can make this transit an especially powerful and

important time in your life. This is also a time for learning and gaining new experience. All this is part of your present need for personal growth, which affects not only yourself, but also the way you deal with the world as a whole. This is one time when persons and resources are likely to be drawn to you, and you should take constructive advantage of them.

You can find out in advance what your transits are going to be. But if you do it on your own, you will have to consult several astronomical tables to find the positions of each of the transiting planets every day and then compare them mathematically to the positions of the planets at the time of your birth.

There's an easier way to learn of your transits. Our IBM System/36 computer will handle all the calculations and provide you with information on all your outer transits based on your exact time and place of birth. With the Astral Forecast you not only receive the most accurate calculation of your personal transits for the next twelve months, you will also receive an extensive printout interpreting the character and significance of your individual transits.

Your Astral Forecast is the most accurate and authoritative guide to the outer transits that you can receive. It is based on the work of Robert Hand, one of America's most famous astrologers, and the author of several astrology books.

Like all Para Research horoscopes, the Astral Forecast is inexpensive. For just $16.00 you can have the same kind of advice that would otherwise cost you hundreds of dollars. This low price is possible because the astrological data is stored in our computer, and can be easily formatted and printed. Also, the mathematical calculations can be done in a matter of minutes. Your only cost is the cost of putting your personal information into the computer, producing one copy and then mailing it.

When you order your Astral Forecast, you receive an unconditional money-back guarantee. This means you can return your Astral Forecast at any time and get a full refund of the purchase price. We take all the risk.

Order your Astral Forecast today. Discover how the transits can bring energy to each part of your personality, fulfill your potential and help you gain more control over your own life.
© 1983 Para Research, Inc.

Para Research, Dept. BT, P.O. Box 61, Gloucester, Massachusetts 01930 Please send me my Astral Forecast. I understand that if I am not completely satisfied, I can return it for a full refund. ☐ I enclose $16 plus $1.50 for shipping and handling. ☐ Charge $17.50 to my MasterCard account. ☐ Charge $17.50 to my VISA account.

Card number		Good through Mo.	Day	Yr.
Mr/Ms		Birthdate Mo.	Day	Yr.
Address		Birthtime (within an hour)		AM/PM
City		Birthplace City	State	
State	Zip	Start calendar with Mo.		Yr.

Don't Let A TERRIBLE THING HAPPEN TO YOU!

SECRET KNOWLEDGE REVEALED THAT HAS BEEN HANDED DOWN THROUGH HISTORY- TO <u>HELP GIVE YOU A RICHER, LOVE FILLED, HAPPIER LIFE.</u>

Will The POWER Of The OCCULT DOLL Work For YOU?

● **OCCULT SUPPLIES**—For centruies it was and still is a tradition that in Secret Ancient Rituals and Magic of Haiti, Africa, and Latin America, dolls and spells were used to carry out every purpose desired. Used for Love, Luck, Riches to gain power. These ancient rituals were rare a constant source of comfort and hope to those who pratice.

We have been making these OCCULT DOLLS and RITUALS for certain customers with Special Problems to see if they were able to help. We are happy to tell you that we feel they have been a great success. Each Doll is made of a certain color with Amulets, Charms, and Herbs sewn in. Believed to attract WHAT YOU WANT. Each Doll is handmade with Great Care by one who knows and believes. Comes with full instructions.

● **LOVE DOLL**
We feel the Most Powerful Love Occult Ritual is done with Red, and special items sewn in. Used to bring a love back to you or get your relationship back to the love and excitement you once had we believe. Comes with special Red tipped pin, powerful instructions.
D300 . . . . 5.98

● **MONEY DRAWING DOLL**
Green Doll handmade with coins and herbs sewn inside. We believe that Green has the power of attracting money to one in need. Strong money directions included.
D500 . . . . 5.98

● **OCCULT RITUAL HANDBOOK**
Everything you always wanted to know about Occult Rituals and Magic—songs, chants, spells for every purpose. Use of Roots, Herbs, Oils plus ceremonial rites and more. The secrets are here.
Bk120 . . . . 4.98

Triple Win BINGO BAG

Did you ever wonder why some people always win at BINGO? Do they have a secret? Now you can have your own secret! Your own BINGO BAG to carry with you.

NOW YOU CAN WIN TOO!
When your numbers are called, you be the one to shout BINGO! You get Bingo Oil, Gemstone, Charm, Seal plus Green Bag and full instructions.
KK795 All 7 items 7.95

LOVE RUB

Rub on your hands or body — or on the body of the one you love. Get what you want and use it wisely.

K371-Red-Passionate Love
K372-Pink-Win love and conquer Evil
K373-Green-Money Drawing
K374-Light Blue-Power to Find a Job

3.98 Any 3 for 11.50

FOLLOW ME COLOGNE

Comes with "LUCKY FORTUNE" A Few Drops Does The Trick. To attract your love, wear this whenever you go out. Sprinkle in your draws also.

K297 Large 4 oz. size

4.98

SPIRITUAL OILS

Used by many thousands of satisfied people because the fragrance charms the senses. Try them today!

2.25 Save 77¢
Order any 3
Only 5.98

K-4 — Attraction	K-14 — Lady Luck
K-100 — Commanding	K-11 — Lodestone
K-2 — Compelling	K-112 — Lovers
K-101 — Concentration	K-113 — Lucky Money
K-102 — Crossing	K-114 — Lucky Hand
K-103 — Dragon Blood	K-9 — Money Drawing
K-16 — Fast Luck	K-7 — Power
K-104 — Finance	K-117 — Protection
K-105 — French Love	K-121 — Spirit
K-106 — Good Luck	K-8 — Success
K-107 — High Conquering	K-122 — Uncrossing
K-109 — Holy Spiritual	K-123 — Van Van
K-110 — Jinx Removing	
K-111 — King Solomon	

SPECIAL INCENSE 2.25

Save 77¢
Order any 3
Only 5.98

Burn incense to attract, to dispel wicked odors. Best incense available, attracting fragrances, satisfying results.

NUMBER IN EVERY BOX
People are used to buying incense with a number. And considering it lucky. We don't claim these numbers as such.

K-77 — Commanding	K-48 — Success
K-42 — Compelling	K-34 — Jinx Removing
K-78 — Concentration	K-84 — Lady Luck
K-97 — Crossing	K-86 — Lovers
K-80 — Dragon Blood	K-87 — Lucky Hand
K-41 — Fast Luck	K-88 — Lucky Money
K-33 — Finance	K-91 — Masters
K-81 — French Love	K-47 — Money Drawing
K-82 — Good Luck	K-39 — Power
K-83 — High Conquering	K-43 — Van Van
	K-35 — Uncrossing

Write to: ANN HOWARD DEPT.SY1 200 West Sunrise Highway, Freeport, N.Y. 11520

$5 Dollar Deposit on all C.O.D. Orders! Prepaid Orders Please Add $1.95 for Postage.
FREE- Latest Catalog-Candles, Oils, Incense, Spells, More. Just Write. No claims are made. These alleged powers are gathered from writings, books, folklore & occult sources. Sold as curios.

"Next to my mother, you have been the greatest inspiration of my life."

You'll be amazed!

When you read what Marguerite Carter has to say about your life in the year ahead you'll be amazed. She delves into the most important areas of your life: romance, money, goals, and significant changes. You'll find out all the wonderful ways you can live a better life when you have your Unitology Forecast prepared for you by Marguerite Carter.

She'll help you.

Marguerite Carter has counseled thousands of enthusiastic followers around the world for decades. She has been the guiding light and helping hand for people from all walks of life: business leaders, hollywood stars and just everyday folks. There is a good reason why they seek her services year after year. They get the help they need in the most important areas of their lives!

'. . . it was amazing.'

People write all the time telling about how Marguerite Carter has helped them.

". . . it was amazing. I just can't believe it." W.C., Canada

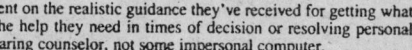

MARGUERITE CARTER

". . . could not put it down until I read it cover to cover." M.L., Illinois.

"Without a doubt, next to my mother, you have been the greatest inspiration of my life. Many others could probably say the same thing." M.A., PA

In letter after letter people comment on the realistic guidance they've received for getting what they want from life. They've found the help they need in times of decision or resolving personal problems. These are judgments by a caring counselor, not some impersonal computer.

Hidden Opportunities

The things you want most may not be out of reach. Marguerite Carter says, "Many people are completely unaware that the opportunities for money, love or advancement are passing them by almost daily . . ." Without knowledge of when the conditions are favorable or unfavorable, the chances for success and happiness are greatly diminished.

Get your Unitology Forecast with special notations by Marguerite Carter. It will be prepared to your specific birthdate information. Remember that you will receive a full year of guidance, regardless of when your request is received, and you'll know that your forecast has come from one of the world's most highly respected astrologer-counselors.

Marguerite Carter • P.O. Box 807 • Indianapolis, Indiana 46206   O-6

☐ Yes Miss Carter, Please send me my Unitology Forecast for the year ahead. Enclosed is my remittance of $9.95 plus $1.00 for postage and handling. (First Class $1.30) Make all checks payable in U.S. funds. Allow 4 weeks for delivery.

Name _____
Address _____
City _____ State _____ Zip Code _____
Birthplace _____
Month _____ Day _____ Year _____
Place _____ Hour _____

ASTROLOGY QUESTIONNAIRE

Help us bring you even better astrology guides by filling out this survey and mailing it today.

A. Book Title (Sign): _____

B. Using the scale below how would you rate this astrological guide? (Place one rating from 0–10 in the space provided.)

Poor	Not So Good	O.K.	Good	Excellent
0 1	2 3	4 5 6	7 8	9 10

Rating

Overall Opinion of book _____

Essay On:
1. Defining Terms _____
2. Your House of The Sun _____
3. The Geometry of Relationships _____
4. Twelve Places at the Table _____
5. Moods of the Moon _____
6. Venus and Mars _____
7. Venus Sign Position Chart _____
8. Mars Sign Position Chart _____
9. The Planets as "Stars" _____
10. Astrotrivia _____
11. Sun Sign Changes _____
12. Your Sign: The Big Picture _____
13. Your Sign: Objectives and Obstacles _____
14. Pairing Off With Your Sign _____
15. Your Sign's Sex Role Dilemma _____
16. Your Sign: Female _____
17. Your Sign: Male _____
18. Your Sign: Help Wanted _____
19. How "Pure" a _____ are you? _____
20. Find Your Rising Sign _____
21. Your Sign: Astro-Outlook for '86 _____
22. 15 Months of Day-By-Day Predictions _____

C. In total about how many astrology guides have you purchased for yourself in the past 12 months?
   # of books _____

D. What topics would you be interested in having Sydney Omarr write about in the 1987 Astrology Guide?
   _____
   _____

E. What is your education?

   1( ) High School   3( ) 4 yrs college
   2( ) 2 yrs college 4( ) Postgraduate

F. What is your occupation? _____

G. What is your marital status?

   1( ) Single   3( ) Divorced   5( ) Widowed
   2( ) Married   4( ) Separated

H. Age: _____   I. Sex: 1( ) Male
                               2( ) Female

Please Print Name:_____

Address_____

City_____ State_____ Zip_____

Phone # ( )_____

Thank you. Please send to New American Library, Research Dept., 1633 Broadway, New York, NY 10019